Why You Like
The Wines You Like

Changing the way the world thinks about wine

By

Tim Hanni, Master of Wine

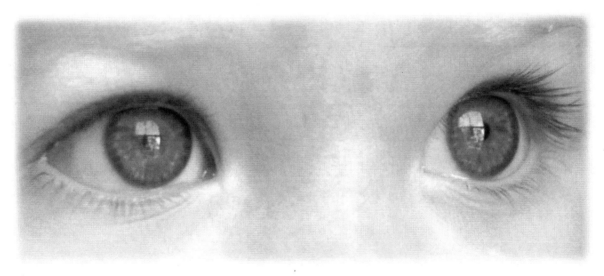

Photo: Rory Webster

"Everything has beauty, but not everyone sees it," Confucius

In loving memory of Dr. Bob Noyes; my friend and mentor.

Dedicated to Kate, Chase and Landen

A special thanks to Dr. Virginia Utermohlen, MD, Sasha Paulsen
and Harvey Posert for their contributions to this project.

Go to www.timhanni.com/book
to access the sensory illusions, videos and other materials that are not
able to be presented book form.

Go to www.myvinotpe.com
to register, take the Vinotype sensory assessment and to receive
personalized wine recommendations.

Acknowledgements

A special thanks for the contributions all of my friends, mentors
and heroes who made my life richer and this book possible:

Sasha Paulsen

Virginia Utermohlen, MD

Harvey Posert

Martha Casselman

Susan Cashin

Sarah Scott

George Taber

Frederic Brochet

Michael O'Mahony

Rie Ishii

Dr. Charles Wysocki

Dr. Robert Noyes

Jancis Robinson

Raymond Sokolov

Yves Durand

Dr. Linda Bartoshuk

John Lawless

Dr. Ian Horman

Dr. Victor Kimura

Chris Cutler

John Stallcup

Albert Cohen

Jerry Neff

Joanne Cottongim

Ed Sbragia

Jerry Comfort

Jane Robichaud

Hugh Johnson

Domenico Corrado

Bern Laxer

Danny Haas

Rick Turko

G. M. "Pooch" Pucilowski

Aaron Kidder

Sue Ann Wercinski

Special Illustrations by Bob Johnson
http://bobjohnsonartgallery.blogspot.com/

Table of Contents

Foreword

By George M. Taber

The people who make history are not afraid to tackle the most sacred hobgoblins of conventional wisdom. Those are people such as Galileo, Gutenberg, or Steve Jobs. They didn't just bend the curve; they set things going in a totally new direction that smaller minds have never even considered. They break the mold. They achieve great things through disruptive change. They know that the most challenging thing in life is a new idea.

It may be just a little early to include Tim Hanni in a class with those august giants. But he is certainly one who dreams of things not done and asks, "Why not?"

I am fortunate enough to have spent many hours with Tim wrestling with some of his ideas while they were still in the formative stage. It was both an exhilarating and an exhaustive experience. With a broad and deep knowledge of wine and food history as well as their complexities, he is not afraid to challenge the way things are done and to suggest alternatives. He's not dogmatic in his beliefs, but he demands that conventional thinkers think again. The payoffs are insights that you would never have considered. You may not agree with all his conclusions, but I promise he will make you think.

Hanni's opinions are not brainstorms that he thought about casually some morning while taking a shower. They are based on solid research, which is often new and little known but comes from professionals with solid credentials. And he has put them up against many serious challengers giving credibility to his conclusions. His once heretical views on radically revising the tenets of wine and food have now been adopted and incorporated into the curriculum of the Wine & Spirits Education Trust.

His views rest on one of strongest résumés in the world of wine and food. From his years as a teenager, when he learned that he could buy French wines in stores if he could just pronounce the names correctly to his experience as a chef experimenting with wine and food combination, his years of wine education at Beringer Vineyards, to his work with distinguished researchers and scientists, Tim has walked the talk.

The full impact of the globalization of wine in the past generation is only beginning to be understood, and it offers great opportunities for everyone from producers to consumers. Wine is no longer a right-little, tight-little world dominated by a few French aristocrats. New people in many fields are opening fresh horizons. Tim Hanni is one of the best of this new generation. So open up a bottle of wine that you've never tried, pair it with an untraditional food, and enjoy a voyage into Tim Hanni's new world of wine and food. You have nothing to lose but your outdated prejudices.

George M. Taber

George Taber was the National Economic Correspondent and Business Editor for *Time* magazine. In 1976 Taber published an account in *Time* about the famous Paris tasting, when unknown California wines bested the best French wines in a blind Chardonnay and Cabernet Sauvignon tasting. Nearly 30 years later he wrote *Judgment of Paris: California vs. France and the 1976 Paris Tasting that Revolutionized Wine* (Scribner, September 2005), a best-selling book selected as the wine book of the year by Decanter, the British wine magazine. He is the author of *A Toast to Bargain Wines: How Innovators, iconoclasts, and winemaking revolutionaries are changing the way the world drinks* (Scribner, November 2011).

Preface

A Man with a Frog on His Head Walks into a Wine Tasting

Say there is a population of frogs living in the forest. One day a group of the frogs ventures into a nearby cave. They decide it is pretty nice with plenty of food and water. Still it's very different from the trees and foliage they are used to. As they move deeper into the cave, they start adapting to the lower light levels. They are now also frolicking on the rocks instead of leaping from tree to tree, and they are eating a new diet of bugs found in the cave versus those that were common in the forest. They procreate and prosper, continuing to adapt and change.

Over time the cave frogs begin to act differently from the forest frogs. Their appearance changes as well. They lose the coloration that was necessary to blend into the flora of the forest and may even lose any skin pigment they once had. After a long time in the deepest parts of the cave they may even lose their ability to see as that sensory function is no longer used or needed. Although they share the same genetic base with the forest frogs it is quite easy to distinguish this new frog phenotype -- they look and act differently. Put into a social situation they would be easy to spot in a crowd of the "normal" frog community to which they once belonged.

If we were to take this story to a fantasy level, one might imagine them extolling the virtues of the cave versus the forest to their friends on the "outside." They might compare and rate the level of comfort, quality of life and superior cuisine they have found. Who knows, they might even come up with a 100 point system to evaluate the food? Forest bugs, they might insist, are for frogs with immature palates; the quality of the cave slugs and insects, while an acquired taste, is vastly superior.

The cave frogs have also developed new survival and defense mechanisms. No longer able to hide behind the foliage or jump from tree to tree, they blend in with earthy colors. They can tuck into tight crevices in the rocks. They can operate skillfully without the need of eyesight and dart into the darkest, deepest reaches of their cave, leaving the predators behind. Now, any trained herpetologist or frog aficionado can easily differentiate the forest frogs from the cave frogs visibly but not genetically.

So it is with the evolution of wine drinkers. The highly evolved wine enthusiasts can be easily spotted across a vast sea of people. They are regaling a group of bored-looking, normal people with tales of fabulous wines, extravagant dinners and wine-related anecdotes about their wine-related travels and travails. They are swirling, sniffing and slurping their wines, usually gesticulating animatedly. While sharing their opinions on wines, wine people, places and rating systems, they speak a descriptive language of fruits, spices and flowers that is mesmerizing for some and stupefying for others. In other words, they behave differently from normal people, and you can learn to spot them from a mile away. This group of wine drinkers would be considered different Vinotypes. They share a common genetic lineage with normal people but have visibly adapted and evolved to their new environment.

Imagine you are a newcomer to this world. You walk into a wine tasting. You observe that everyone is holding their glass by the stem. Better get with the program! And look how they swirl the wine. You start tentatively, making little circles with your glass on the table and finally, voila! You are swirling wine!

Notice how they do not just sniff above the glass. You have to bring your entire face down and inhale slowly and deeply. Check – I got it.

Someone you admire comes up and asks, "What do you think of this wine?" Your first response is truthful: "Wow, it kinda sucks."

He responds, "Are you crazy? This wine is $200 a bottle and got 95 points – it is clearly the best wine here."

Note to self: Shut up and watch other people to see if you should like it and if anyone asks, declare, noncommittally, that the wine is "interesting." When you are told about the intense and concentrated flavors of ripe black cherries, fenugreek and smoky French oak, you learn to nod knowingly to show you are part of the in-crowd.

Ascension of a wine drinker: from wine enjoyer to enthusiast to connoisseur to wonk to expert to geek.

Over time your confidence as a wine expert soars. You start learning this new wine lexicon. You can swirl the glass with either hand, both clockwise and counterclockwise. When you take wine into your mouth, you swish it like mouthwash and lean your head a bit forward so you can suck air through the wine to gain every molecule of taste and aroma possible. You lament to anyone within ear shot that the poor host is serving the wines in the wrong choice of glassware and the food they have selected is really not suited to the wines at all. Don't forget to regale people with your recent trip to the wine country or about the wine you found mismarked at the wine shop that you picked up for a steal.

Now you are confident. You despise the poor newbie who uses the word "interesting" to lamely avoid commenting on the quality of a wine. Maybe you are making your own wine. Someone hands you a glass, asks your opinion and you can spout off a description of exotic fruits and spices that would make Carmen Miranda proud. You can cite comments from at least three major wine critics.

You are at a party. A wine expert, you can be easily distinguished by your traits, your behavior with wine, by the language you speak. Someone again hands you a glass of wine and asks, "What do you think of this wine?"

Put on your serious wine face. Swirl the glass a few times, bury your face in the glass and take a long, deep draught. Sip, swish and suck air. Contemplate a moment and — wait for it — you declare: "This wine sucks. Who would even release a wine this bad?"

And you are told, "This is your wine. It is from the bottle you brought yourself."

No problem! You have created your defense mechanisms and are well practiced in ways to deal with dangerous situations. After vigorously swirling the wine again, you return to another long, slow smell and thoughtful, brow-furrowed contemplation. Smile now and declare, "Ah, the wine is starting to open up now and show how wonderful it is with more aeration…"

You have evolved and become a new Vinotype. You have adapted and changed just as the frogs in the cave have adapted to their environment. Your demeanor, behavior, language and preferences are visibly different even though your genetic makeup is still exactly as it was before you started mutating.

This is the state of wine today, and I wrote this book to disrupt this wine status quo. It is intended to empower wine consumers by providing a new understanding of personal wine preferences and insights into the wine preferences of others. It is intended to act as roadmap for exploration and discovery on your own terms and as a handbook for wine professionals to better understand the personal preferences of others and the means by which wine professionals can better serve anyone who likes wine.

Wine in the U.S. is enjoying the greatest popularity in history. It is being produced in every state and not just California, Washington and New York. Healthy, vibrant wine industries are emerging Virginia, Ohio, Missouri and Indiana.

Around the world, great and wonderful wines are being produced in Europe, Australia, New Zealand, South Africa and South America. Wine production is re-emerging in Eastern Europe, the Baltic and regions considered the cradle of wine: Turkey, Syria and Israel. Japan and China are experiencing a growing development of vineyards and wineries. China looms as a potential powerhouse for both consumption and wine production. It and other Asian countries offer the potential for an explosive, global expansion of wine popularity.

There are minuscule wineries that produce tiny quantities of wine and mega-wineries that produce millions of cases. And the quality of wine being produced, at every level, has never been better. There is something for everyone in terms of flavor, style, variety and aesthetics.

Wine consumers have never had more wine options, information or availability. It is estimated that in the U.S. market there are nearly 100,000 different wines available at any given time and the number is rapidly rising. The accelerated expansion of new and traditional producing regions, combined with the common strategy for large wineries to generate a proliferation of new labels, will ensure there is no lack of options for a long time to come.

Along with the extraordinary expansion of wine production, changes in how we communicate present new challenges. The Internet has certainly transformed how wine is sold and bought. It has altered how wine consumers research and learn about wines. It has also had a dramatic effect on how like-minded wine lovers convene and share information and on how people with opposing views argue and attack each other. The role of the wine critic has evolved, and blogs, wine message boards and online publications allow anyone to become a wine pundit.

It's no wonder that when consumers are polled, the adjectives they most often choose to describe their feelings about wine is "confused" and "overwhelmed." What has not evolved or improved is a deeper understanding of the spectrum of people who love and drink wine. A better understanding of consumers will in turn provide a better means to guide them to discover the wines that they genuinely enjoy and will suit their personal preferences.

Why is it that something that can provide so much pleasure has become the source of so much intimidation and anxiety?

Volumes of wine information are circulated with greater velocity and fervor than ever before while the quality of the information disseminated has degraded. Misguided assumptions, myths and lore have become "truths." From the misguided notion that sweet wine drinkers are unsophisticated and should learn to prefer dry wines to the idea that red wines are best served with meat, these statements have been repeated and unquestioned for so long that they are accepted as conventional wisdoms or immutable truths. I am now inviting everyone to question the assumptions, bust the myths and restore reality to wine lore.

My long and passionate affair with wine began as an enthusiast and evolved into a career. I mutated from a wine enjoyer to enthusiast and connoisseur. From there I became an ardent student, expert and wine professional. Even during my stint as a certifiable wine "geek" I was baffled by my perception that information I was presenting — food and wine pairings, for example — provoked different reactions from different people. The same wine, or combination of wine with food, might prompt reactions from delight to disgust.

To discover why people had such different reactions set me on a personal journey that turned into decades of research, talking to everyone from scientists to consumers around the world. Much of my appeal for change in the way people communicate and interact around wine lies in the understanding I have gained in how differently our perception can vary from one person to the next. Fundamental differences in our physiology help to explain preferences in everything from thermostat settings and levels of noise to the irritation some people get from the tags in clothing. While some people can delight in intense, high alcohol wines, for others these same wines are unpleasant; they will gravitate to sweet, low-alcohol wines to avoid what they perceive as intolerable bitterness and burning sensation.

Passionate and well-intentioned wine enthusiasts, myself included, are guilty of perpetuating inexcusable misjudgments about wine consumers based on flawed or distorted information; one of the most prevalent is that people who like sweet wines are unsophisticated and will, in time, "mature" to a preference for drier wines as if they are somehow immature for having a preference for sweet wines. In fact, this person is what I call a Sweet Vinotype, one of four basic sensory sensitivity groups, and is made up of individuals possessing the highest perceptive acuity. Discovering your Vinotype is the beginning of finding wines you will love and of understanding why someone else may have a completely different perceptive experience with the same wine.

Wine is due for an overhaul in how we talk about, market it, and above all, learn to enjoy it. This has led me to create the New Wine Fundamentals, which I refer to and outline in this book. My hope is that if you are new to wine, you will find here a roadmap to discovering the wines you love with confidence and without apologies. If you are in the wine industry — as a winemaker, a retailer, a sommelier, wine writer, or a member of a tasting room team — you will find better ways to serve your clients and help their love of wine to flourish and offer a more personalized and intimate means to explore and discover new wines.

My understanding of how this all works has completely changed so much of what I thought I knew about wine, wine with food and, more important, about the people who consume wine. There are hundreds, if not thousands, of books written about wine and pairing wine with food. There is no book written, to my knowledge, about the wine consumers and the factors to understand why you like the wines you like and other people like the wines they like.

You will not find wine recommendations or guidance on what wine to serve with which food *per se*. I wrote this book more to deepen our understanding of human nature than to understand wine itself. I hope you will enjoy the information, demonstrations, insights and stories. If this book instigates a greater awareness of the reasons that contribute to our diverse personal preferences, and more understanding and tolerance between people with different points of view about wine, then this book has served its purpose.

Chapter 1: Power to the People!

"To effectively communicate, we must realize that we are all different in the way we perceive the world and use this understanding as a guide to our communication with others."
Anthony Robbins

Albert Einstein said, "Insanity is doing the same thing over and over and expecting different results." If one turns to more formal sources, insanity can be defined as "an extreme folly or unreasonableness" or "something utterly foolish or unreasonable." The wine industry is, and has been for decades, on a mission to make wine less intimidating for consumers. The means of accomplishing this mission is through wine education and extolling the virtues of wine and food pairing. I assert that more wine education and the escalation and complexity of wine and food pairing is not the answer to making wine less intimidating. Thus, relying on more wine education and more focus on perpetuating the myths of matching wine and food is fits Dr. Einstein's definition of insanity.

Now, before you come after me swinging wine bottles, I am not accusing wine enthusiasts, zealots and pundits of being any more, or less, insane than any other individuals in our modern society. People are crazy about all kinds of things: music, art, cars, handbags, electronic gadgets — you name it. When people get crazy about things they often do crazy things, at least in the eyes of people around them, e.g. spending crazy amounts of money for things, spending inordinate amount of time focused on something, planning around the object of your obsession. And anything as diverse and varied as wine, with its associated history, tradition, sciences, rituals and range of products, is certainly subject to its own specialized form of insanity.

A characteristic of insanity is delusions! And I propose the wine community is guilty of being delusional, participating in extreme folly and operating under the specter of widespread collective delusions that form the basis of information being disseminated via wine education and concepts of pairing wine with food.

I do not think wine education is bad but I do believe much of the information is in serious need of revision. I do not think pairing wine with food should be eliminated – but I do believe it is in dire need of an overhaul in thinking.

Sir, if you knew anything about wine and food...

Another prevailing delusion today on the part of a great many wine experts is that everyday wine consumers are incapable of determining for themselves what good wine is or is not.

It was a scenario to strike fear into the hearts of wine lovers everywhere. I was sitting next to a good friend at an impressive dinner at a multi-Michelin-starred restaurant. The guests included sensory scientists and a number of great chefs who had all taken part in an international symposium celebrating the 100th anniversary of the formal proposal of the existence of umami, now considered one of the five basic tastes, along with sweet, sour, salty and bitter. The menu was 10 courses. Each course was accompanied by a wine selected by the sommelier as the appropriate choice for each dish.

After the second course, my friend turned to me and said, "The wines they've selected for us are really too strong for my taste. Would you mind ordering something for me that I would like better?"

No problem! I was, after all a wine expert, a Master of Wine and certified wine educator. Moreover, I knew the lady and her tastes quite well. I summoned the sommelier and asked, "Do you have a wine by the glass that is really light in intensity, maybe just a touch off-dry and lower in alcohol?"

"Sir," he replied, "we have selected the best wines to pair with each of the dishes."

"I understand," I said, determined to be amicable, "but my friend would really enjoy something lighter and more delicate."

"Sir, if you knew anything about wine and food you would realize these are the best wines to accompany the dishes."

Uh-oh, I had been dissed.

The New Wine Fundamentals Mission:

The New Wine Fundamentals is an education process that begins and ends with the wine consumer. This book represents the introduction to the New Wine Fundamentals principles, and my intention is that this becomes the new starting point for any other wine education or training programs. Here is what this mission is intended to accomplish:

- Encourage a more vibrant and diversified wine market with greater opportunities for wines of all types and styles, and from all regions of production.
- Match wine to the diner, not the dinner.
- Create a unified educational platform that provides a new foundation for anyone interested in, or with a passion for, wine.
- Incorporate Vinotyping into all existing wine education programs.
- Establish a zero tolerance policy for those who do not respect the personal preferences of others.
- Eliminate arrogance and inappropriate judgments often imposed on, or directed towards, wine consumers.
- Mark the beginning of a new wine era celebrating both the diversity of wines produced around the world and the diversity of people who love wine.

Still, I asked to see the wine list. As the sommelier went to get it, my friend elbowed me in the ribs, demanding, "Show him your freaking business card!"

But I just ordered a glass of wine that she loved.

The woman was Lissa Doumani, who, with her husband, Hiro Sone, owns Terra, a Michelin-starred and highly popular restaurant in St. Helena, the heart of the Napa Valley. They also own Amé, their second Michelin-starred restaurant in San Francisco. Lissa is Terra's pastry chef; she's nicknamed the Pastry Princess. She is also the daughter of Carl Doumani, who owns Quixote Winery and was the founder of Stags' Leap Winery, where Lissa grew up. She is a woman who knows her way around the world of food and wine, and so she had enough confidence to ask for a different wine, without being the least worried by waiter's snooty looks. Still, a highly trained professional at a top-flight restaurant was reluctant to bring her the wine she wanted because it wasn't "the right choice."

I know that the sommelier was only doing his job, at least as it is understood in today's wine climate. But was he really doing the best for his customers? For every Lissa, there are thousands of people sitting in restaurants, at dinners or visiting tasting rooms who are far too intimidated to ask for what they would really rather have: a glass of light, delicate or even sweet wine. There are so many of them, in fact, they constitute one of the four basic Vinotypes: A Sweet Vinotype who simply finds the powerhouse, intense, high-alcohol wines to be intolerably burning and bitter .

All too often, however, today they become the victims of well-trained, well-meaning wine aficionados. In fact we have reached a point in the wine industry where experts not only evaluate, judge and criticize wines: they go so far as to judge and unfairly criticize the people who like wines they deem unacceptable.

I know about this overt disapproval act because for a long time I was a big part of the problem. I was a

OMG - tell me you didn't order THAT wine!

wine geek, working in the Napa Valley and conducting wine seminars around the globe. I was teaching the art of wine appreciation and creating wine pairings. I was also frequently wondering what in the world was wrong with the people who didn't like the wines that I found orgasmic or didn't agree that the wine and food pairing I created was rapturous. The nerve of those pesky people! What was wrong with them? Didn't they know anything?

And they, too, often end up wondering, "What's wrong with me?" because they don't like the wine an expert tells them is fabulous or they find a food and wine pairing downright awful. Instead of discovering the many pleasures wine has to offer they opt to order a cocktail rather than facing the risk of embarrassment. The wine industry loses a sale and a potential wine lover is dissuaded from consuming wine.

Don't believe me? Walk into almost any high end winery tasting room or fine dining establishment, especially a restaurant selling "great steaks" and be so bold as to ask for a glass of White Zinfandel. More often than not you will be met with some form of disapproval for your obvious lack of taste. (The other side of the coin is to ask for a glass of an intense, rich Cabernet Sauvignon with a delicate piece of fish. In either case you may be subjected to overt disapproval for your indiscretion.) I often simply ask about White Zinfandel when I am dining out just to see what kind of reaction it elicits — like this one:

Arriving at a hotel late in the evening for a wine conference, I was dining alone. I asked the waitress, "Would the White Zinfandel go well with my steak?"

"No," she counseled me, "a Cabernet Sauvignon would be a much better choice."

"Do you like Cabernet yourself?" I asked.

No, she admitted, she did not. She told me, in fact, that she hated wine. I pressed the issue and it turned out that she did love one kind – sweet wines. She was too embarrassed to say so, but she loved the very wine I had ordered, White Zinfandel. She had been taught that it was bad wine and certainly should not be ordered with red meat. Hmmmmm.

What happened to old fashioned notions of hospitality, to the idea that "the guest is always right?" Is there some sort of wine exemption for the guest being right? What, in fact, has happened to the wine industry? "Sir, if you knew anything about wine," indeed.

Wine and Hospitality

Although today sweet wine drinkers all are too often dismissed as unsophisticated, there actually was a time — not too long ago — when sweet wines had a respected place at the table: They weren't just dessert wines, but were offered as choices throughout a meal "if the guest prefers." This is one bit of wine history overlooked — or forgotten or unknown — as wine experts try to tell people what they should and should not like. What we have lost is the tradition of hospitality

Guests and Hospitality

Guest, n. (www.dictionary-reference.com)

1. a person who spends some time at another person's home in some social activity, as a visit, dinner, or party.
2. a person who receives the hospitality of a club, a city, or the like.
3. a person who patronizes a hotel, restaurant, etc., for the lodging, food, or entertainment it provides.

Hospitality, n. (www.dictionary-reference.com)

1. the friendly reception and treatment of guests or strangers.
2. the quality or disposition of receiving and treating guests and strangers in a warm, friendly, generous way.

— truly understanding and catering to the desires and needs of guests. I am asserting that anyone who serves wine when they entertain, works as service professionals or sommeliers in restaurants bars or recommends and sells wines in stores is engaged in the service of guests is in the hospitality business. I will even go so far as to expand this to online Internet sales sites, wine bloggers and wine pundits. When I say "serving" guests, the context is about being of service to the guest, not the service of the wine, which involves the art, protocols and rituals of selling, presenting, opening and pouring of the wine.

The word guest *geist* originally meant a stranger or unknown being or spirit. It is closely connected to the German *geist,* or spirit. Someone who visited your home or inn was thus an unknown spirit you were taking in. The word "host" comes from the Latin, *ghotis,* and is now defined as a person who receives guests, or strangers. A *poltergeist* is literally a loud guest or ghost – a stranger or spirit making loud noises. "They're heeere," as they say in the movie ***Poltergeist***. Just as an aside, if the guests tried to leave a place that welcomed strangers for a fee without settling the bill, it was common practice to keep a member of the party as collateral until the payment was made. This is where we get the term "hostage: *A prisoner who is held to insure that another party will meet the specified terms of an agreement."*

True hospitality is the art of making a guest or stranger feel warmly welcomed to a hostile (another word derived from the same etymology) or unknown environment. Vinotyping is a way to get to know people better and treat everyone, even strangers, in a warm, generous way.

Ending the "tyranny of the minority"

I say it is time to end the existing "tyranny of the minority" of wine gatekeepers and turn the power of choice over to wine consumers. It's time to expand the enjoyment of wine and to foster a greater understanding of people's preferences, interests and passions. It's time to change the wine conversation, to disrupt the archaic and often fallacious information that is accepted as conventional wisdom in the wine community today.

This is not to imply that the authority of any of the critics, writers, evaluators, experts or pundits is lost or diminished. It means that the different forms of describing, evaluating and rating wines peacefully coexist: points, puffs, medals and descriptive prose. It means that all forms of describing, evaluation and rating wines can peacefully coexist; all the while fostering a greater understanding of why personal preferences can be so different and how to better serve all wine consumers — ultimately, providing them with the right information, recommendations and wines they will love.

In short we would be working together to restore a greater sense of hospitality to the wine community, eliminate the specter of the stereotypical wine snob and offer a greater diversity of effective, personalized ways to guide consumers to wines they will love.

Over the years information about wine, wine consumers and the enjoyment of wine with food has become so twisted and corrupted that it is far too intimidating and daunting for millions of consumers. It's time to re-engage millions of disenfranchised consumers who love wine but feel uncertain about their personal preferences and intimidated by the rules and values of wine experts.

Wine Snob Denial

Most every wine snob I have ever encountered, myself included, is in complete denial that he or she is a snob. Often when someone makes the declaration they are not a snob it is the first indication that they are a snob indeed.

Snob (freedictionary.com):
1. one who tends to patronize, rebuff, or ignore people regarded as social inferiors and imitate, admire, or seek association with people regarded as social superiors.
2. one who affects an offensive air of self-satisfied superiority in matters of taste or intellect.

The following diatribe is taken from the website of a wine snob in denial. Note that the article starts with clear rejection of the notion that the writer is a wine snob followed by the blatant air of rebuff for the most popular wine in America. In turn they forward misinformation like this commonly held theory on why Americans like sweet wines (in spite of the fact that the French historically loved sweet wines).

"I also happen to love wine, and have always been mystified by stuffy wine snobs who talk about fermented grape juice as if it were some celestial beverage that could only be understood by chosen, higher authorities. Just to let you know, I hate most California Cabernets, so if that's your poison, don't expect to see glowing reviews of them here. Too many Americans grow up eating fast food and drinking soda pop. American people expect a beverage to be simple and sweet. Thus wines 'made for made for immature American palates' have sugary fruit, a face-slapping dose of oak, not much acidity nor complexity, and a nonexistent finish."

The wine industry acknowledges that consumers are overwhelmed and confused. One of the on-going calls to action is the need to "educate" wine consumers if we want to continue to expand the enjoyment of wine. This "need for education" is not a good sign for consumer products.

There has been one attempt after another to address consumers overwhelmed by the vast array of wine products. The battle cry of "make wine more simple" and all of the attempts to eliminate the angst around wine continues today, just it has for decades. So why does the problem persist?

Even with the best of intentions, many wine educators and hospitality professionals are running on a bad operating system. If the experts on geography were still operating under the delusion that the world is flat, their attempts to better educate people about geography would be challenging at best. The solution would not be offering more information and more details about a flat world. The solution would require updating an antiquated paradigm. Much of the information and language about wine has been corrupted and distorted over time. More action using bad information will not generate the global explosion of popularity wine is poised to enjoy.

Wine consumers today need a new foundation of information so that they will no longer feel insecure or embarrassed about their wine preferences. It's time to restore the rights of all wine consumers to be able to discover and freely express their preferences, to ask for wines that meet and exceed their expectations. And it's time to train wine professionals who are willing and able to engage with consumers on a personal, respectful level. Better understanding what factors drive personal preferences, attitudes and behaviors would mean wine experts; critics, pundits and professionals, can better communicate with and serve wine consumers.

Balance is in the eye of the beholder

Wine flavor "balance" is subjective. Wine experts often refer to the need for wines to have a certain "balance," and this often depends on the type, variety or the style of any given wine. Yet even the experts frequently disagree on what balance is or is not for specific wine or even in general terms. When it comes to the consumer's ideas of balance, there is no uniform agreement on what constitutes good, or appropriate, balance of flavors.

Here is what might be considered an acceptable definition of "balance" for wine:

> **Balance:** A wine has good balance when the concentration of sweetness, fruit, alcohol, level of tannin and acidity are in harmony.

There is no universal agreement for the constitution of a balanced wine, not among wine experts, not among wine consumers; and certainly the divide between experts and consumers can be enormous.

Some people love wines that are considered very fruity while others who find these same wines unpleasant. There are people who demand high levels of astringent tannins and others who find even slight amount of tannins unpleasant. Acidity in wine can vary a great deal and what is acceptable to one person is very sour to the next. Sweetness is not even mentioned in this definition – basically discounted in general with the modern delusion that dry wine is good wine and sweet wines, for the most part, are unacceptable (see the side bar, "What, me a snob?" for reference).

There is nothing inherently wrong about having an opinion or point of view on what "balance" is or is not in wines. What this book intends to change is the idea that there is a "better" or "best" balance and to remove the judgmentally descriptive language that is often associated with the evaluation or critique of wines. It is also important to recognize that some wines are balanced or exhibit characteristics that may be considered a technical flaw in a wine and that someone else finds wonderfully balanced and delicious. Our perceptions and expectations can vary that greatly.

What is The New Wine Fundamentals definition for balance?

> **Balance** is the subjective interrelationship between sweetness, acidity, alcohol, tannins or bitterness and intensity that provides the overall flavor profile of a wine. Good balance is determined by personal preferences and expectations.

This new definition also leaves a lot of room for general and collective interpretation for different types of wines where balance is a defining trait of the wine. Examples, in relative terms, may range from

- Cabernet Sauvignon (dry, moderate acidity, high alcohol, high tannins/bitterness and high intensity)
- French Chablis (dry, high acidity, moderate alcohol, slight tannin/bitterness and moderate intensity)
- White Zinfandel (moderately sweet, moderate acidity, low alcohol, no tannin/bitterness and light intensity).

Wines that exhibit really wild fluctuations in styles can be duly noted:

- Riesling (from very sweet to dry, typically higher acidity, low to moderately high acidity, sometimes slight bitterness, a light to moderate intensity)
- Red Zinfandel (from moderately sweet to dry, moderate to higher acidity, moderate to very high alcohol, light to high tannins/bitterness and light to high intensity)

This is not very far off from what most wine people would consider a reasonable way to broach the subject of wine balance. Here is where things differ between the New Wine Fundamentals (NWF) tenets and Conventional Wisdoms (CW) descriptions which are verbatim wine descriptions:

- Any given wine is never "too sweet" unless in the context of a personal opinion (or by the general agreement of a collective of experts for a given style of wine).

- NWF: This wine is very sweet, much too sweet for my personal taste, but I know that it would appeal to people who love a wine like this.
- CW: I classify White Zinfandel as a bubble gum or beginner's wine.
- Arguments over alcohol levels would be tempered by an understanding that there is disagreement over what is appropriate and simply good or bad. One could say, "This wine has a lower alcohol that I personally love but I know other people favor a much higher alcohol for this type of wine."

If someone then knows the baseline for a wine variety or type from a given region of production we can have a new conversation – without the unnecessary derogatory remarks or judgments. It also enables a comparative, nonjudgmental description to be used when comparing different wines, helping consumers (and experts) discuss wines without having to prove there is a better or best balance, just different.

Personal opinion could and should be a part of the conversation but should not be as arrogantly judgmental or stigmatizing as it is today. Any personal opinion, professional or otherwise, should be tempered by a better understanding of personal perceptual subjectivity and expectations.

What's your Vinotype?

After nearly 20 years of researching consumer wine preferences, behaviors and attitudes I've identified four distinct groups that I call Vinotypes. A Vinotype is defined by a combination of physiological factors that determine your general level of sensory sensitivity and psychological factors that affect your preferences over time – learning, life experiences combined with cultural, social and peer elements of fashion and propriety.

Vinotype is a direct play on the word "phenotype," which means an organism that exhibits genetic traits that have evolved as it adapts to a different environment. Vinotype captures the essence of the factors that determine wine preferences: the inherent genetic make-up of individuals combined with the adaptations that may occur due to environmental influences — like a normal person going to wine classes, learning the wine lexicon and evolving into a wine geek. This process will be explained in detail, along with instructions to more precisely determine your Vinotype later on in the book, but I thought it important to give a quick introduction to the concept.

Personal wine preferences are determined by a combination of your individual sensory sensitivity quotient (which, by the way, does not render you more or less capable as a wine expert or taster) and the memories and expectations you have developed through learning, life experiences, culture or society and the like.

Vinotypes are defined by the following criteria (and will be covered in greater detail in Chapter 4):

Sensitivity quotient
+ Genre (aspirations, learning)
+ <u>Favorite Wines</u>
= **Your Vinotype**

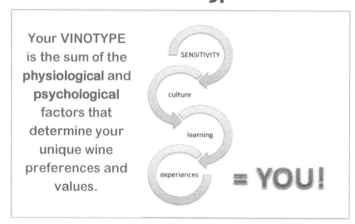

Your VINOTYPE is the sum of the **physiological** and **psychological** factors that determine your unique wine preferences and values.

- **Sensitivity Quotient (SQ):** This is literally your level of perceptive sensitivity that determines the range and intensity of sensations your experience. Individuals range from the most sensitive, (Sweet SQ and Hypersensitive SQ) to people with moderate sensitivity (Sensitive SQ) to those who are able to tolerate intense stimuli (Tolerant SQ) that more sensitive people find irritating or even painful.

- **Genre:** Vinotype genres are categorized by common wine values, the wine-related groups or environments you gravitate toward and also your position on, or aspiration for, wine learning. Your genre is a category defined by things such as your level of enthusiasm, passion, aspirations, learning or expertise. Your genre is often changeable over time – a nanosecond or years. There are genres for wine consumers: the Yum-Yuk crowd (wine is yum or yuk and that's all you want to know and we have a site just for you – www.yumyuk.com) enthusiasts and collectors, and also for wine professionals, such as the critic, sommelier or educators. For the record, if you say, "I don't need no stinking genre – you can't put my preferences in a box," that is actually a genre and there are others like you.

- **Wine preferences:** This is simply the flavor styles or types of wines you know you like and enjoy on a regular basis. If you have no idea at all what wine you might like, we can start at your sensitivity quotient and go from there. If you love everything under the sun, that is certainly not a problem and the sky is the limit. You may also fit into the, "My preferences vary on occasion, mood and the food I am eating." Any and all variations are welcome, as they say, and simply a part of your personal Vinotype.

Here are just a few Vinotype examples to demonstrate how the combination of sensitivity, genre and wines you tend to like on a regular basis work together. Remember the point of this is to improve communications about wine preferences and lead to a way to get personalized, smarter recommendations for anyone who is interested in exploring new wines.

Sweet Wonk who loves Rieslings: "I am learning to enjoy dry wines more and more and am taking wine classes. I do like a lot of wines from around the world but not the really strong red wines. My range of preferences is growing but I still tend to gravitate to the more delicately styled, and especially sweet, wines."

Hypersensitive Enthusiast who loves Cabernet: "I try to go to the wine country whenever I can, started out drinking light whites but have gravitated to red wines – but I like them really smooth and balanced, not the really tannic, high alcohol styles."

Sensitive Professional who loves obscure wines: "I love just about any well-made and honest wine but have a penchant for Grüner Veltliner and Chinon. I'm studying for my sommelier certification and work in a restaurant. I am learning from my mentors and love my career and the interactions I have helping guests explore new and different wines."

Tolerant Connoisseur who love collectable wines: "I love big red wines, the bigger and harder to find, the better. I have a bumper sticker that declares, 'No wimpy wines!' I read the Wine Spectator, follow Robert Parker and the 90 point system is my guide for quality. Did I tell you I have a big wine cellar filled with expensive wines?"

Sensitive Geek that likes wine that make a status statement: "I only drink the finest and most obscure wines in the world and know more about wine than most anyone on the planet. I loathe people who are unsophisticated about wine or the art of pairing wine and food, so I try to educate people with immature palates so they can lead a more fulfilled life."
NOTE: This may seem like an oxymoron but the "sensitive" part of this Vinotype is a sensory phenomenon, not an indication of a sensitivity to other people's feelings. One of the traits of a true geek is they are unaware they have overstepped the boundaries of acceptable social behavior.

The list of Vinotype variations goes on and on, and the variations are limited only by the number of humans on earth! In the world of the New Wine Fundamentals and Vinotypes no one is the "right" type — and no one is wrong.

Time for a new wine conversation

The time is ripe for the critical re-thinking of, and challenge to, many commonly held beliefs or Conventional Wisdoms about wine. It is time to start an empowering and constructive way to communicate about our personal preferences and values. "The times they are a changin'" and it's time to introduce some positive change and start a new era that supplements and balances traditional wine education with greater learning and understanding about wine consumers and why people like what they like.

The <u>disruptive change</u> I am proposing is intended to help provide the foundation for a new conversation for wine. Here are some of the common beginnings to many wine conversations. (The change, as will be seen later, lies in the responses that are provided to these questions.)

- What wine do you like?
- Who can I trust to help me find a wine I will like?
- Will this wine be good with my meal?
- How can I learn more about wine without feeling stupid?
- Why don't I like the wines the experts (or my friends or my spouse) like?

The goal is to have people possess a new confidence about their current wine preferences and make sure if they ask for help, wine and hospitality professionals are prepared to understand and guide them intelligently to other wines they will love – without judgment. Evidence that this mission has been accomplished will come when people can freely and confidently express their wine preferences without judgment, reproach or admonition. We are there when it becomes common knowledge not only that people perceive things differently, but how these differences vary from one person to another and what this means in terms of wine personal preferences.

Another objective is to provide new means to enable people to find the answers for themselves if they choose to go on a wine discovery expedition. Along the way I hope to clear up the myriad of misassumptions, myths, confusing language and contradictory values and information surrounding the enjoyment of wine so we can return to the true history and traditions of wine, to redefine and clarify important words in the wine lexicon used to communicate about wine.

How can we have a breakthrough in taking wine enjoyment to a whole new level? How can new, emerging wine regions and traditional wine regions making wonderful and distinctive wines around the globe all gain greater acceptance and market visibility? The answer is to turn our attention to celebrating the diversity of wine consumers. The wine industry and consumers alike can benefit by creating a new system to leverage this understanding of personal preferences and by learning to match the wines — and wine information — to the people who will enjoy them the most.

Here is how the new conversation might go: "Can I help you find a wine? Do you know your Vinotype? If not I can help you figure it out. It is really easy and then I can make sure to recommend a wine you will really love!"

Many people may say, "Hey, I already ask the right questions and know how to make great choices."

My assertion is that while this is very often, maybe even most often the case, there are so many misconceptions, so many myths and lore that every conversation about wine can benefit by learning about Vinotypes, understanding the factors that provide our personal preferences, revising the entire conversation about wine with food and removing the stigmas associated with certain wines.

The subject of wine has provided me with a seemingly endless realm of joy and exploration. I stand testament to the fact that one can spend their entire lifetime learning about the appreciation, history, sciences and cultural aspects of wine and never fully quench a thirst for knowledge

This is why I've created the New Wine Fundamentals and written this book as the foundation for the New Wine Fundamentals curriculum; it's about more people enjoying a greater diversity of wines from all areas of the world. The information in this book is the preface to the New Wine Fundamentals and intended to become the requisite "Wine 101" for other wine education programs.

Power to the people? Don't consumers already have power? Let me explain. The power I am proposing comes in the form of wine consumers becoming the insiders on the real story about wine. It comes when consumers can demand wine on their own terms, whether it's White Zinfandel, a nice glass of Chardonnay, Pinot Noir, or Chateau Lafite Rothschild, or a glass of something from an obscure grape variety made in an even more obscure region. Power to the people comes when they can do away with "wine and food pairings" and drink the wines they like with the foods they enjoy. It comes with the end of the tyranny of a minority of wine experts that have come to dictate the styles of wine that are deemed most appropriate.

This is also an invitation for wine experts to update their files on the true history and tradition of wine and gastronomy while helping to create a wine industry focused on a higher level of hospitality and service for all wine consumers. It is a "back to the future" opportunity to readdress traditions and customs of European wine cultures and revise some critical errors that are being perpetuated about what people really drank and the role of wine with food.

What's so funny about peace, love and understanding?

Your sensory sensitivity traits show up early in life and have an impact that goes far beyond your wine preferences. Children with attraction to, or avoidance of, certain foods like ketchup tend to be early signs of someone with very high perceptive sensitivity. Included are people who are inclined to like greater amounts of salt, sugar and sourness. These individuals are frequently trying to deal with the acute sensitivity to bitterness, smells and food textures that other children are often oblivious to, or at least find much easier to tolerate. We tend to punish children by telling them they have to sit and finish their foods while the "good" kids can play. Children with sensory sensitivity will often crave strange things like pickles – even like to drink pickle juice! They are also pre-disposed towards hyperactivity and attention deficiency as they perceive, and are distracted by visual, touch and sound sensations most people do not even notice.

Children who are picky eaters or love salt or ketchup tend to have high perceptive sensitivity.

Understanding differences in our sensory sensitivities and perceptive predispositions thus goes far beyond the enjoyment of wine. It offers the opportunity for understanding all sorts of behaviors and attitudes and also avoiding unintentional misassumptions that crop up throughout our lives. We just cannot imagine how different the world we live in can be due to these perceptive differences.

I was talking recently with Olga Karapanou, a smart and passionate young Greek woman and a winemaker for the Sonoma wines for E&J Gallo Winery. Olga holds many certificates for wine knowledge and wine service and is studying to become a Master of Wine. I am proud to be her mentor as she prepares to take the Master of Wine examination. We were discussing my work on differences in perception and she told me the story of her experience growing up with an uncommon condition called synesthesia, a condition in which one type of stimulation evokes the sensation of another, as when hearing a sound produces the sensation of an odor or, in Olga's and her sister's case, visualizing letters or words in color. She did not discover that everyone did not experience this phenomenon until she was 22 years old and it was a tremendous relief to find out synesthesia is known and shared by others and does not mean there is anything "wrong" with her. I asked her to write about her experience:

"As kids, my sister and I used to play the 'color game.' She would ask, 'What color is Saturday?' I would say 'Black.' My sister would say 'No, it is red.' She saw the letters and words in color as well, just not the same colors. We would frequently argue about the color game and these arguments would escalate until they became a fight.

"It wasn't until I was 22 years old when I discovered the color game had a name, synesthesia, and both my sister and I had this neurological condition.

"My discovery that I was different began at the age of 20. By that time I had realized that not everybody sees the same colors with the same words. I asked my best friend, 'What color do you see for the word Monday? She replied back 'What do you mean? Monday cannot have a color.' So while I was explaining what I meant, I realized she had no idea what I was talking about. My sister and I started asking other people and the response was the same. We started realizing that the colored letters and words was our own little world – we could not tell if there was something wrong or if we just invented it.

"Research we did at that time was unfruitful, so we decided to just quietly live with it – maybe afraid of what we would discover? One day two years later my best friend sent me an email saying: 'Hi, I have a gift for you' and below was a link to the synesthesia website being forwarded as a chain email. It was almost a relief. Out of all the things that could have happened this was definitely a huge relief for us and the most fun option.

Sometimes our perceptive differences are very minor and sometimes they are enormous. I firmly believe the world would be a better place in so many ways if all humans had a better understanding of the factors behind why we like what we like, why we believe what we believe and why we perceive the universe individually, and uniquely, the way we do. Children grow up being punished for having acute perceptive sensitivity — they are easily distracted, can't sit still and have picky or weird food habits. We admonish them and unintentionally begin the stigmatization with the groupthink, "You sit at the table and finish your vegetable. The other kids can all go out and play. Why can't you be a good child and be more like them?" Back to wine, the people who typically have the greatest sensory acuity are stigmatized and persecuted just as they were from a young age.

My advice is that we also learn to recognize and understand perceptive sensitivity traits in other people. If you have a child (or a spouse, significant other or friend) that you may have complained to, or even punished, because he or she loves salt, is very picky and can't eat anything unless it is covered in ketchup, go apologize to them. Tell him or her you are sorry that you now have learned and understand what their world must be like. Offer to help them find the new ways to deal with the bitterness in food, scratchy clothes and frequent distractions that they experience due to their perceptive sensitivity. Then start to explore ways to help them develop a healthy attitude for trying new things and allowing decisions what is good or not while directing them to a diet that is nutritious and healthy.

CLOSE-UP OF THE TIP OF A TONGUE SHOWING AN ABUNDANCE OF TASTE PAPILLAE

This is a close-up of the surface of the tongue of a hypersensitive taster.

The large rounded bumps are the fungiform papillae, which house the taste buds. The black dots on the top surface of the bumps are the taste pores, entryways to the taste buds.

Photograph by Tim Hanni

And be wary of thinking that what you are doing and saying to protect a child means what you intend for it to mean. For example, when my hypersensitive, ADHD, brilliant son, Landen, was very young he loved salt so much he put it in his chocolate milk. His greatest gastronomic discovery was that the top of the salt shaker could be unscrewed and provide unfettered access to the seasoning. I remember when it first happened and he look up at me, shaker in one and the top in the other, with a wide-eyed and joyful expression of surprise as if he hit the mother lode or just gotten a pony for Christmas.

Wanting to address his picky-eater issues I would set him on the counter while I cooked and give him opened jars of herbs and spices to smell. Once, while not paying close enough attention, I heard him exclaim, "uh oh" and turned around to find he had tilted back his head and poured cayenne pepper down his nostrils. Not good. I turned him upside down and flushed out his nasal passages. Luckily it did not require a trip to the emergency room but it was a close call. To this day he hates anything peppery.

That being said, he is gastronomically adventurous overall. When he was about 4 years old I taught him how to surreptitiously spit out food he did not like. To engender a spirit of trying new things he always had permission to try something and then discretely eject the food into a napkin if he did not like the taste or texture in any way. You cannot imagine the difference this can make, and to this day he will at least try just about anything.

The other thing to keep in mind is that the message we think we might be sending can be completely misconstrued. Sitting up on the counter from an early age it was my duty to warn him that the stove was hot – don't touch! I would pretend to touch the stove and burn myself saying, "Ow, the stove is hot – don't touch it!"

Years later a guest at a dinner party we were having asked Landen, "Your dad is a really good cook, isn't he?"

Landen's answer? Having seen me" burn" myself so many times to demonstrate the need for safety, he declared, "Naw, my dad is a really stupid cook. He keeps burning himself on the stove over and over."

The point of this "new conversation" is to understand and accommodate our palatal and preferential differences and to assure that we are all on the same page with the conversations we are having. Make sure that the points we are making in wine education are forwarding the information we are trying to convey. If you are a wine educator and say something to the effect, "trust your own palate," do not turn around and contradict yourself as we typically do in wine education.

"Did you like the wine dinner you went to last week?" someone may ask.

"Naw – it was OK but they took away my favorite wine as soon as the course it was supposed to 'match' with and the rest of the wines for the night were not at all to my taste."

Wine can be an object of zealous passion and discussion but let's not overlook the value of equally regarding wine as wine as a simple and delicious beverage to be enjoyed on any person's terms.

Time for a new wine and food conversation

I am convinced that almost all wine and food matching occurs primarily in the fertile imagination of usually well-meaning and earnest wine and food enthusiasts and professionals.

This is not to say that people do not experience what they would describe as good or bad experiences with combinations of wine with food. This point is that it is subjective. When an expert is asked to recommend a wine and food "match" they conjure up the dish ingredients and then mental list of metaphorical wine descriptors that fit then come up with their choice. The process is not based on any reality, just our fertile imagination and personal wine favorites. Note there is nothing wrong with this: Just what the heck is a poor consumer supposed to do if they do not like the style of wine recommended with a dish or don't buy into the wine and food matching ritual?

Match the wine to the diner, not the dinner

Here is a quick look at what is to come later in the book in Chapter 7: Wine and Food.

1. Always choose a wine in the realm of a something you would enjoy in the first place. If you hate high alcohol Zinfandel, White Zinfandel, Pinot Grigio, Cabernet Sauvignon or whatever, it probably will suck with your food (or without).

2. The more emotionally you are tied to wine and food matching, the more likely the imaginary wine and food matches you conjure up will work together. This is a psychological phenomenon and self-fulfilling prophecy of wine and food matching, not an experiential reality.

3. The more Hypersensitive you are the more likely you are to get a bitter reaction from strong wines (high extract, higher alcohol) with foods with lots of umami. A tiny addition of lemon and salt will cure most negative reactions but you don't tend to favor huge reds or oaky whites in the first place; stick to the wines you love the most.

4. The more Tolerant your sensory sensitivity, the more you will love big, extracted reds with whatever the hell you are eating. You are less likely to get any bitter reactions that other people complain about. You just want big, red wines and you know who you are! A delicate Riesling with sushi is not in the cards for you.

5. If you love the metaphorical matching of heavy wines with heavy foods, searching for that orgasmic synergy when the wine and food elevate the experience to a whole new level; complement and contrast the flavors and textures, keep on doing that. Just understand that the experience is personal, subjective and mostly all in your head!

It is time that to radically address the role of enjoying wine and food together. Things are completely out of control and the misinformation, false premises and misunderstandings are at an all-time high. If you are willing to play along with me, try this bit of homework I assign when I conduct wine and food workshops:

Consciously try to order the wrong wine and food combinations.

For many years I have been making it a point to order the wrong wine with a dish, or vice-versa, whenever I have the opportunity and encourage others to do the same. When I have guests at my house for a meal we make this a game. If I am dining out I will ask, "What wine would be terrible with this dish?" and then order a glass. I find virtually identical success trying the wrong combinations versus trying to find the "right" matches. The rule is that the wine needs to be something that you would like on its own flavor merit. Of course wine you hate will in all likeliness be horrible regardless of the food.

Try a Cabernet Sauvignon with your Sushi (if you love Cabernet Sauvignon). Have your favorite Chardonnay with a steak. You will find the people who passionately love Pinot Noir will find a good Pinot Noir delicious with all sorts of combinations. The Sauvignon Blanc aficionados will often be delighted to see how great their favorite wines blend with lamb, steak and about anything you can come up with. Do you really love sweet wines? Order a sweet Riesling, Moscato or White Zinfandel with your pasta, salad, roast beef or fish.

We make it out that there is some specter of "wine and food disasters" looming that can befall the poor, unsuspecting consumer if they make the mistake of ordering or serving the wrong wine with the wrong food. This is in fact a very rare occurrence and the exercise of trying bad matches will demonstrate the fallacy of this thinking in a heartbeat.

Go ahead — spend a week, a month or the rest of your life, diligently trying the wrong wine with your food, or vice-versa. You will be surprised at the success you and your guests will have finding delicious matches you never imagined.

Here is some data about wine and food matching from a study conducted by Dr. Virginia Utermohlen MD, my research colleague and mentor, and me in 2010. You will find more details from our study in Appendix 2: Vinotype facts and figures.

The respondents were primarily core, everyday wine drinkers. It is obvious people love the idea of matching wine and food and would like to learn more, but very few love the idea or feel confident about their ability or consider wine and food matching "very important." It is interesting to note the "very important" category is dominated by Sweet Vinotypes, the people that are told the wines they like do not go well with most foods!

Percent of each Vinotype sensitivity group for the following attitudes towards wine and food pairing:

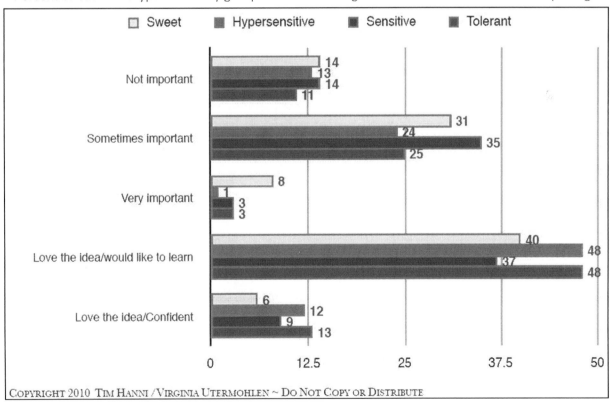

Chapter 1 Q&A

Question: What do other wine experts think of your concepts?

Answer: It ranges from agreement and active participation in the continued research and forwarding of the concepts all the way to abject hatred and open hostility. The great news is the tide is turning toward more of the latter and less of the former!

Here is an excerpt from British Master of Wine Jancis Robinson's Purple Pages blog after I, along with several of my mentors from the sensory sciences field, provided a presentation to 250 experts from around the world at the Masters of Wine International Symposium in July 2006, demonstrating the extreme variations in sensory sensitivity and perception from one person to the next:

Shocks for the Masters of Wine in Napa...
Jancis Robinson MW, OBE

Tim Hanni MW organised this session [at the 2006 Institute of Masters of Wine International Symposium] and made us all do the 'PROP' test whereby we put bit of paper soaked in a key compound [6-n-propylthiouracil] identified as a taster marker to see which of us were hypo-tasters, normal tasters and hyper-tasters according to whether it tasted of nothing, slightly bitter or unbearably bitter respectively. I had never done this test but hoped I was, like most of the population, a normal taster as this would be most useful professionally. I discovered I am a hyper-taster ('supertaster' is a rather misleading alternative term) which may explain why I go for more subtle flavours than those who are, for instance, hypo-tasters who need lots of everything to make an impression.

The main point of the session was to suggest that there are all sorts of populations of people who will perceive wine differently, thanks to our own sensitivities and preferences, and that the wine business is crazy to act as though one message, or even one sort of wine, suits all.

Source: Jancis Robinson MW, OBE, the Purple Pages, JancisRobinson.com, July 2006

Question: How do I know that your information is any different or better than another wine expert's opinions, recommendations or point of view?

Answer: Only time, discussion and careful examination of the evidence I present will determine whether this information is any more, or less, valid than the prevailing information on wine preferences and the enjoyment of wine with food.

Question: Are you inferring that wine experts are delusional?

Answer: Yes, but I am inferring all humans are delusional as well. Being delusional is a part of being human and nobody is exempt.

Question: What has been your biggest challenge in trying to establish your ideas and generate the change you are asking for?

Answer: The biggest challenge has been creating what is called "stickiness" – the ability to have the change implemented and then stick. This is part of what I discovered when I started learning about disruptive change and collective delusions. It is much easier to revert back to the Conventional Wisdoms of wine than to try to initiate change and different ways of thinking. We tend to get sucked back into the delusions! This will provide a great segue to the next chapter on paradigms and disruptive change. This is a quote from Tim Starkey who you will hear more from in the next chapter:

"There is always an 'old guard' that will fight against change and if necessary persecute the agents of change in order to hold on to the familiar (or to the personal advantages they derive from the existing frame)."

Notes: _____

_____

_____

_____

_____

_____

_____

_____

_____

_____

_____

_____

_____

_____

_____

_____

_____

_____

_____

_____

Chapter 2: The World Is Flat and Other Delusions

In ancient times, people believed the world was flat. This was not considered speculation but common knowledge. At the time it seemed plausible enough. How did people know? Just ask the experts — the map makers. Yep, the world is flat; just look at the evidence. Here is a map and picture of how it looked according to

1922 illustration from the Swedish & Norwegian magazine Allers Familj-Journal

the experts of the era. Not only that, there were dire warnings of what might befall those impertinent souls who did not heed the warning from those who were knowledgeable about such things! Those failing to adhere to the conventions of the prevailing collective wisdoms could fall over the edge of the world or be devoured by sea serpents.

This kind of widely held misconception is a classic collective delusion. If the experts on geography were still operating under the delusion that the world is flat, their attempts to better educate people about geography would be challenging at best. The solution would not be offering more information and more details about a flat world. The solution would require updating antiquated paradigms.

Paradigms and resistance to change

Following is an article I find particularly insightful regarding change and the very natural tendency to resist new ways of thinking, technology or paradigms. Resistance to change runs the gamut from music to religions to governments to literature to computer operating systems to ways to raise our children to television programming to new shoes.

Paradigm Shifts & the History of Science

Timothy W. Starkey, Ph.D., ABAP

- You might be wondering why, when science is finding so many better ways of doing things, we don't just go ahead and do them. Old paradigms die hard... they (we) resist changing the way we see things... we tend to prefer the older, more comfortable ways of looking at our world. We prefer to focus on the picture "within the frame" and not the frame itself. **There is always an "old guard" that will fight against change and if necessary persecute the agents of change in order to hold on to the familiar (or to the personal advantages they derive from the existing frame).**
- Some theorists believe that all major scientific discoveries are preceded by a paradigm shift (a monumental change in theory or knowledge that forces change in a scientific discipline).
- Almost every significant breakthrough in science is preceded by a break with tradition (e.g. the old or previous paradigm).
- Throughout history, scientific breakthroughs have been ridiculed at the time and the scientists who made them have been persecuted and sometimes even threatened with execution (e.g. being burned at the stake during the Inquisition)
- For example, after 1,500 years of geocentric paradigm, a scientist named Copernicus (early 1500s) dared to say that the earth revolved around the sun (heliocentric paradigm). This was considered heresy and Copernicus was threatened with death unless he recanted (which he did) because it contradicted the Bible's teaching that the earth is the center of the universe.

The inmates are running the asylum

I have accused the wine community of being insane and said that one of the symptoms of insanity is the manifestation of delusions; this is because closely held tenets about wine, wine consumers, the enjoyment of wine with food and even a lot of the supposed history and traditions of wine are nothing more than collective delusions with little or no basis in reality.

What are some of the more prevalent collective delusions about wine? Here is a short — and incomplete — list to kick things off:

- Dry wine is good wine and sweet wine is for novices.
- You cannot "taste" wine when you have a cold.
- It is important to pay attention to matching your wine and food.
- Americans grew up drinking soda pop and that is why they like sweet wines.

- Women are better tasters.
- Consumers inevitably turn to dry wines as their palates mature.
- If a wine comes from the same place as the food they will be a better match.
- More sensitive tasters have better palates for wine tasting.
- Red wine goes with red meat (or white wine goes with fish).
- Wine should never be mixed with other ingredients.
- You can taste the soil in some wines.
- Wine experts are more objective about wine.
- People who put salt on their food before tasting it have no taste buds.
- Heavy wine is best with heavy food, like the combination of steak and red wine or a sturdy white wine with grilled sea serpent.

Anatomy of a collective delusion

I used to teach the phenomenon of the tongue/taste map to all of my wine classes. This was in spite of the fact that I, like the author of the article below, did not perceive the tastes in the appropriate places. I just figured there was something wrong with me or my palate. Yet up went the slide with the commentary, "You taste sweet on the tip of your tongue, salty on the sides, sour a bit back and bitter on the back of your tongue." Here is an update from a very credible source, shortened to focus on the significant points, but this is a perfect example of a challenge correcting a persistent collective delusion.

The Tongue Map: Tasteless Myth Debunked

Christopher Wanjek

Date: 29 August 2006

The notion that the tongue is mapped into four areas—sweet, sour, salty and bitter—is wrong. There are five basic tastes identified so far, and the entire tongue can sense all of these tastes more or less equally...

You might know the map: The taste buds for "sweet" are on the tip of the tongue; the "salt" taste buds are on either side of the front of the tongue; "sour" taste buds are behind this; and "bitter" taste buds are way in the back. Wineglasses are said to cater to this arrangement.

The tongue map is easy enough to prove wrong at home. Place salt on the tip of your tongue. You'll taste salt. For reasons unknown, scientists never bothered to dispute this inconvenient truth.

The map has frustrated many a grade-schooler, including me, who couldn't get the experiment right in science class. I failed for insisting I could taste sugar in the back of my tongue.

In fact, there's more to taste than sweet, sour, salty and bitter. Most scientists agree that there's a fifth distinct taste, called umami, identified by a Japanese scientist named Kikunae Ikeda in the early 1900s (and ignored by the West for most of the twentieth century). This is the taste of glutamate. It is common in Japanese foods, particularly kombu, a type of sea vegetable similar to kelp, and in bacon and monosodium glutamate (MSG), which Ikeda isolated and patented. There's considerable debate about the existence of a sixth taste receptor for fat, too.

…There were variations in sensitivity to the four basic tastes around the tongue. (Wineglass makers rejoiced.) But the variations were small and insignificant. (Wineglass makers ignored this part.) Collings found that all tastes can be detected anywhere there are taste receptors—around the tongue, on the soft palate at back roof of the mouth, and even in the epiglottis, the flap that blocks food from the windpipe…

… Why textbooks continue to print the tongue map is the real mystery now.

Source: http://www.livescience.com/7113-tongue-map-tasteless-myth-debunked.html

Does the concept "collective delusion" mean anythin' to ya?

Let's examine the pervasive and persistent collective delusion that heavy foods, like grilled meats and stews are best with heavy wines. "Heavy wine" is a metaphorical description often applied to intensely flavored, dry red wines. A wine like White Zinfandel would be considered a light wine and certainly is considered by wine insiders as an inappropriate choice of wine to "go with" a substantial dish like a steak.

But did you know that in truth White Zinfandel weighs more — is, in fact, heavier than the most intensely dark and tannic Cabernet Sauvignon? White Zinfandel has a greater specific gravity, because it has more sugar and less alcohol than Cabernet Sauvignon. Therefore it weighs more or is, by common definition, heavier than a typical Cabernet Sauvignon.

This is simply one of the most prevalent of the many, many collective delusions around wine. Not only is the misuse of the word "heavy" part of the delusion, the whole idea that red wine is "better" because of the steak, that it is

In spite of conventional wisdoms, White Zinfandel is in fact "heavier" (weighs more) than Cabernet Sauvignon

"traditional" to serve red wine with red meat are ripe for a little disruptive clarification, which we will get to in the chapter on Food and Wine Un-Pairings.

Let's try another exercise. How many collective delusions can you spot in the following story:

The woman in the tasting room at Robert Mondavi Winery was making her first visit to the Napa Valley. "So far, everything has been very nice," she told the associate at the counter. "But" — she hesitated here and looked apologetic — "my husband said you have a wine here that I might like. It is — I think he said it is a sweet merlot?"

She was, in fact, asking about the Mondavi Moscato d'Oro, a luscious, golden-hued wine with 9 percent residual sugar.

"I do like sweet wines," she admitted self-consciously as he opened a bottle to pour her a taste. "I know that as I get better at drinking wine, I'll like dryer wines. I'm working on it. I don't like wines as sweet as I used to."

Then she tasted the Moscato d'Oro. "Oh," she sighed contentedly. "I like this."

Clearly she had accepted the prevailing attitudes about sweet wines and people who like them. Imagine her surprise, in learning that Moscato d'Oro is one of the most popular wines at Mondavi, the top request for visitors. "Robert Mondavi used to freeze it in the summer and make slushies out of it," the winery guide pointed out. She looked astonished but encouraged: If the great Robert Mondavi liked it, then it must be OK for her to like it too.

Whether or not she goes on to teach herself to prefer dry wines, or she follows her own inclination to ask for sweet wines, I hope it was, for her, a disruption in a collective delusion that was getting in the way of her enjoyment of wine.

What if we could replace "You can't possibly have that Moscato with your steak," with, "Terrific – that gives me a great clue as to what you love and I have just the wine for you if you are interested trying something new and different."

This does not mean that anyone who loves an intense red wine is in any way discouraged from ordering what they love the most. In keeping with the true traditions of wine and food, this would mean it is entirely appropriate to simultaneously offer an intense, concentrated and tannic red wine for anyone who would prefer. Or anything in between the two extremes, "What do you like — dry or sweet, red or white, still or sparkling?"

There is no Santa Claus

Remember that collective delusions are often simple, everyday beliefs. Where there are collective delusions there is the potential for a phenomenon known as disruptive change. Disruptive change occurs when new evidence or collective behaviors are introduced changing or collapsing a collective delusion or altering a groupthink.

Santa Claus is a collective delusion that seems like reality to children. Most parents don't think twice about perpetuating the myth so the concept also fits the definition of groupthink: a Collective Wisdom that most everyone really knows is not true but it is a part of a societal or cultural norm. Many common rituals and beliefs fall under the heading of a groupthink. For example, most people in the US and many "western" cultures participate in propagation of the Santa Claus deception without cause or concern. Disruptive change occurs when you introduce evidence that that collapses a collective delusion to someone who really believed the deception was real.

For my son Landen this happened when he was eight years old. My wife, Kate, and I had an agreement with Landen, that if there was something he really, really wanted to know the truth about he could ask, "OK, give it to me straight," and we would tell him, as best as we knew, the truth (even if that was that we didn't know, like when he asked what happened at the end of life). We found this approach opened up all sorts of great dialogue and discussions between a child and his parents.

One evening, when, as I was putting him to bed just before Christmas, he asked the inevitable. "Dad, give it to me straight, is there really a Santa Claus?"

"Do you really want to know the truth?" I asked.

"Yep. I want to know," he said.

"You are really, really sure?"

"Yes, I really want to know the truth," he insisted.

"Collective Delusions" and "Groupthink"

Collective: of or characteristic of a group of individuals taken together

Delusion: a mistaken or misleading opinion, idea, belief

Collective Delusion: a mistaken or misleading opinion, idea or belief of a group of individuals.

An important element of a collective delusion is exhibited in a group dynamic that is called "groupthink."

Groupthink is defined in Merriam-Webster's dictionary as "a pattern of thought characterized by self-deception, forced manufacture of consent, and conformity to group values and ethics."

Suffice to say that a lot of the beliefs, opinions and ideas of the wine collective and wine industry fall into the realm of collective delusions and groupthink.

NOTE: Collective delusions and groupthink are a normal part of the human experience. They are NOT necessarily good, bad or evil. These are simply ways in which we rationalize and describe our existence and try our best to share experiences.

"All right then, I am sorry to inform you that he is all made up," I admitted. "There is no Santa Clause,"

"I knew it!" was his response. "I knew you were lying to me! My friend Jason said there was no Santa. I believed you all along." His reaction was pretty much along the lines of the bottom-row middle frame in the picture on the next page. Sternly upset but not really angry, "curt without being obsequious" (the favorite wine description of Garland Duke, my good friend and tasting partner, may he rest in peace).

Here are a number of possible reactions people might have in relation to "disruptive change" and the collapse of a collective delusion. You can simply imagine these reactions superimposed on various wine writers, experts and critics in reaction to this book:

This was Landen's moment of disruptive change. He had heard rumors that there was no Santa Claus but wanted to find out from a more reliable source. "Why do people make things up like this?" he asked.

This turned into a long and wonderful conversation about religion, controlling children through long and isolated winters, hope and expectations. It is amazing what comes up when you collapse a delusion and discuss why it exists in the first place. People often fear that if we assail a long-held convention, some dire consequence will occur. That is usually just another delusion popping up.

It has been much like this scenario in my curious questioning about wine and wine preferences. Encountering nagging questions or vague ideas that something is not quite right, I set out to see if there is another way of looking at things. I have been working with sensory scientists, researchers and specialists for nearly 20 years now, and for the most part researchers with little or nothing to do with wine, identifying collective delusions and turning to more reliable sources to find the best and most accurate information.

A delusion can be defined as having the following qualities:

- Certainty: A delusion is held with absolute conviction that it really, really is true.
- Incorrigibility: A delusion is not changeable by compelling argument or proof to the contrary. It's not empirically proven or provable. "Just ask anyone," or, "I experienced it myself so it must be real" is usually the response to "How do you know?"
- Impossibility or falsity of content: A delusion is indeed implausible, bizarre or patently untrue.

To qualify as a collective delusion, versus a plain-old delusion, two or more people must share the delusion.

Collective delusions are also "individually rationalized," meaning that each person in the collective has an impetus to keep the delusion alive. It may be as simple as wanting to appear to be part of the in-crowd or just going with the flow. It could be that an individual has something at stake professionally and the delusion provides something of value. People who have invested a lot of time and effort in becoming experts in a subject are unlikely to want to concede that the paradigm was flawed. The people who offer the greatest resistance to disruptive change are those who are in a position of

Lofty aspirations, oenobabble and a flock of geeks

God had a way to deal with overzealous geeks: There were some people who decided to build a city with a lofty tower to get closer to God. They apparently set their aspirational sites too high and were struck down and rendered incapable of communicating. According to sources close to God at the time, he said, "Come, let us go down and confound their speech."

This same phenomenon often affects people who aspire to wine-godliness.

Wine geeks are known to babble on about wine in a manner that is virtually unintelligible to normal people. (The word babble means to utter a meaningless confusion of words or sounds and comes from the Hebrew *babhel*.)

Thus I offer the formal definition for Oenobabble: To utter a meaningless confusion of words or sounds pertaining to wine (Greek *oinos*, wine) + Hebrew *babhel*, meaningless words.

Another relevant concept is the Ivory Tower syndrome. This may or may not be related to the tower of Babel but this seems like a good place to interject the idea. An Ivory Tower is considered a place of attitude or retreat, especially a preoccupation with lofty, remote, or intellectual considerations rather than everyday life. People who speak oenobabble tend to convene in Ivory Towers.

What do you call a bunch of wine enthusiasts with lofty aspirations? A flock of geeks. If they are on the ground I guess they are a gaggle of geeks.

power or authority that may be compromised if the collective delusion is exposed.

Collective delusions are also noted to be "mutually assured," meaning the concept is prevalent, widely held as true. This ensures that the delusion persists over time. People may lean towards a disruptive view of the belief but are inevitably pulled back into the delusion by the mutually-assured dynamic. It can take a very, very long time, and much empirical evidence to change a collective delusion. Map makers did not want to become globe-makers – plus how stupid would they look after telling everyone that the world was flat for so long. I suspect they would say, "Let's kill this 'world is round' crap or we will all look like idiots" at map-making conventions in the world-is-flat days.

A new "operating system" for wine

The wine industry spends an inordinate amount of focus, time, effort and money to "educate" consumers about wine. Now, don't jump to the conclusion that I am saying wine education is not important or should go away. What I am saying is that in many industries, such as electronics, the need to educate potential product users can be a sign of a real problem. Sure, people need to know how to use products and some people may want to learn all about the inner workings of a device, but a need to "educate" people can also point to problems with ease of use, and thus impact the market potential of a product.

Take computing as an example. Before the advent of the graphic user interface, or GUI (pronounced "gooey") technology, anyone who wanted to compute was required to learn long strings of code to perform simple tasks.

For example, if you wanted to open a folder using DOS commands here are the "simple" instructions you would need to follow:

In your command prompt, for example C:\, you can use the DIR command to view the contents of a folder. This command has several parameters, or options, you can employ. You can type "DIR /S" and hit enter, this will show the entire contents of the drive your command prompt shows, and includes all contents of all subdirectories as well. This gives you a lot of data, if you do it on your C drive especially! so you probably want to use the pause option as well. To do this, you would type "DIR /S /P" which will now span all subfolders and pause every 25 lines, you hit any key to proceed to the next screen. If you would like to learn more about the DIR command, you hit "DIR /?" and it will display all the different options you can use with this command. To change to another folder, to make your prompt show that you are in another directory, you use the CD command, For example type in "CD \WINDOWS" to Change Directory to the Windows folder in the C drive. You use the MD command to Make Directory, this will create a folder INSIDE THE LOCATION DISPLAYED IN YOUR PROMPT. So if your prompt says "C:\Windows\>" and you type in "MD Stuff" you will create a folder called Stuff inside the Windows folder on your C drive.

Whew. How many people would follow this to the end of the instructions let alone get excited about learning to use a computer?

GUI technology was created to make interface is a little easier and allow almost anyone to be able to compute simply:

> Point your mouse at the little picture of the folder you want to open and click the little button thingie twice on the folder picture. To open the program or document you want inside the folder click on the little picture of the document with the name you want.

Look at me! I am computing!

I am old enough to know how the computing experts reacted to the disruptive innovation of icons, mice and the possibility for easier computing for all. There was resistance from the people who had invested the time and effort to learn the language, codes and protocols necessary to compute with these mysterious systems. The ability to compute meant power and those who held the keys were reluctant to turn computing over to the masses. "This dumbs down computing," was often the rationale provided from the computing insiders. "We don't want everyone to be able to compute – that would be crazy!" Yeah, right.

Look at what has happened to computing since then. Within 50 feet of me are at least 10 devices that incorporate the elements of the transformational technology that experts resisted fewer than 40 years ago. The GUI interface fits the definition for "disruptive innovation." It offered many advantages to the prevailing technology and was simple and easy to use. I contend that it is time that this kind of transformation, or disruptive innovation, takes place with wine.

The real solution for expanding the enjoyment of wine is introducing a new operating system and consumer interface. It will require a deeper understanding of the people who consume the product, not a deeper knowledge of the product itself. It must be simple and easy to use but not "dumb down" the subject for anyone who cares to deepen their understanding and knowledge on the subject.

I suspect that the wine wonks who are reading this book are already squirming. "Oh no, we have to ensure that the wine pairs properly with the food," is racing through your minds. Or: "Wine anarchy is no solution — we have to educate consumers and guide them, illuminate them so they can distinguish quality and appreciate the intricacies, propriety and aesthetics of wine."

I say, maybe not. Maybe we are missing something really important, something really big. Maybe there is a better way to approach making wine more fun, less pretentious and eminently more enjoyable for more people.

In short, it is time for more than a little disruptive innovation in the world of wine.

The once and would be of wine

Once upon a time wine was one of the only reliably safe beverages to drink for millions of people. It was an indispensable staple of the table to be shared by families and communities.

Grapes are the one fruit that "goes bad" really well! Early in my wine career I read a description of wine that went something like, "In its simplest form wine is just grape juice that has not finished going bad." I love that quote! But seriously, grapes have everything needed to turn into wine provided the grapes are ripe and are a reasonably good variety suited to "positive spoilage." All you need is some grapes and a container to put them in and nature, along with a lot of luck, will do the rest.

Natural enzymatic fermentation starts the process and bursts the grapes (called carbonic maceration), exposing the juice to the yeasts that are naturally found on the waxy cuticle of the skin. Yeast fermentation takes over with carbon dioxide emitted to prevent oxidation, the tannins in the skins and stems provide more antioxidant protection and also help clarify the wine and voilà — you are a vintner!

I like to imagine a tribe of early humans coming across wild vines, heavily laden with ripe grapes, and picking as much of the crop as they could to carry back to their cave. I see them putting the grapes into a natural indentation in a rock, a natural bowl if you will, and then getting called away to chase down a mastodon that had been spied nearby. There is a call to arms and the entire clan takes off to capture the beast.

After possibly weeks of tracking and a monumental battle, the triumphant hunters return with their trophy. Time for a celebration and some mastodon on the barbecue! They start the fire and start butchering the mastodon. Someone decides some nice grapes would make a lovely addition to the menu. Wait a minute – we have some in the cave! When they look into the rock indentation where they had left the fresh grapes, they find they are all mushed and have completely transformed. "Ugh, grapes gone bad," they may have declared.

Then one of them may have put a cupped hand into the mush only to find the juice was relatively bright and clear and this juice was not at all objectionable to the taste. In fact, the juice is pretty dang good.

As they drink and share this new beverage they start to dance, snuggle and act a bit crazy.

What wine goes with wooly mammoth?

"This must be the beverage of the gods!" they decide. "And do you notice how well this traditional local variety pairs with the local cuisine? I give it 92 points, finding the flavor rich and elegant. This wine is curt without being fawning or obsequious…" OK, I am getting carried away.

What is wine to you? Is it a simple beverage to enjoy with relish or does it represent a wonderful journey of exploration and discovery? Is it a cherished acquisition to be sought and collected?

Wine can be any of the above. In this new paradigm for wine, the consumer comes first, and anyone who interfaces with consumers, in stores, wine classes, online and in restaurants, recognizes and understands why you like what you like. It is a paradigm where wine experts can provide you with recommendations for wonderful wines to explore and discover that are custom-tailored to your unique sensory physiology and expectations. Sweet or dry, delicate or intense, pink, white or red, with or without bubbles. Nice and yummy or 95 points and highly extracted. "Want to know more about this wine? Well, let me tell you…"

Giving power to the people creates wine community that can understand, embrace and cultivate anyone who cares to enjoy a nice glass of wine. Where would we be today if someone hadn't taken the risk to propose a different way of looking at how computers work and finding a way to make computing and easy for everyone?

And please don't get me wrong. I love wine education. I am, in fact, a certified wine educator credentialed by the society of Wine Educators. I love wine. I was also guilty, at one time, of being one of the stuffy wine snobs who talked about fermented grape juice as if it were some celestial beverage that could only be understood by chosen, higher authorities. But I am getting over that! And I've gone through every phase of a wine lover on my own journey to where I am today, losing my delusions along the way.

Chapter 2 Q&A

Question: So do you think you are exempt from collective delusions?

Answer: No way. I have perpetuated my fair share and even probably invented a few of my own. Collective delusions are all around us and not necessarily bad unless they get in the way of progress. Remember my background is deeply rooted in the Conventional Wisdoms and there are many that will remain for a long time.

Question: You seem to have been talking about these concepts and this change for a long time. What is different now?

Answer: Many of the disparate areas of my research have finally been completed. My epiphanies occurred over a period of decades. What I am proposing seems to many people like a sudden and massive shift but in truth end goal of simplifying things for consumers became more complex, and took much more time, than I ever imagined! Every time I unlocked a new door to look behind for information I would find 5 new doors that I had not even considered.

Question: So you are asking everyone to abandon current wine education and throw out the old wine books?

Answer: Not at all. These concepts could comprise the "new wine 101," if you will, for anyone who is interested in learning more about wine. First, learn about the basics of perceptive individuality, your personal preferences and Vinotype. Gain a greater awareness of the differences between you and other Vinotypes. THEN get on with the traditional wine education and follow your personal preferences, interests and passions. If anything needs to be thrown out it is the stigmas associated with certain wines and the stigmas associated with people who like those wines and the attitudes that keep the stereotypical association between wine, elitism and arrogance alive.

Notes: _____

_____

_____

_____

_____

_____

_____

_____

_____

_____

_____

_____

_____

_____

_____

_____

_____

_____

Chapter 3: A Funny Thing Happened on my Way to the Master of Wine Examination

Many people who criticize my work (and believe me there are a bunch of them), argue that my beliefs and approach to wine, and wine with food, represent a break with tradition, but it is, in fact, a return to classic traditions. The principles of the New Wine Fundamentals, particularly the right to personal choice and the tenets of Flavor Balancing as compared to food and wine pairings, have been around for a long time and started to become lost about the time of World War II.

I come from a classical, traditional background with wine and food. A professional chef by training, I enjoyed working for many wonderful years as a wine retailer, conducting a lot of business in rare wine acquisition, sales and consumption. I have been learning and teaching about wines for more than 45 years. Working in the Napa Valley in the 1980s, I had gained international acclaim as a "wine and food matching guru." My close friend Joel Butler and I were the first Americans to earn the credential Master of Wine.

I extolled the importance of serving the precise wine with the right dish in the pursuit of the magical synergies that are the Holy Grail of pairing wine and food. But the more I learned about wine, the more I noticed the differences of opinion between people, everyday consumers and experts alike, about how they described and evaluated wines and combinations of wines with food. It often seemed as if they were not even on the same planet in terms of how they described flavors or wine and food combinations. Different people, having the exact same wine or wine with food, frequently would come to opposite opinions. As I became determined to learn more about this, I was faced with more and more evidence that maybe these tenets and truths were not all they were cracked up to be. The changes in my attitudes about wine, and wine with food, were punctuated by numerous epiphanies that were more like being thunderstruck.

A geek is born

For all intent and purpose, I was a wine geek from the get-go. I was a teenager in the mid-'60s, when I discovered wine, specifically red wines from Burgundy, France, which are made from Pinot Noir grapes. I especially had a penchant for the wines from the Burgundian village of Volnay. These were my father's favorites and hence became mine.

A member of the Chaine de Rotisseurs and the Physicians Wine Guild, Dad did a lot of entertaining and event planning for the Dade County Medical Association in Miami. He loved to cook "gourmet" meals and these provided me with an early environment for learning about the rituals of dining and fine wines. I adopted his passion for cooking as well as for fine French wines. He let me take tastes of many different wines. I was spellbound. I cannot remember a single wine that I did not like.

Not only did he love to cook, but we also used to frequent the restaurants of the classic 1960s hotels like the Fontainebleau, Doral and Eden Roc. Back then, if it was fine dining, the restaurant had to be French.

For my 14th birthday in 1966, our family went to La Parisienne Restaurant on Miami Beach, and there we ate snails for the first time. This started as a dare between my brothers and me but it turned out we loved them. They arrived bubbling in the garlicky butter with fresh parsley and lemon juice, and I sopped up every drop with the crusty French bread. I was off to a great start in culinary adventures.

The entrée my father ordered was rack of lamb *á la bouquetiere,* and I was awestruck with the presentation. The vegetables were beautifully arranged around the lamb on a silver platter, and the individual ribs tipped with fancy paper crowns. There were colorful clusters of green broccoli, orange baby carrots trimmed to identical size, perfect whole mushrooms and neatly arranged asparagus spears. This was all framed by a border of *duchesse* potatoes that had been piped through a pastry bag and placed under the broiler until they were delicately browned. The waiter carved the lamb rack into cutlets table side, and arranged them with the vegetables on our plates. My father ordered a bottle of his beloved Volnay from Burgundy, and we were allowed to have a glass as well. "Wahoo," I thought. "This is living!"

By the time I turned 15, I was learning to cook and reading books about the history and traditions of the French wine regions. Of course, you could not read about the wines without encountering a detailed account of the gastronomy. I learned about the great gastronomes in history. Prosper Montagné, Auguste Escoffier, Antonin Carême and la Varenne became my culinary heroes. Their names were more meaningful to me than sports heroes, like Johnny Unitas or Yogi Berra, were to my brothers. Yes, I was quite the young geek! For my 15th birthday I got an omelet pan — I swear. All the other kids in the neighborhood were out riding their bikes or throwing around the pigskin, while I was in the kitchen whipping up a Gruyère omelet. Thanks, Mom.

An old copy of the encyclopedic **Larousse Gastronomique** became my bible. My copy was the 1961 Crown edition, which was the first English translation of the monumental work, and not the more modern and watered down (but certainly more practical) version. I could spend hours perusing the pages and reveling in the lore – entries about sumptuous banquets, biographies of culinary superstars, and the vague, sketchy recipes that often seem insane by any standard today. One of my favorite recipes is for meat extract, which calls for a calf (or one-quarter of a beef carcass), two dozen old hens, a couple of sheep and a large pot. Large pot — no kidding. The trivia and information in this book, which you can find on Amazon.com, is wonderful for anyone with a penchant for learning about pre-World War II wine and food. It is not only a great resource, but a lot of the information is really a hoot!

Another seminal book for me, written by an American in 1958, is Waverly Root's *The Food of France*. The book divides France into three primary domains, based on the principal fat used in the region: olive oil, butter or lard. This ingenious approach demonstrates how climate and terrain dictate what can be grown, and how regions at opposite borders can share common elements used in defining the cuisine. Where you have mountains and colder climates, lard is the only logical choice – olive trees don't grow and cows are not practical for the terrain. Where olive trees flourish, you will be in a much warmer climate. Leeks, garlic and fresh herbs are bountiful, along with the rice and even the similarity of fish species that come from the warmer Mediterranean waters. Find arable land and a cool climate such as in the north, and voilà – butter and cream. Compare a Mediterranean fish soup, redolent with olive oil, garlic and saffron, with one from the north containing butter, cream and possibly potatoes, and you'll easily see how long ago the regions shaped the cuisines. This book was instrumental in creating the sense of connectedness between products and places for me.

A nice bottle of Burgundy, please

The thing that really sealed the deal for me came in high school. I learned if I asked for French wine by name in a liquor store they would never ask for identification to see if I was 21 years old.

In 1969 I was 17 years old and a senior in high school. Rick Huckabee, Joe Weiss and I rode our bikes to a Seven-Eleven store located nearby in South Miami at the corner of 87th Avenue and Sunset Drive. Our mission was to score a six-pack of beer. You could find a six-pack of Busch Bavarian beer on sale for about 79 cents back then. Our strategy was to see if we could find someone of age who might sympathize with our plight and ask them to pick up a six-pack, give them a five dollar bill and an invitation to, "keep the change." Our first "mark" brushed by, admonishing us, "You kids are too young to drink," and took off with our five bucks.

Five bucks down but still resolute, I took our last five dollars, went across the street to a real liquor and wine store. I strode to up to the clerk with every ounce of maturity I could muster (which was not much). "I would like to find a nice bottle of wine for dinner," I declared.

The clerk glanced up from his newspaper, took a drag of his cigarette and looked me over suspiciously. "Yeah, what did you have in mind?" he asked.

"A nice Burgundy – a Corton would be nice," I said. I knew my Dad liked Corton, a high quality red Burgundy, and that it fit my needs of being two syllables and relatively easy to pronounce.

He came out from his cubicle and went over to some wines laid neatly in a rack and said, "Here ya go – knock yourself out."

I selected one that looked pretty, paid the $3.50 it cost, and was delighted to hear the invitation, "Come back again," as I left with a brown-bagged bottle. After I got home and looked it up, I learned it was a 1964 Corton Grand Cru, produced by Jaboulet-Vercherre. I scored and the clerk even invited me back and thanked me for shopping with there. You betcha.

This, I thought, is so cool! And my friends were amazed and impressed. We had a cookout at our house with steaks on the grill and fine wine. Huckabee decided to fire up the dying coals a bit without first taking the steak off the grill. The pyrotechnics were impressive but the beautiful New York strip steaks ended up reeking of lighter fluid. My date was Marge Davis; she never went out with me again. It must have been the wine.

But I had figured out that if I said, "A nice bottle of Corton, please," I was in. My expertise was understandably limited and my ability to pronounce the wines in French was limited to two syllables. I focused on the reds of Burgundy, my father's favorite region. We would buy a couple of bottles of two-syllable Burgundy, do a little shopping at a gourmet store and then head off to the beach with our booty.

We organized fancy cookout dinners at Crandon Park on Virginia Key. We set our beachside picnic table, shaded by the palm trees and Australian pines, with a tablecloth and silver candelabra. We cooked escargots, bubbling up in their shells with garlic and butter in a Dutch oven, and grilled duck over the charcoal. Other picnickers would look up from their hot dogs and hamburgers when we announced things like, "Time to open up the Beaujolais and let it breathe." People around us flipping burgers and drinking beer thought we were nuts; we thought we were cool.

This was my shtick through high school. I learned that if I could cook and provide wine I could get a date. This formula for attracting the opposite sex worked perfectly for me for many years. Just ask my wife, Kate.

The connoisseur

Somewhere around 1972 I discovered there was something called "bad" wine. In my naïve enthusiasm I relished every wine I could get my hands on. Each wine was a revelation and I was always eager to get back to the wine books to look up and read about the wines I'd scored.

I had just started my pastry apprenticeship at the Sonesta Beach Hotel on Key Biscayne in Miami. I was passing by a Big Daddy's liquor store on the Miracle Mile in Coral Cables when a basket of wines in the window caught my eye. Written by hand in magic marker on the bright orange cut-out sign was "Chateau Calon Segur, $3.88 a bottle."

I had heard of that one and I recognized the elegant label with an outline of a big heart. I went in and bought all nine bottles – my largest wine purchase ever — and took the wines home. I looked up the Chateau in one of my Father's wine books. It turned out the Comte de Segur used to own the great Chateaux Lafite Rothschild and Margaux in addition to Calon Segur but "his heart was always at Calon Segur." Cool. That explained the heart on the label.

I opened a bottle of my prize with my less-than-sophisticated friends and marveled at the look, smell and taste of the wine. Wow – this was incredible. Or so I thought until friends of my parents, an attorney and his wife, came over for dinner. He was reputed to be a wine connoisseur. All that my brothers and I knew he was pompous; we called him, "Freddie the Jerk."

When dinner was served, I ceremoniously opened, decanted and poured the wine. Freddie the Jerk sat squarely with his left hand in a fist on the table, his right hand grasping the stem of the wine glass. He

Chateau Calon Segur label
"My heart is at Calon-Segur"

looked awfully serious, almost dour. He swirled the wine, put his face in the glass and inhaled deeply. When his face emerged, it was scrunched up into a full-blown frown, and he shook his head from side to side in disapproval. "Such a great estate and such a horrible, horrible vintage. This is crap. How can they even release such a horrendous wine?" he declared.

I was crestfallen. What? I loved the wine! Look at that pretty, pale orange color. The smell was so intense – just like my mom's nail polish when she was getting dressed to go out. Later I would learn those are not the things you look for in this kind of wine. It turns out the entire vintage year of 1968 had been declared "atrocious" in the Bordeaux region by my now-guru and hero Michael Broadbent. In 1960s there were five suspect vintages, the year in which the grapes for a given wine are grown: 1960, 1963, 1965, 1968 and 1969. Many of the greatest of estates produced wines that were of such a low quality that you would be hard pressed to find a wine so poor almost anywhere in the world today.

What I wonder is who drank all of the really bad wines (by today's standard) that used to be produced? There were veritable decades when even the top wine estates and Chateaux in France, let alone the small producers of everyday wines, made wines that would not be considered commercially sound by any of today's standards. And what foods did they serve with them, bad food? "Here, try this old, moldy food in a nail polish sauce to marry perfectly with the grapes ruined by rains and poor weather with a piquant acetone quality from fermentation run amok." Maybe a steak doused in lighter fluid would be the perfect match. Get it, "match"? Hmmm, that sounds familiar. (Pun intended.)

As a result of the Freddie-the-Jerk episode I learned to pay more attention to the color, smells and tastes of wine. I learned to watch and listen to the experts closely so I could figure out what was good or bad and which words to use for describing different types of wines. Learning what I should and shouldn't like, I was formally on my way to becoming, simultaneously, a wine connoisseur, wonk and geek.

One of my first formal job applications was for Crown Liquors. They were looking for a sales person to work in their store in Kendall, in south Miami. I was a frequent customer and knew they had a nice wine selection with plenty of two-syllable French wines for me to buy. When I handed in my application the manager noted I was not old enough to drink. Oops. That was a problem.

On my brothers' 21st birthday (twins, 14 months older than me), dad took us to the lavish Club Gigi for dinner and a Las Vegas-style show at the Fontainebleau Hotel. My brother Jon, who has never shown any interest in wine then or now, decided it was his turn to order the wine on this birthday. It had always been me, my dad or Jon's fraternal twin Chis who had the wine ordering honor. It was a ruse. He told the sommelier that he would like a nice bottle of Chateaubriand, knowing that this is a cut of filet of beef and not a wine. The sommelier nodded and walked away and no one laughed – my dad was chasing down the sommelier to cancel the order that sounded almost identical to Chateau Haut Brion, a wildly expensive and rare Bordeaux wine that in 1970 was over 100 dollars a bottle, easily equal to about $1,000 by today's prices!

I decided to become a chef and I started to build my culinary repertoire and experience by working in hotels and restaurants. I spent ten years working as a chef. While I focused on French cuisine I also mastered the art of *garde-manger*, cold foods preparations, and was charged with creating a Danish table of more 50 items nightly. Next I moved to Atlanta to reformat Chinese restaurants and learned to run a three wok station — quite a feat to be sure.

Differences between everyday consumers wine experts

The brains of people who become more interested, aspirational, emotionally or professionally engaged in wine become completely reprogrammed.

This falls under the heading of Cognitive Psychology that is, according to the Merriam-Webster Medical Dictionary, "a branch of psychology concerned with mental processes (as perception, thinking, learning, and memory) especially with respect to the internal events occurring between sensory stimulation and the overt expression of behavior - compare behaviorism."

It is a process where the brain associates sensations to different benchmarks of values or meaning through experiences, observation and learning. In simple terms, our brains become scrambled and our behaviors change as we become trained to be more expert.

For example, one of the things commonly taught in both consumer and professional wine studies is how to detect and recognize various wine flaws. You will probably experience defective wines, or even specific compounds, containing the sensory properties associated with flaws. This will forever change how you evaluate wines.

It is plausible to consider that many experts at the highest level no longer look for what is enjoyable or pleasurable in wine – they have become wired to ferret out what is wrong, not right, with every wine they evaluate. This is the highest form of wine geekdom one can aspire to!

I worked my way up to become an executive chef, and all the while my passion and curiosity for wine continued to grow. I left the kitchen to become a retail wine manager in 1979 for Happy Herman's in Atlanta, Georgia. That name really conjures up fine wines, right? All the same, I became immersed in wines from all around the world and built a sizable business as a vendor for some of the rarest and hardest-to find wines in the world. I was like a kid in the proverbial candy store — getting paid to drink and learn more about my favorite subject, wine. A diehard Francophile in terms of my wine preferences, I was confident of my knowledge of the classic wine and food matches. I could dazzle people with the regional rationale and all of the pseudo-sciences that explain why certain wines match best with certain foods. I became so good at this that I became internationally recognized as a wine and food guru.

I lived in the delusion that I really understood wine and food affinities and matching based on region and tradition. It went something like, "The reason oysters have such a perfect affinity with Chablis is due primarily to the calcareous soils of the region, which we all know are the Paris basin Kimmeridgean limestone deposits of early brachiopods and ancient oyster beds from the Cretaceous era, impacting the vine and shaping the aromatic minerality and affecting the acidity of the Chablis, which illustrates the synergy of the land and the vine in creating gastronomic harmony."

But something was eating at me (figuratively speaking), and deep down inside, I was also feeling more and more like something was wrong with a lot of the principles and premises for my wine and food matching wisdoms. As my exposure to the world of wines began to expand, I began to note the many inconsistencies in my own stories, as well as in the information I used to teach others the "art" of wine and food.

Sure, the bistros in Paris served fresh Bélon oysters with the traditional crisp, dry wines of Muscadet. This particular wine was served in the bistros as a matter of fashion and convenience. A restaurant or bistro featuring the Bélon oysters would proudly feature the wines of the area and very likely be owned and run by an individual or family from the French province of Maine. But if you found the traditional Muscadet or other wines they might offer too dry and acidic, it was equally fashionable to order a Kir, a mixture of dry white wine and crème de cassis, and enjoy the wine sweetened, with a blush of color.

Digression – did you know the region of Maine, France, which lent its name to the State of Maine in the US, was famous for a fish soup that was made with cream and cooked in a special cooker called a *chaudiére,* or kettle, giving rise to the famous chowder of New England?

And while the combination of Muscadet and Bélon oysters may have been the local pairing of the coastal regions where they share a common origin, if you went to the Bordeaux coastal region of Arcachon Bay, where you will find an equal passion for their local oysters and their local wines, it was customary to enjoy your oysters with local red wines and little salty lamb sausages. And if you look carefully in the pages of *Larousse Gastronomique*, you will find a wine and food chart, added to the original text in the 1961 translation, that shows intensely sweet wines, even Chateau d'Yquem, recommended to be served with hors d'oeuvres, fish and crustaceans!

The geek

By the late 1980s, the wine industry in the U.S. was taking off, and the apex of action was the Napa Valley of California. When Beringer Wine Estates offered me a job as director of communications, I moved from Atlanta to the Napa Valley, and I was in hog heaven.

Beringer Winery, and its then Nestle-owned Wine World Estates, was a rising star in the international wine scene, and the organization was simply the best. The construction of the Hudson House Culinary Center on the Beringer Estate was nearing completion, and this was to become my new playground for entertaining and conducting educational programs.

Unlike France or Italy, wine was not part of our culture. For those who hadn't grown up with wine but were greatly interested in it, there was a huge gap in knowledge. With my background in the culinary arts, wonderful trivial knowledge of classical cuisines and mindset deeply rooted in French and rare wines, I was considered a veritable "wine and food matching guru."

One of my first responsibilities was to conduct wine and food training for the School for American Chefs, the centerpiece program launched in conjunction with the opening of the Hudson House. This was a two-week program for small groups of chefs from around the country. The amazing Madeleine Kamman, a culinary teacher and food historian, was the program director.

I would meet with the incoming groups and spend the first day immersing them in the intricacies of wine and food and dazzling them with my knowledge and prowess. I was deeply enmeshed in the Conventional Wisdoms of wine and matching wine with food. To put icing on the cake (my apprenticeship was in pastries) in 1990 I became one of two Americans to successfully pass the examination and earn the Master of Wine credential. Uh-oh, now I had become a credentialed wine geek.

As I conducted my wine and food demonstrations around the world and with many different audiences, however, I ran into a problem. The dang chefs, the emerging and ensconced experts on the American wine and food scene, would not cooperate.

I'd begin with a wine. I'd pour tastings and ask the participants, "What do you think?" Some loved it; some hated it. Hmmm.

Next I'd provide what I considered to be a truly delicious wine and food pairing. Arguments would frequently erupt between the participants. The disagreements were so intense it was as if they were not even tasting the same things. Some participants raved about it; others would wrinkle their noses and shudder with disapproval. They were that polar in their perspective.

"Jeez, what is wrong with these people," I wondered. Being the expert, I would explain to the naysayers why the combination was correct and implore everyone to try the combination again. Same results. Disagreement.

I would next launch into the rationale for why it was a "good" match, citing the complex interrelationship of the ingredients, the tradition, the regional affinities and the descriptive similarities of flavors between the wine and the food. Still, some said it was magical; others said it was horrible.

The conversation became personal: "What's wrong with you? This combination is great!"

"No," some of them said, "it is not. It is bitter and horrible." Inevitably many of these tastings and meals turned into arguments, like bad kids fighting at the card table in the living room that the mother had set up to separate the troublemakers who could not behave themselves at the adults' table. Is this what people had in mind when they talk about wine as the "civilized" beverage, the source of harmony at the table for family, friends and community? I don't think so.

At Beringer Winery I was working with a core group of chefs like Jerry Comfort and Sarah Scott, plus a range of sensory scientists who had become my mentors. We were all constantly questioning the core principles of wine and food matching, and we were subject to one epiphany after another.

We would take wine and food conventions and put them to the test. Time after time we found there was no basis, either experiential or historically, for a rule. During one of the sessions we discovered that making a rich beef stew with a reduction of an acidic white wine was much more pleasant when served with the Beringer Private Reserve Cabernet Sauvignon than the same dish made with a reduction of the same Cabernet Sauvignon we were serving. Slap. We cracked up one time when we all seemed to slap ourselves in the forehead simultaneously. Thus the flatheads were born. (There was a lot of forehead slapping going on, and the action continues unabated today.)

In the early 1990s, I joined a group called The Wine Brats. The charter of the Wine Brats was to change the stuffy nature of wine tastings, rebel against the wine lexicon and make wine more fun and attractive to younger consumers; yet it wasn't long before organizers recognized an unhealthy trend developing — a new generation of wine geeks and wonks was emerging that was becoming just like the geeks and wonks from previous generations — just more of the same old stuff.

We decided to create a "Wine Geek Rehab" program. At events, or wine raves as they were called, we had a table that was identified as a Wine Geek Recovery station. Pamphlets were handed out to participants and listed the early warning signs of becoming a geek: speaking in a strange and unintelligible language; slurping and sucking air while drinking, taking on an attitude of superiority – you know the classic signs of a geek. If you observed a friend sinking into the depths of wine geekiness you were instructed to take them to the Rehab table. There was a list of steps for recovery that started with:

1. First you must recognize that there is a higher power.
2. The second step is to get that you are not that higher power!

Make no mistake about it – I loved my years as a geek. I reveled in the tastings of new wines, rare vintages and the fantastic dinners. I loved, and still love, soaking up wine history, tradition and science. When I started travelling to different wine regions I was like a kid at Disney World. And I wanted more. I wanted to reach what I thought was the pinnacle – to become a Master of Wine.

In 1989 I applied to the Institute of Masters of Wine to see if I met the requirements to take the examination and earn the credential Master of Wine. I submitted a requisite essay (Winemaking, Science or Art?), participated in a blind tasting and was accepted to "sit" the examination as an international candidate.

In May of 1989 I travelled to London to take the exam. To say I failed is putting it lightly. There was a handful of Americans that year and we were all unsuccessful. The then-chairman of the institute, David Stevens MW, used to tell the story that my papers were so bad that he had pen in hand trying to find civil words to the effect, "Dear Mr. Hanni, please stay away for some time before your next attempt…a long time."

David never wrote or sent the letter. I returned to Napa convinced I had the knowledge to pass the examination and needed some help learning to write more cohesively and coherently. I decided to take a writing class.

I did a little research, found the writing class that sounded perfect and signed up. I signed up for, and attended, the wrong class. For 3 days.

Illustration credit: Bob Johnson

The seminar you are looking for was last week in San Jose

The class I signed up for was for electronic engineers. My radical change in perspective about wine, wine with food and the personal preferences of wine consumers came about because of a mistake I made signing up for the wrong writing seminar.

I knew I needed some help in writing coherent essays before I took the Masters of Wine examination again. I signed up for a three-day writing seminar. When I showed up at the registration desk, however, I was told, "The course you wanted was in San Jose last week. This is a workshop to help electronic engineers learn to communicate more clearly at a technical level and to better communicate through sales and marketing."

Oops. Well, I was checked in at the Stanford Court Hotel for three days — what the heck. These three days changed my life and I may never have passed the Masters of Wine examination had I not chosen to stay.

I was the only "wine guy" in the class of 80 engineers. This meant I was really popular as a partner in the many exercises requiring two or more people. The exercises started with things like, "Make a list of 10 essential technical words that are used day in and day out in your work and then write how you would define those words on a separate piece of paper. Exchange your list of words with your partner and write your definition for the same words. Then compare the definitions to the ones you wrote originally."

The words on my partner's list included words like heuristics, analogue, optoelectrics and nan gates. Huh? My list of technical terms for wines seemed simple enough: taste, flavor, aroma, bouquet, body, match, pairing, dry, weight and complexity, all from my everyday conversations about wine and matching wine with food. As it turns out, these words were as foreign to my partner as heuristics and optoelectrics were to me.

As a result of this exercise it became crystal clear to me that although I was a world-class wine wonk, the definitions I used were certainly not part of non-wine users' vocabularies. And I had to admit that a lot of the definitions I had adopted, and even taught in classes to others, were either completely vague or even nonsense.

The other really important thing I learned in this workshop was "the art of critical thinking" to identify a problem and find new, better solutions. For example, critical thinking can be employed to resolve a conflict between two engineers who have differing points of view on how to solve a problem or create a product. Critical thinking can also be used if production and marketing need to rethink a product feature to make the smartest decision that will benefit the end user. The computer mouse is a great example of what can come of identifying a problem (complex protocol and computer language) and finding a better solution that will improve ease of use and potential expansion of sales (the mouse and cursor).

The first step in critical thinking is to identify the conflict or problem. The different points of view are considered, and the evidence supporting each is collected and analyzed. After noting what can't be substantiated, you look for other valid points to throw in the pot before you readdress the problem to see if you can find a resolution. Applying this to my wine research would eventually lead to the New Wine Fundamentals. Meanwhile, other things were happening in my life, too.

Mom, meet my new boyfriend

At Beringer a group of us formed a garage band and played at parties and wine functions. I rewrote the lyrics to "Route 66" with a vinous twist. Instead of "get your kicks on route 66" it was now "get your wine on Highway 29." Bob Janis, my partner in crime, added "Silverado" (the road running parallel to Highway 29 in the Napa Valley) to the tune of "Desperado." (There is a video of our band, Kate Hanni and the Toasted Heads, at the www.timhanni.com website if you are interested).

Looking to record some of our songs for a Beringer sales meeting, we hooked up with Bob Foley, a brilliant winemaker and equally great guitar player, recording artist and all-around musician. Bob said he knew of a really good female vocalist who was in search of a band. After one practice together, we agreed she had immense talent (frankly, too much talent for my guitar playing) and should join the band.

Her name was Kate, and we were soon in love. She is now Mrs. Kate Hanni. All it took was a few years, some fancy cooking, a hot tub in the vineyards and lots and lots of wine. It did not hurt that I could take her on trips to fabulous destinations around the world to attend killer wine and food events.

But back in the fall of 1991 my new girlfriend Kate and I were headed to Eureka, California, to spend the Thanksgiving holiday with her mother and step-dad. This was the inevitable trip to "meet the parents." Kate was particularly nervous because I was a noted wine expert, and her mother, Joanne, was a White Zinfandel lover. I told her, "I have no problem with that; people have all sorts of personal preferences." Besides, working with Beringer, I could get all of the Beringer White Zinfandel I wanted free of charge. But Kate was worried nonetheless.

When we showed up on Joanne's doorstep, I had a leg of lamb in one hand and a case of White Zinfandel tucked under my other arm. Joanne took in the scene, brushed right by Kate, stretched out her arms, and while hugging me said, "Welcome to our home. Let me show you the kitchen." Kate was left standing outside with the luggage while I was led away, arm in arm, by Joanne.

I got to know Joanne over the weekend, and she did not fit the wine industry stereotype of an uneducated, unsophisticated and immature White Zin drinker. She had a Ph.D. in economics, golfed in amateur events all around the country and had comfortably retired with relative wealth. Our holiday meal was spectacular, and we offered everyone a choice between White Zinfandel or Howell Mountain Merlot. As Joanne tasted the Merlot and I could see her nose wrinkle with displeasure. "Hey, what's the problem," I thought, "more for me!" Over the course of the weekend I began to really get something was very, very wrong with the way the wine cognoscenti judge wine consumers by the wine styles they may love.

What was going on here? Joanne was certainly not a novice, immature, uneducated or a beginning wine consumer. Wait a minute! Maybe the clichés and stereotypes about White Zinfandel drinkers were a big mistake? Insert slap on the forehead here.

Just to finish up this story, I proposed to Kate on a trip to London. She said yes.

The road to recovery

During this period of my life I had another really, really big epiphany. I mean it was a dandy! It was the realization that I needed to address a generations-old problem with alcoholism. The epiphany was not that I was an alcoholic. There was little doubt about that in my mind. The epiphany was that I had met and married the woman of my dreams and this new relationship would end up badly, just like all of the other relationships in my life. The "geek recovery stations" at the Wine Brats events proved to be ironic. I stopped drinking in December of 1993 and entered a rehab program in early 1994.

I do not want to make light of my alcoholism or my on-going recovery. It turned out to be the biggest contribution to my wine career than I ever could imagine. Here I was, newly promoted to the position of Director of International Business Development with Beringer Wine Estates and had just a couple of years earlier earned the coveted Master of Wine credential. During a session with one of the counselors I asked the big question, "Do you think I can continue to work in the wine industry?"

"Would you be willing to leave the wine business if your sobriety depended on it?" he asked.

"Yes," I answered without hesitation.

"If you had hedged or hesitated the slightest I would have said not, but your answer was so resolute that you would be willing to give up your career it just might work," he said.

I won't go into a lot of detail but suffice to say I have never had a relapse nor have I ever resented or doubted my decision. I found that there are many recovering people in the wine industry, in every conceivable position. Some make it work for them, others do not. I talk to people from around the world who contact me about their drinking issues and to concerned families with loved ones who face the same challenges with drinking that I do. I share my story and also clearly communicate that I can only offer a retelling of how it was for me before I confronted the issue, during my recovery and what my life looks like now. My program for recovery is mine alone and is in no way recommended for anyone else – if you have a problem you should seek qualified, professional help and work the program they prescribe.

For the record I do very infrequently taste and rigorously spit wine when it is required for winemaking or product development projects. I do not taste wines to critique, evaluate or offer tasting notes. It is my program and it is NOT recommended for anyone else in, or considering, recovery from alcoholism unless you have discussed the option with a qualified recovery professional administering or monitoring your personal recovery program.

The importance of being clear about my recovery, and why it should not be taken as a sign for others who are in recovery to follow without professional guidance, is punctuated by a situation that occurred with a dear friend of mine who is also a notable wine personality in recovery. We had joined forces to put together a spectacular auction lot for a community fundraising effort. It was a night of rare wines, dinner by some of the most notable chefs in the world. I was the wine geek *du jour* in charge of leading a "tutored tasting" of the wines with the guests. I was carefully spitting as I went along and doing my geekly best to impress everyone with my insights, knowledge and metaphorical descriptions. The evening was great and everyone was happy.

A month later I got a call from my friend. He said, "We gotta talk. How about getting together for a cup of coffee?"

It turns out that knowing I was a fellow recovering person and could taste and spit, he thought it was reasonable to assume that he could taste and spit too. He started slowly, tasting and spitting at the winery during production tastings and then on VIP tours with special guests. Then he decided it was OK to taste and spit at wine dinners and events. He started planning where he could taste and spit next. He noticed he was tasting more and spitting less. That's when he gave me a call. It was a miracle he caught himself spiraling back into a relapse and reached out to me. From that point on I have taken my sobriety and the challenges of others who choose not to drink even more seriously.

Many people have attacked my theories for instituting positive change in the wine industry by inferring I have had a relapse or questioned my authority because, "He is a recovering drunk." Remember back in Chapter 1 there was a section about resistance to change when someone is trying to introduce disruptive change into a fast-held paradigm? Here it is to refresh your memory: "Throughout history, scientific breakthroughs have been ridiculed at the time and the scientists who made them have been persecuted and sometimes even threatened ..."

The good news is that everything is dandy at my end. As a matter of fact, if I had continued my drinking ways I never, ever, would have had the clarity and new perspective that comes from being a spectator at wine events rather than a participant. Maybe makes me the real-deal wine spectator?

Needless to say, things started to look really different for me after I quit drinking. It was amazing the new perspective I had as the most sober person in the room! I still went to tastings, conducted wine education classes; my curiosity about wine and gastronomy now turned even more toward understanding human behavior, wine preference variables and answering the "unanswerable" questions and dissonance that had been dancing in my head for years.

And on the up side – I am now the best designated driver you will ever find in the wine country!

Wait a minute - this combination sucks!

Not long after getting out of recovery and sometime after meeting my White-Zinfandel-loving mother-in-law Joanne, I was conducting a wine and food pairing seminar back at Beringer. Something really odd thing happened. I had prepared a dish to demonstrate a sure-fire wine and food combination: a ragout of lamb and wild mushrooms which would of course pair perfectly with an intensely flavored Beringer Private Reserve Cabernet Sauvignon. I took a bite of the dish and sip of the wine. It was terrible. The wine became bitter, thin tasting and nothing at all like what I had said the combination should deliver. Wait a minute, I thought, this wine and food combination sucks!

It finally became clear that it was possible that any number of people may be eating the same foods, drinking the same wines and having completely different sensory experiences. I mean, I already knew that people have their own opinions and experiences, but it struck me differently this time.

And why shouldn't they? We all like different foods. Some of us have a sweet tooth; others can live without sugar. Some prefer highly spiced foods; others can't tolerate a hint of spiciness. Some people love the herb cilantro; to others it tastes like soap. Some take their coffee strong and black; others need to add cream and sugar just to drink it. And there are those who reach for the salt shaker before even trying a dish while others complain the dish is already over-salted.

Why was wine treated so differently? In answering this question, I set out on a journey that has led me around the country and the world, from Ohio to China, from Texas to Turkey. I delved into scientific research to try to understand the physiology of preferences. I've talked to people who make wine, sell wine, and most of all to people who buy, and want to enjoy, wine.

Since then my insatiable curiosity and research have occupied me for the past 20 years. I have spent a lot of time critically rethinking much of what I had held for so long as sacred and seemingly immutable Conventional Wisdoms and taking a balanced approach that has actually deepened my knowledge, love and enthusiasm for wine. You might say I've come full circle.

Chapter 3 Q&A

Question: How can you be a wine expert if you don't even drink?

Answer: Simple – I know a lot about the subject! My focus has turned to researching the factors that contribute to personal wine preferences and revising the misinformation that has become so imbedded as Conventional Wisdoms in our education programs. I do not rate wines or make wine recommendations. I help people discover more about themselves and educate the industry on how to be of better service to wine consumers.

Notes: _____

Chapter 4: What's Your Vinotype?

If the shoe fits...

Forrest Gump's mother had a saying: "Momma always says there's an awful lot you could tell about a person by their shoes. Where they're going. Where they've been."

The same can be said about wine. There is an awful lot you could tell about a person by their wine preferences. What is their sensory sensitivities, what flavors do they savor most, how seriously do they take all the fuss about wine and even what wine regions have they have fisited?

But imagine going to buy a pair of shoes the same way people buy wine:

Shoe expert: Hi! Welcome to the Shoe Emporium. We have all sorts of shoe styles and designs from all over the world and for every occasion. I will be your shoe consultant. Just to assure you that I am qualified for the task, I am a Master of Shoes. This means I can be given a shoe blindfolded and tell you just by smelling and feeling it what style it is, where it was made, what materials were used and often even identify the shoemaker by name!

Customer: I need something that is sort of smart that I can wear to work or to a casual occasion – not too expensive. I kind of like Italian shoes.

Shoe expert: Here is one that fits your needs perfectly. We just had a shoe fitting and experts tried more a thousand

Vinotype Definition

phe·no·type
- The set of observable characteristics of an individual resulting from the interaction of its genotype with the environment.

vi·no·type
- The set of observable characteristics of a wine-imbibing individual resulting from the interaction of its genotypic sensory sensitivities in a wine-related environment.

Sensory sensitivity: The intensity and range of sensations an individual experiences.

Vinotype genre: A collective of people who are in general agreement based on wine education, confidence, expertise and aspirations.

Personal wine preferences: The expressed likes and dislikes of wine types and styles, music, food or art.

different shoes and this was rated 99 points and given the Best of Show award at the Milan International Shoe Competition. Try it on.

Customer: But it's a size 11. I wear size 8.

Shoe expert: Obviously your foot is not mature. A knowledgeable shoe-wearer would recognize immediately this is a great shoe. Maybe you should become more educated about shoes? We have classes. Do you know the history of the heel and the various materials employed to make them over the ages?

Consumer: No, I just want a comfortable pair of shoes.

Shoe expert: I am so sorry, but this is the shoe we deem best. As you become more sophisticated, as your feet mature, you will learn to recognize the quality…

There is another part about the shoe analogy before I dive into the physiology of sensory and perceptual sensitivity and how it relates to wines that you may, or may not, find comfortable or appropriate.

As your foot matures you will learn to appreciate these shoes...

Ever buy, or have to wear, shoes that don't fit? Most everyone has. People even buy shoes that don't fit with the delusion that, "they will stretch." This fits our definition of a collective delusion. Here are some other delusions that might compel us to purchase uncomfortable shoes:

- They make you look thinner.
- My wife says, "Honey, you look so hot in those shoes I want to jump your bones when we get home." (my delusions, thank you)
- This is the last pair (scarcity is a powerful influencer).
- I need them for a special occasion and won't wear them much. They'll be OK.

If I am a bit dressed up and walking out of our house in the shoes I want to wear, Kate, my wife, will ask snidely, "You aren't going to wear THOSE shoes, are you?" Nope, just seeing how far I can get. On go the spiffy, stiff, uncomfortable shoes that elicit the statement, "Much better."

Off we go. I am having a great time. An attractive young wine wonk is talking to me, telling me how wonderful it is to meet a Master of Wine. I am playing it up, trying my best to be witty and put on an attractive air. By the way, I am not paying attention to my feet and the pain is non-existent. That is until I see Kate coming at me with "that" look. The one she gets when she sees me flirting with another woman.

Suddenly I notice again that my feet hurt. I mumble something like, "So nice talking with you, I have to sit down for a bit, my shoes are really uncomfortable." My attention has shifted and now I notice my feet.

Attention and distraction when tasting wine influence our perception as well. Environment, focus and attention greatly alter our sensory consciousness which is also one more reason why professional wine tastings are not in sync with the reality of how normal people drink wine. I will dig deeper into the influence of environment on the experience of wine later in the book. It is an adaptation phenomenon and something called Vinotype plasticity – the ability and degree to which a wine drinking organism can adapt in a given environment. We are all constantly adapting, all the time.

Meet Virginia Utermohlen, MD

I had been researching the mysteries of food and wine preferences on my own for nearly a decade when I met Dr. Virginia Utermohlen, M.D., from Cornell University. It was becoming clear to me that I was going to have to go outside of the conventional wine boundaries to explore the question of taste preferences. In January of 2006 I was perusing the Internet for information about sensory sensitivity, when I came across an article written by Dr. Utermohlen based on a study correlating the roles of restaurant professionals to a set of sensory sensitivity markers.

She wrote: "The National Restaurant Association Show provided us an opportunity to explore taste sensitivity among people involved in the food business. We found that chefs and food preparers had, on the average, significantly higher responses to the 'coolness' of mint than did restaurant managers and most everyone else. Overall, we have found that people of different taste sensitivity tend to approach decision-making in differing ways, even problems concerning issues that have nothing to do with flavor or food."

I was fascinated. It seemed that we were thinking along the same lines in terms of the interrelationship between sensory sensitivity, preferences and even behavior. After looking up her biography on the Cornell University web site I was sure I had to connect with her. Her website is www.tastescience.com and you can go there to learn all about her, her research and background.

A board certified pediatrician, she had received numerous awards for her work and her teaching. With her appointment at Cornell in the Division of Nutritional Sciences, she focused her work on how taste and smell sensitivity relate to personality, food choices, eating attitudes, behavior and even choice of profession.

I called her up and we talked for a long time. I should note, by the way, that Virginia would soon become the poster child for the Vinotype who loves great sweet wines: She finds most dry wines unbearably strong and bitter. For her alcohol levels over 12 percent are hot and unpleasant. Highly educated, sophisticated and interested in food and wine, she's another of many men and women I've met who

Perceptual Sensitivity

Following are a number of conditions related to perceptual sensitivity. It is interesting to note that the conditions are often related to mood or environment.

Hyperosmia: Heightened sensitivity to smell.

Hypergeusia: General food fussiness or extreme sensitivity to food textures.

Photophobia: Light sensitivity.

Hyperacusis: Sensitivity to sound volume or certain specific sounds like lawn mowers, radio/TV, leaf blowers, household appliances, etc.

Seasonal Affective Disorder: Mood swings, sadder or happier, related to dark or overcast days.

Pain threshold: The level at which you detect pain, sometimes mood-related.

Tactile defensiveness: Touch sensitivity - tags in your clothes, seams in your underwear or socks.

Vistibular (motion) sensitivity: Increased car or sea sickness, roller coasters, etc.

Synesthesia: an involuntary neurological condition in which people "smell" colors or sounds, or see numbers inherently colored.

"Synesthetes often report that they were unaware their experiences were unusual until they realized other people did not have them, while others report feeling as if they had been keeping a secret their entire lives, as has been documented in interviews with synesthetes on how they discovered synesthesia in their childhood." Source: Wikipedia

completely debunked the prevailing image of sweet wine drinkers.

We began corresponding and then collaborated on a survey study correlating wine consumer preferences, behaviors and attitudes, which we published in the early fall of 2010 and a synopsis of the report is reprinted in Appendix 7: Vinotype Facts and Figures in this book. The information for obtaining the complete report can be found at www.timhanni.com. Working with Virginia added impeccable credentials, a new dimension and understanding plus a much greater degree of competence to my work.

Our study was done in conjunction with the Consumer Wine Awards at Lodi and it provided us with tremendous insights on the way in which sensory sensitivity factored into not only wine preferences but confidence selecting wines, frequency of wine consumption and alternative beverage selections.

As I learned more about the genetic variables that determine individual taste sensitivity combined with changes in wine preferences that occur over time, it soon became clear that the commonly held idea that somehow "our palates mature over time" was related to environmental interactions, such as observation and learning in different cultural and social situations. It had nothing to do with our "palates" per se.

As we explored the combination of physiological and psychological factors that create our personal preferences, I had to look up something pertaining to genetics and there I came across the word "phenotype." That's when it hit me – Vinotypes: the genetic traits of an organism, in this case one who drinks wine, combined with how they adapt and change in different environments. This explained so much!

We published a paper together, which asked, "Why does physiology matter?" The answer to this question is straightforward: Our sensory physiology dictates how sensitive we are to different tastes and flavors.

The total number of taste buds in the tongue ranges from fewer than 500 for some people to more than 11,000 for others according to credible estimates. It is easy to imagine that the person with more taste buds will get stronger taste messages than the person with fewer, and, typically, this is the case. It is important to note that more taste buds does not equate to a "superior palate" or better ability to taste wine. It does mean that people with different sensory physiology may experiences sensations differently. Research clearly shows that many people sense different compounds that other people are incapable of sensing at all.

Simply put: Some people have more taste buds than other people, and some people get a stronger message from wine — of acidity or alcohol, for example — than others. (The complete paper is published in the Appendix.)

Discovering how different people respond to sensory stimulation soon took us far beyond wine preferences. As you will see, all sorts of behaviors correlate to the factors that determine our Vinotype — everything from having to cut tags out of clothes to having linear or non-linear ways of thinking. Arguments about settings for thermostats or television settings, being a picky eater, even preferences about underwear may all relate back to your Vinotype.

The basic assessment consists of various questions that help us determine your physiological boundaries – your sensory sensitivities and tolerances. Next comes your genre, which is an expression the elements you value about wine. The final step is to simply declare the kind of wines you favor – be it sweet and pink or intense and red, or anywhere in between.

The result is your Vinotype – the unique combination of sensitivities and values that comprise your personal wine preferences. Your Vinotype becomes the means by which you can discover a doorway to people who have similar proclivities, as well as the means for wine and hospitality professionals to get a clear sense for making smart, personalized wine recommendations for you.

The easiest way to begin in understanding Vinotypes is to find out your own. The following assessment will help you determine your own Vinotype and also to think of other people in your life and their Vinotype.

A grossly oversimplified Vinotype sensitivity self assessment

I hate oversimplifications and generalizations and find many people feel the same way about these schlock "self-assessment" exercises, but keep in mind that this is just the first step: Cognitive psychology plays an essential role in determining your true wine passions and preferences. This assessment focuses primarily on your sensory sensitivity quotient.

Give it a go if you care or go to www.myVinotype.com to take the online version. And don't forget, this is only the sensory sensitivity part of your Vinotype.

ADDITIONAL IMPORTANT AND REDUNDANT NOTE: Your answers will reflect both your intuitive responses combined with adaptations you may have made over time, such as how much salt you use, your attitudes about artificial sweeteners, etc. Try to answer the questions based on what you intuitively like or dislike, not what you think about in terms of philosophical, spiritual or from a health implications of the ingredients or questions.

1. **Gender**
   0 Male
   3 Female

2. **Salted snacks such as nuts, pretzels, potato chips**
   0 I find most snacks too salty.
   1 Yeah, I like salty snacks.
   3 Yum! I am addicted to salty snacks.

3. **3. Salt preferences (try to answer by your taste preference, not from a health standpoint)**
   0 I find many foods too salty.
   1 Food usually tastes fine as is and/or I add a modest amount of salt when I cook.
   1 I avoid salt for health reasons (but if you really want to add more, select how much!).
   2 I usually add a little extra salt to my food, or would like to but don't for health reasons.
   3 People give me a hard time for adding too much salt.

4. **Coffee or Tea**
   Describe the perfect cup of coffee or tea:
   0 I like it very strong (espresso or black tea: English Breakfast tea).
   1 I like it strong (Starbucks, Peet's or Earl Grey tea).
   2 I like it medium (the weak coffee served at work, green or herbal tea).
   3 Coffee tastes so horrible I can't stand it.

5. **Sugar in your coffee:**
   0 I drink coffee/tea with no sugar.
   1 A touch.
   2 One teaspoon or the equivalent.

3 Two or more teaspoons.

6. **How do artificial sweeteners in diet sodas taste? (Try to answer by your taste preference, not from a health standpoint.)**

    0 No taste problem (whether or not you choose to use them).

    1 Don't know — I've never tried a diet soda in my life.

    1 Taste funny, but not too bad.

    2 I can tell a big difference but have adapted OR some are much better than others.

    3 Yuck! They taste horrible.

7. **Cream/Milk**

    0 I drink coffee black.

    1 Touch of cream or milk.

    2 Moderate cream or milk.

    3 Lots of cream or milk.

8. **Do you enjoy coffee with steamed milk or flavoring such as almond, vanilla, Irish Cream?**

    0 No!

    1 Cappuccino, latte, or *café au lait* - but not flavorings

    2 Sometimes.

    3 Yes.

9. **Bonus question: do you an occasional drink of straight Scotch, Cognac or Armagnac?**

    -3 Yes!

    0 Sometimes.

    1 No way.

Now add up your score to get your Sensitivity Quotient score. This score will determine into which of the four taste sensitivity groups you fall. The groups, from most sensitive to least sensitive, are: Sweet, Hypersensitive, Sensitive or Tolerant. In the general population about 30 percent of people fall into the Sweet category, 25 percent into Hypersensitive, 25 percent Sensitive and 20 percent into the Tolerant group. Keep in mind that the more experienced and confident you are around wine, the more you will have already developed strong wine preferences through those personal experiences of life and learning.

- Taste SQ score 15 to 25: Sweet
- Taste SQ score 15 to 25: Hypersensitive (the main difference between you and a Sweet Vintoype if you prefer mostly DRY wines)
- Taste SQ score 5 to 15: Sensitive
- Taste SQ score -3 to 7: Tolerant

Read on to find out what this means for you. And don't forget to take the answers "with a grain of salt."

Why the coffee questions?

For most people coffee is an acquired taste. Some people, especially the most sensitive category, are so affected by bitterness they can never get past their natural avoidance disposition. Others find they can deal with the bitterness as long as it is suppressed via the addition of cream and sugar.

There are others, like me, who grew up in a macho environment that pretty much demanded you drink coffee black – like a professional kitchen in the 1970s. Even today when I conduct Flavor Balancing workshops for culinary professionals, a major portion raise their hands when I ask, "Who drinks their coffee black?" compared to a group of consumers. And also keep in mind that coffee is becoming similar to wines in terms of a specialized language and fast-changing coffee culture. There are coffee geeks to be sure!

Why the salt questions?

The misconceptions about salt preferences and ignorance bear repetition – a craving or need for unusually high quantities of salt is a sign of having more, not less, taste sensitivity. The association with salt and negative health impact make it difficult to get a straight answer about whether people simply like the taste of salt or not. In fact, if you hit all of the traits of a Sweet or Hypersensitive type and do not use, or dislike the taste of, salt you may find that you grew up in a household where it was withheld due to a medical condition of a family member – dad, mom, grandma or grandpa had a heart condition or hypertension or high blood pressure, and many people subconsciously associate the salty taste with this. Or you may have the medical condition yourself and have "disposed of your taste" (remember this is the opposite of "acquired a taste") for salt.

Take it "with a grain of salt"

If you love salty snacks or reach for the saltshaker before you even taste your food, conventional wisdom says that you have dull or underpowered taste buds that need a boost to get enough taste. In fact, just the opposite may be true.

The bitter-suppressive qualities of salt have been known for centuries, and studies suggest that you may love salt because of your sensory hypersensitivity and the need to suppress that bitterness you experience.

And don't forget it is easy to "dispose of" your taste for salt. You may love salt intuitively but over time reroute the sensation to associate with hypertension, high blood pressure and heart disease. This would have you learn to dislike the taste over time.

What is the height of perceptive ignorance and arrogance? Restaurants sometimes remove the salt with the misassumption that the Chef has seasoned the food perfectly for everyone.

For you Sweet and Hypersensitive Vinotypes who still love your salt? Just take it with a grain of salt, and tell them to bring you the shaker.

Do you admonish or think badly of people who reach for the salt shaker without tasting their food? Are you a restaurant that has removed the salt shaker from the table? Well, cut it out!

So what's the deal with artificial sweeteners?

The different compounds used as artificial sweeteners elicit very different sensations for people. Tolerant tasters, who usually can give up sweet things with relative ease, often find that the artificial sweetener alternatives are fine for the most part. Maybe they find them a little different but what are people complaining about? Some are OK with one type but not others. Some people cannot stand any of them and describe repulsive chemical and metallic taste. Some will say "They are disgusting," based on their distaste for the concept, not the sensation. And finally every now and then, I hear, "I don't know, never tried them."

Results of the grossly oversimplified Vinotype sensitivity assessment:

YOUR VINOTYPE = SWEET

People in this segment are physiologically among the most sensitive. If you are in this segment you are probably acutely sensitive to light, sound, touch, smell and taste. The thermostat is rarely right (too cold), you may be frequently irritated by tags in your clothes and please, fer chrissake, turn down the TV! Picking the right sheets and pillowcases for Sweet types is a really big deal. Getting the thread count and feel just right is imperative!

These consumers are highly sensitive tasters who want sweet tastes to mask bitterness and alcohol — higher alcohol content not only increases the sensation of burn for these consumers, but it also increases the perception of bitterness. They love fragrant sweet wines that are typically low in alcohol and impeccably made. Not slightly sweet – pretty darn sweet. And they want sweet wines with the foods they love most, including steak or anything else!

Their preference for sweetness extends to other bitter beverages: They take their coffee — if they drink it at all — with lots of cream and sugar. If you take away cream and sugar for their coffee they will simply stop drinking coffee, just as they will stop drinking wine when in situations where dry wines are *de rigueur*, as our research shows.

They tend to use lots of salt in food, also to mask bitterness. They tend to dislike more foods and to be conservative about their wine choices — they stick to what they know. Sweet wine fashions may come and go, but sweet wine consumers are here to stay.

In our survey, 21 percent of the women and 7 percent of men were in this segment.

Interesting fact you can check on yourself: If you are a Sweet type, there is a high probability that your mother had morning sickness or serious heartburn with you.

YOUR VINOTYPE = HYPERSENSITIVE

Hypersensitives comprise the largest segment on our studies, 36 percent men, and 38 percent women. Like the Sweet tasters, Hypersensitives live in a vivid and intense sensory world of taste, smell, light, touch and sound, and living in this sensory cacophony is a challenge. Hypersensitves are often artistic, and may have attention deficit disorders. Hypersensitives love fragrances and revel in aromatic memories.

If you are Hypersensitive, you avoid strong flavors and are physiologically predisposed to find more intensity and complexity in wines that less sensitive tasters — especially the Tolerant crowd — deem "too light" and "weak." For you, high alcohol levels burn and bitterness is extremely unpleasant, which also explains the fiercely differing opinions between Hypersensitive and Tolerant wine critics about alcohol levels and intensity for many wine styles.

Hypersensitives love the flavors they experience from Pinot Grigio and really appreciate the trends that provide slight sweetness in traditionally "dry" wines like Chardonnay, Sauvignon Blanc and even red wines. They are also favorably inclined to love Riesling in the 1.2 percent to 2.5 percent residual sugar range, and light, fragrant red wines that are low in alcohol and devoid of the reductive or other aromas that constitute "complex" wines for less sensitive tasters. Hypersensitive Vinotypes can be very receptive to rose wines, but the drive to make rosés more "serious" (reductive aromas, oak aging, etc.) makes these wines less pleasurable for this group. Red wines must be impeccably crafted, lighter in intensity and alcohol levels, phenolics (the dissolved solids in wine that are responsible for color and also bitterness) and acidity must be carefully kept in a delicate balance.

The big difference between Sweet and Hypersensitive Vinotypes is that Hypersensitive Vinotypes tend to prefer dry, or just off-dry, wines on an everyday basis. Their favorite wines tend to be more delicate and very, very smooth while also being lower in alcohol. They may even like intense red wines but not with a lot of oak or heavy tannins —smooth and rich, baby. The Hypersensitive Vinotype is a bit more likely to "talk dry and drink sweet," looking for those wines that have a slight bit of residual sugar. The smoothness is a key wine attribute for them.

YOUR VINOTYPE = SENSITIVE

Sensitives go with the flow. Maybe they take their coffee with cream or a touch of sweetness, but they'll enjoy black coffee if the wind is right. This type is very open to trying new things, and variety is the spice of their lives. If you are a Sensitive Vinotype, you are frequently the mediator in family, marriage or business disputes. You're a team player and everyone wants you on their team. You tend to be more adventurous in both food and wine choices. Because of the wide range of things that appeal to you, decisiveness is not your strong suit. How should I take my coffee today? What wine? You tend to see things in the big picture.

Sensitive types consumers comprise about one-quarter of our survey respondents. They are, by far, the most compliant segment because of their predisposition to enjoy a wide range of flavors. They will be satisfied with more delicate wines yet are also able to tolerate, if not fully enjoy, the full-blown, high intensity wines of the Tolerant world.

It is very likely that early in their "ascension" to fine wines they may indeed be lured to the simplicity of the 100-point rating system, and the "more is better" way of comparing wine value, only to tire of high intensity, tannins and alcohol over time. As they grow more confident they will seek wines that they consider better balanced (relative to their standards of balance) and less over-blown and over-the-top.

Sensitive types are among the most adventurous wine lovers and open to all sorts of flavors and wine styles from delicate to robust and love a wide range of mostly dry white and red wines – and even many rosés and sparkling wines. They do have more limitations on bitterness and tannins — they are not typically looking for the oaky monsters but really impeccably balanced, smooth. The word "complex" is usually important as a wine description for this type.

YOUR VINOTYPE = TOLERANT

Tolerant Vinotypes don't understand what all of the fuss is about with more sensitive segments – those wimps! Damn the torpedoes; set the thermostat colder and turn up the volume on the TV!

If you are a Tolerant Vinotype, you love all things bigger, faster and stronger — it equals better. You tend to be a linear thinker, with a tendency to gesticulate with your hand in a linear way to make a point. You're decisive and bottom-line oriented. You might even speak loudly to compensate for not being able to hear very well. Tolerant types see things in black and white, quite literally. They are most likely to have a bumper sticker that says, "No Wimpy Wines." It is little wonder that the 100 point wine rating system often makes the most sense to Tolerants.

Big, red wines are the favorites. Intensity is the name of the game, and the bigger the better. Although they are the antithesis to the Sweet types, Tolerants also want the wines they love where and when they choose, whether it is with seafood, steak or salad. Just as long as it is red.

According to our research (see Appendix 2) the Tolerant segment is two-to-one male: 32 percent of men and 16 percent of women were in this category. Clearly the red wine set, Tolerant consumers love intensity in wine and are often able to "tolerate" many flavors that more sensitive tasters find intolerable, such as Cognac, Scotch, strong black coffee, cigars and big red wines.

Tolerant Vinotypes find that high levels of alcohol taste "sweet" and seem to be oblivious to high levels of bitterness and tannin. Current practices in wine merchandising promote wines that appeal to these consumers, yet interestingly, this is not the segment with the highest percentage of wine professionals.

We have discovered that a larger than expected number of wine professionals secretly find themselves in the too-often despised and stigmatized Sweet segment. A study we conducted in the U.K. showed that as wine professionals retired. a very large percentage went back to drinking sweet wines! Out of the cave, back into the forest.

A world of diverse Vinotypes and life experiences

A lot of readers are already saying to themselves, "What a load of crap — I don't fit any of these groups listed above." Not to worry, there is a place for you in all of this. And along the way, you'll come to better understand others who may not share your preferences and to connect with those who do.

Remember, this is just a quick introduction. There are many variations on this theme, and each of the sensory sensitivity groups are further defined by wine interests, education and aspirations. Later we'll get to the concept of "neural plasticity," which explains how changes occur in our preferences over time. This goes for wine, as well other many things — it's the inside scoop on acquiring and disposing of tastes through observation, learning and adapting to new environments.

Please pass the hot sauce

Do you love, even crave, really, really hot, spicy foods. Like, REALLY hot? While not considered clinically addictive, the chemicals responsible for the hot, burning sensations in chilies, wasabi and the like are known to trigger the release of euphoric chemicals into the bloodstream for certain individuals.

Early in my observations this seemed to be another contradiction. One would likely conclude that the Tolerant Vinotypes would be the ones that could tolerate the intense burning in spicy foods. More often than not it was the Sweet and Hypersensitive Vinotypes who had a strong penchant for the high levels of heat in their foods. It would seem these are the people who would be least likely to crave the heat.

It turns out there is a payoff I had never considered! For some people the hot and burning sensation triggers the release of endorphins and other euphoria-inducing chemicals into the bloodstream.

"Endorphins are neurotransmitters produced in the brain that reduce pain," says Alan Hirsch, MD, neurological director of the Smell & Taste Treatment and Research Foundation in Chicago. "They have also been known to induce euphoria." Drugs such as morphine, heroin and cocaine are classic endorphin-releasing entities, according to Dr. Hirsch.

While some of us just find the burning sensation irritating and unpleasant someone else may be experiencing a *Harry Met Sally* moment. The idea that you should not have certain wines with spicy foods is moot to someone who has a smug grin on their face and is enjoying a strong, dry wine with their hot, spicy food.

The thing to keep in mind is that the more involved you are with wine, the more likely it is that your likes and dislikes have already changed. In short — you have developed stronger opinions and the means to find the wines you like the most.

Think of Vinotyping as the means to understand personal sensory sensitivities and our differences in perception in a way we can custom fit wine recommendations to different individual. This provides a much better level of understanding and communication for wine professionals before they go blasting off with their personal preferences without considering the preferences of others and asking them where they might like to go!

Exploring and Discovering Wines

Embarking on an expedition of exploration and discovery is pretty intimidating if you believe that terrible perils lay ahead. Now imagine you have an expert who is supposed to help get you to your destination and you discover your guide still thinks the world is flat. He may warn you of the dangers of setting off on your own and that without expert guidance you may fall victim to dire consequences..

This is what a lot of wine experts, pundits and geeks do. It is mostly unintentional – just part of the wine collective delusions and groupspeak. Articles and wine blogs are filled with examples warning of wine perils and *faux pas* including making the wrong wine choice, ordering something considered unsophisticated or, horror of horrors, ordering the wrong wine and food combination.

Preparing for an expedition

ex·plore *v.*
1. To investigate systematically; examine: *Explore different styles of wines*
2. To search into or travel in for the purpose of discovery: *She was exploring the wine list for new wines to try.*

discover *v.*
1. To be the first to find or find out about: *I discovered a new wine that I want to share with other people.*
2. To learn about or encounter for the first time; realize: *She discovered the pleasures of wine.*
3. To find after study or search *I discovered I liked certain red wines as long as they were really smooth.*
4. To reveal or make known *My job as a wine expert is to help you discover wines you will love.*

If you DO choose to go on an expedition for exploring new vistas, what would you need? Here are the basics:

1. You need to know where you are when you set off – your point of embarkation, if you will.
2. It is best to have a destination in mind – it can be quite specific, or you might want to just leave it open-ended and see where you end up.
3. It is important to have a guide, map or navigational resources that will help you pinpoint your intended destination.

This is where the value of knowing your Vinotype comes in handy. It is even more valuable if you ensure the any "guide" you engage, such as someone in the wine section in the store where you shop or the sommelier or service professional in a restaurant, understands the Vinotype principles. You can also look for Internet sites that have a way to filter wines by your Vinotype so you can peruse information about your wine options with greater confidence or join a wine club that can personalize your wine shipments to your Vinotype specifications. D**o not be embarrassed or timid in sharing your personal wine preferences whatever they may be!** If you declare you like a certain wine and get an arched eyebrow or snigger from any wine expert or "guide," tell them to get with the program. Order the wines you love, demand that wine professionals focus on YOU and eat the foods you really want with the wine you want. You are the holder of the new, inside information. They are operating under an old and passé paradigm. This is executing the Power to the People part of the New Wine Fundamentals!

Here are a few examples of how the beginning of a new wine exploration might look:

- I am a Hypersensitive Vinotype who loves Pinot Grigio, an enjoyer who just knows a good wine when he tastes it. Can you help me find something special for tonight?
- I am a Hypersensitive Cabernet lover and enthusiast who really loves traveling to and exploring the California wine country. Do you have something red, really smooth and a bit different for me to try from South America?
- I am a Sensitive Vinotype, a professional sommelier, wonk and borderline geek love just about any well-made and honest wine but have a penchant for Grüner Veltliner and Chinon. I would really like to try something completely new and different.
- I am a Tolerant Vinotype, a connoisseur with a passion is for obscure dry wines from classic regions and I am a member of the ABC (Anything But Chardonnay or Cabernet) movement. What do you have in the way of a full-bodied white for me to try?

The wine guides of the future will ALWAYS listen to your needs and take you where YOU want to go.

- I am a Sweet Vinotype and becoming more of an enthusiast. Can you recommend something that is sweet but different? I am in the mood to experiment a bit.

Remind your guide, if you must, that this is **your** journey. Demand that wine professionals learn where you want to go and are able to get you to the wine destination you choose.

Not everyone wants to go to Paris

Many retail consultants, sommeliers, wine educators and wine articles start out with the well-intended and over-zealous generalization to the effect, "Everyone who likes wines wants to be taken on a journey of discovery. They want to explore the history and tradition, wine regions, experience new flavor sensations and discover new wines."

Nice thought, but not everyone may want to go on this ride. Not to deny that many people do want to go on an adventure, but many people just want a wine that tastes delicious on their terms and with whatever food they are eating. Wouldn't it be nice if the first thing all wine people did was ask, "Where do you want to go?"

I was at a lecture and heard the following story about "Taking Someone to Paris." The presenter started with the premise that if you asked people the question, "Would you like to on a first-class, free trip to Paris?" You may be hard-pressed to find anyone who would say, "No." From this most people could confidently assume that everyone would want to go to Paris on these terms.

A man was walking along on Times Square and came across an elderly woman who was clearly terrified by the cacophony of people, sounds, lights and cars. He politely inquired, "Can I be of assistance? You seem to need some help."

She replied, "Thank you so much, you are very kind to offer. I need some help to get across the street to visit my sister. This is all a bit intimidating and bewildering to me."

So, with every good intention, the well-intentioned and generous man decided to take this elderly woman not just across the street but all the way to Paris. They flew first class, drank Champagne and ate caviar. On arrival they visited the Louvre, the Champs Elysées and saw the Eiffel Tower. Over a magnificent meal at a 3-star restaurant he turned to her and asked, "Aren't you glad I took you on this wonderful adventure? Don't you just love Paris?"

She replied, "Thank you so much. I am embarrassed to say that although you have most kind I am very intimidated and not really pleased. This is much different than what I really expected or needed. Paris is just not to my taste. I really just wanted to cross the street and visit my sister."

This story is for the many expert, well-intending wine professionals and educators who firmly believe that everyone who enjoys wine wants to be taken on a journey filled with discovery. Maybe yes, maybe no. The point is: Let's teach everyone involved with learning about wine that before taking someone on a flight of vinous discovery, please first have the courtesy to find out where they might like to go.

If you are a wine enjoyer and someone does not seem to understand where you want to go, you can tell them, "I get that you are passionate and enthusiastic about wine but please settle down. I don't want to go to Paris right now. I just want to cross the street and visit my sister. And it would be nice if you could help me find a nice bottle of wine to take her – she is a Hypersensitive Vinotype and likes something white, dry, light and delicate."

Not everyone may share your passionate wine interests.
Illustration courtesy of Bob Johnson

The Great Cabernet Debate: Polarized points of view

People who have been around wine at a high level for a long time know just how polar the opinions over wine quality and value can be. It can become seriously ugly and I have even witnessed arguments nearly coming to blows over who is right or wrong. My wife will verify I was nearly attacked by an angry table full of wine people at a dinner in Orlando, Florida, when I inferred that when people come to my house for dinner I ask what people love the most, open lots of wines and let everyone freely explore the options – without any regard to wine and food matching.

Here are two opinions from wine writers, both of whom are highly qualified and expert wine judges (and two of the best wine writers and true wine journalists around), who both wrote articles about the quality status of Cabernet Sauvignon in California in the same week in early 2010. Note one was writing about Napa Valley Cabernets more specifically and the other the wines from the entire state including the wines from the Napa Valley.

In one corner we have Steve Heimoff writing about the current state of Napa Valley Cabernet Sauvignon:

Steve Heimoff: Napa Cabernet: As good as it can get?

"Well, these certainly are wines that have become spectacular in recent years. You really do have to wonder where their evolution will take them. I know some people who don't like the Napa cult style, which is based on super-mature grapes (with consequent low acidity) and generous dollops of new oak. They're entitled to their opinion; I happen to like it."

Source: http://www.steveheimoff.com/index.php/2010/01/19/napa-Cabernet-as-good-as-it-can-get/

Dan Berger: The collapse of Cabernet

In the other corner we have this quote from an article by Dan Berger that appeared almost at the same time as Steve's article:

"For more than a decade, I have hoped for a miracle. Then last week I realized the worst: Cabernet Sauvignon has changed so appreciably that I fear we'll never see it in the way we once did...A long book could be devoted to this sad tale of decline."

Source: http://napavalleyregister.com/lifestyles/food-and-cooking/wine/columnists/dan-berger/dan-berger-the-collapse-of-Cabernet/article_704bc688-0712-11df-a231-001cc4c002e0.html

Both Steve and Dan are right in their assessments - from their personal points of view. They simply do not recognize that they are describing the wines having perceptive differences that are as distinct as the three blind men in the Sufi parable - each is trying to describe an elephant from their distinctly different points of view and actual sensory experience. More on that later!

Consider for a moment that on one end of the spectrum we have Dan Berger, a hypersensitive taster whose tongue, general taste sensitivity and wine preferences I have personally painted blue, analyzed and photographed, writing about his very real and very passionate views on what Cabernet should or should not be. His hypersensitivity provides experiences such that high alcohol burns and many modern Cabernets and other wines which he finds are over-blown and over-oaked are not enjoyable for him with, or without, food. For Dan, and anyone else with his sensitivity and values, his point of view is dead-on correct: "There are complicated reasons for this turnabout, but the bottom line is that we may have lost Cabernet for all time. I can't drink them young; I can't imagine they will age well, and I cannot figure out why so many people are still buying them." Spoken like a true and passionate hypersensitive expert! And perfect advice for other hypersensitive and many more sensitive tasters. This is why I urge all highly sensitive Vinotypes of the enthusiast, connoisseur, wonk and expert genres to tune in to his great articles and books.

People at the less-sensitive to tolerant end of the spectrum will more predictably love the high-alcohol, oak and intensity that have come to define great Cabernet for the Robert Parker or Jim Laube (the terrific Cabernet specialist for the Wine Spectator) crowd. And with food as well! The alcohol tastes "sweet," the oak and tannin are not at all overbearing and, in fact, the very same wines are perceived as smooth, rich and balanced. This level of extract and intensity is the source of "great" for many tolerant tasters.

I can pretty much surmise that the getting to the source of these differences in opinion lies in better understanding the vastly different experiences from people at different ends of taste sensitivity continuum. I have surveyed and tested thousands of people. I know that people like Tim Mondavi and Jancis Robinson, along with Dan, are at the hypersensitive end of the spectrum and predictably in the same camp with Dan on the unpleasant direction things have gone with "too much" oak, "too much" alcohol.

Steve responded to one of my comments on his own blog, "But is a hypersensitive palate necessarily a good thing in a wine critic? I don't think so." My response, as you know by now, is that hypersensitivity is neither good nor bad. Different sensitivities are often the source of a lot of unpleasant, and unnecessary, disagreement between wine critics and experts.

Perhaps in the future we may see articles like, "Hypersensitive Vinotypes may find the higher alcohol and extreme amount of oak becoming popular in modern Cabernet Sauvignons not to their taste while the tolerant Vinotypes are celebrating the rich delicious flavors that these wines exhibit. We urge the more Hypersensitive and Sensitive Vinotypes to explore the wonders of Pinot Noir, Barbera, Temrpanillo and other wines that typically exhibit less tannin, alcohol and oak…" And who knows, we may even find the emergence of an expert, authoritative and passionate voice writing expressly for the Sweet Vinotypes of the world!

Find the right Vinotype to be your guide

Imagine a future where retail wine consultants, service professionals and writers know how to ask the right questions to lead to wine that will meet and exceed your expectations time after time. In this future an expert could ask you, "What kind of wines do you like the most?" and you would not hesitate to confidently and explicitly tell then exactly what style of wine you prefer with no fear of scorn or disparagement. This does not exist in the wine world today.

If you wanted to go on a trip to explore the Costa Rican rainforest you would probably not want to hire an expert on leading expeditions to Antarctica to be your guide. So why would anyone want to seek advice from a wine expert who does not have expertise on your personal preferences and desired wine destination? You need to be able to find a wine retailer, Internet wine sales site, wine club, restaurants and winery tasting rooms where people understand your personal needs.

Since this is just the beginning of the New Wine Fundamentals and Vinotype revolution, it may be challenging to find the right guide until these concepts become better established. I like to think finding someone who understands this new way of connecting with consumers is analogous to trying to find the appropriate guide to an uncharted territory. But hey, I am delusional just like everyone else!

There are people who love the idea of just heading out with no particular destination in mind. They are excited to just pack up and head out to see where the road leads. Many Vinotypes love to just to go on a ride and live vicariously through the lives of wine experts. If you fit this description, certainly don't stop doing this! Wine experts love the customers who ask, "What have you tried lately that really excited you?" This really allows an enthusiastic wonk or expert to share their passions and discoveries. If you are the enthusiastic wonk or expert just make sure to get permission to before launching off on an exotic expedition.

Speculating about wine pundit Vinotypes

In this section I will outline a few of the people I know and respect who write about wine and make wine recommendations in syndicated news articles, newsletters, and blogs. I cannot do justice in covering the entire range of great wine reviewers available today, but as you read these "reviews of the reviewers" see if you can find the clues to what kind of wine maven you should be on the lookout for to match your own Vinotype.

Finding access to the actual wines recommended by wine writers and bloggers can be a real challenge and, as I will note, some of my favorite reviewers and writers are from different parts of the world. There are just so many products available and the selections differ widely from one area to another – even different stores in the same town. That is why it is so important to find a retail wine consultant you can trust. You need a guide that will put your personal preferences first and who will talk with you on your terms, dedicated to exploring the world of wines on your conditions.

Please note that I am not necessarily saying that I know the exact Vinotype of each of the people I am introducing in this section. I am speculating that if you find your Vinotype in the heading then this is a wine writer or reviewer I seriously recommend you check out.

For the Sweet Vinotypes who love White Zinfandel and Moscato:

I am sorry to say there is no wine writer, as yet, who has your interests at heart. The collective delusions of the wine community have become so jaded about sweet wines and the people who love sweet wines that there is no writer or blogger that I am aware of that is capable of reviewing and recommending wines expressly for you! My hope is that very soon someone will step forward and declare, "I am a Sweet Vinotype and dedicated to the millions of sweet wine drinkers who have been erroneously disenfranchised by the stupidity of the Conventional Wisdoms of the wine cognoscenti."

Today's wine experts have been taught to recommend drier wines when you want sweet. The focus will shift to what the Conventional Wisdoms dictate and that they are doing you a favor by selling you a "more complex wine that pairs better with food." Run away and find another guide – this person is trying to sell you size 6 shoes to fit your size 8 feet!

There is an opportunity for someone to step forward, really break up the tyranny of the minority and become the unabashed advocate and wine reviewer for Sweet Vinotypes. If someone does decide to become the Ponce de Leon for sweet wine drinkers let me know! I will post your contact information on my website.

For the Hypersensitive Vinotypes with a passion for bubbly and adventure:

Sarah Abbott MW, a fellow Master of Wine and goddess of wine education and learning, is one of my favorite examples of how both psychological and physiological elements come together to form an individual Vinotype. She harbors a very distinct Sweet Vinotype inner child. She is hypersensitive to everything in her environment, and she loves wine.

She is mad (not in the angry way, but in the enraptured way) about sparkling wines, Champagne in particular. Her passion for adventure led her to Italy where she tasted the famous Barolo wines of the Piedmonte region. Barolos are notoriously intense, strong red wines -- incongruent with Sarah's level of sensitivity. All the same, her experiences led her to acquire a taste for Barolo. Sarah started to associate the smells and tastes of Barolo with the wonderful experiences she had this region; the wine now stimulates those positive memories and so it is a favorite. Yet the uber-sensitive Sarah's specific stylistic preferences do not necessarily match those of Barolo aficionados, typically the Tolerant Vinotypes. The difference is that, whereas a Tolerant type may favor the big, tannic and more heavily oaked examples of modern Barolo, Sarah searches for the softer, lighter styles, still true to her Sweet self. She is based in the UK so keep in mind that her recommendations may take a little work to find in the US.

http://www.sarahabbottmw.com/about-wine/

For the Hypersensitive Vinotypes who are insanely enthusiastic and want to go on a wild ride:

Gary Vaynerchuk is one of my favorite figures in the wine industry. We met at an event in Houston and I conducted my "Dr. Phil" version of the Vinotype assessment. He is an over the top Hypersensitive. In fact, I had him call his mother to apologize for the horrible morning sickness he put her through (correlated to hypersensitivity of the fetus). Gary is involved in many projects and less in wine these days, though his work lives on. There are hundreds of his videos still available and he is one of the few people in the wine business who is crazy enough to make me look relatively sane.

www.winelibrary.com

For the Hypersensitive Vinotypes looking for an adventurous sense of tradition and unbridled passion:

Dan Berger should appeal to any Hypersensitve Vinotype who loves a really wide range of wine both classic and off-the-wall recommendations. A passionate and outstanding wine writer, he doesn't understand why people get so excited by the high alcohol, overly intense and heavily-oaked powerhouse wines – either red or white - that get so much attention today. And he certainly cannot imagine how anyone can enjoy these wines with food. He loves wines with "classic" and elegant style. He also is a great champion for the varietal and regional wine "orphans" as modern wines become more homogenized and similar in style. He is the author of ***Beyond the Grapes: An Inside Look at Napa Valley*** and ***Beyond the Grapes: An Inside Look at Sonoma County***. His newsletter is more directed to the Wonks, Experts and Professional Vinotypes and his widely syndicated columns should appeal to anyone.

http://www.vintageexperiences.com/

For the Sensitive Vinotypes who are younger, hip and looking for a fresh voice:

Joe Roberts has a blog I love. His tag line says it all: Serious wine talk for the not-so-serious wine drinker. He writes for Playboy Magazine now and also has a book, ***How to Taste Like a Wine Geek: A practical guide to tasting, enjoying, and learning about the world's greatest beverage***. What I particularly admire about Joe is the range of wine styles and prices he covers – the mark of the true Sensitive Vinotype. His blog is also interactive with lots of comments and discussions available for participation by any Enthusiasts and Wonks.

http://www.1winedude.com/

For the Sensitive Vinotypes who appreciate a wide range of wine diversity, elegant writing and elegant restraint in wines:

Jancis Robinson MW, OBE, is a famed English wine writer and appeals to people across a wide spectrum of Vinotypes. Her passions range from dry, delicate and fragrant; she shows great reverence for sweet wines yet is able to take delight in rich, powerful reds – up to a point! People who have grown weary of the high alcohol, intensity-at-all-cost wines will find her recommendations more towards rewarding the restrained and understated styles that often get lost in the 100 point chase. She is truly a grand adventurer and is responsible for some of the greatest books on wine of our time.

http://www.jancisrobinson.com/

For the Tolerant Vinotype who seeks clear and authoritative voice:

Steve Heimoff loves intense, extracted and rich wines and this is not to say he does not recognize and appreciate delicacy and finesse in many wines as well. He will appeal to Tolerant and many Sensitive Vinotypes that love wines from all around the world and particularly intense red wines, like Cabernet Sauvignon from the Napa Valley. His genre is professional wine writer, blogger and wine critic and he combines the 100 point rating system with vivid wine descriptions. He is a trained journalist and a really engaging writer on a wide range of wine-related topics. I particularly admire the way he uses critical thinking to compare and contrast wine attributes rather than asserting any one wine or wine style inherently better than another and to celebrate the diversity that is available to today's wine consumers.

http://steveheimoff.com/

For the Tolerant Vinotype who wants the 100 point rating system:

Robert Parker forever changed the role of the wine critic and established the pervasive 100 point wine system that has become the standard for rating wines. The 100 point Parker system is reliable, replicable and appeals to highly aspiring Sensitive Vinotypes and is the international gold-standard for the Tolerant Vinotypes. It is interesting to note that in the earlier issues of the Wine Advocate there was a lot of pushback about his reviews for the more delicately styled wines of Burgundy and the decision was made to find a different Vinotype to cover those wines. Bob has announced that he is stepping down as editor of the Wine Advocate and it will be interesting to see how this effects the ratings as different, but similarly inclined, Vinotypes will assume many of his duties as he scales back, Parker is not retiring and will remain as CEO and chairman of Wine Advocate's board. In his note to subscribers, Parker said he plans to keep reviewing wines for the publication.

https://www.erobertparker.com

The list of great wine writers, critics and bloggers goes on and on. The ones noted above are just a representative sampling covering a wide spectrum of options and noting the different Vinotypes they may appeal to the most. Explore the options and find the guide, or guides, that are right for you!

Let your palate be your guide

This is such a lame cliché in the wine community I just had to say it. If wine people really thought this was true there would be no condescending sneers when people share honestly about their favorite wines, and wine intimidation would not be an issue for consumers. The full saying goes something like, "Let your palate be your guide as long as you don't like THAT swill."

Now is your time to take control. Find your favorite wine and stick to your guns. Look for your own and very personal wine "AHA!" moments. For many people the "aha" moment of declaring their wine independence comes with discovering a favorite wine: a new Moscato, favorite White Zinfandel or Grand Cru from Burgundy that only a few insiders would ever recognize.

If you haven't found that "AHA!" wine yet keep exploring. It just might be that all the collective delusions we've been dealing with in the wine industry have prevented you from discovering it. There you may stand, seemingly the only person in the crowd who isn't fawning over that intensely bitter and unpleasant Cabernet or listening to some yahoo complaining about a "wimpy" Riesling you find delicious. It's time to start exploring the direction and destination of your choosing and with confidence — knowing that you're following own unique roadmap to enjoying wine. You will know it when you find it.

A new 100 point wine rating system for everyone

Years ago, during a restaurant roundtable discussion in the Napa Valley, the topic of the 100-point rating system reared its head. A lively and increasingly heated debate ensued about the value of this and other point-based wine evaluation scales. The arguments centered on whether or not this, or any other, system, system was relevant, reliable and consistent. Needless to say, there was a great deal of wine consumption going on at the meeting. It became increasingly obviously the issue was not going to be resolved anytime soon and the debate over the validity of the 100 point system rages on to this day.

So I started critically rethinking the existing 100 point model. The first thing I considered was the goal of a rating system. One thought was wine rating was used as a benchmark of quality and/or value to forward wine appreciation and provide consumers with information to make smart wine buying decisions. That seemed fair enough.

Next was taking a hard look at the word *appreciation*. If this was indeed the goal of the wine rating system it would be necessary to clarify the definition.

Appreciation can be interpreted as recognizing the value of something, especially of aesthetic quality, like music or art appreciation. This definition is based on something gaining a greater value through learning and observation. You learn to appreciate a symphonic piece just as one can learn to appreciate certain wine qualities by learning more and detecting different attributes, discerning nuances and perceiving wine differently.

Appreciation can also be defined as an increase in monetary value. A house may (or may not) appreciate in value over time. The value of a stock can appreciate. In this case the property or product is looked at from a benchmark point of value and then is said to appreciate or depreciate in relationship to the benchmark: This house was worth $750,000 and has appreciated in value to $1,000,000.

The opposite of appreciation is depreciation, defined as the loss or reduction of value or a property or goods: This piece of machinery was purchased for $100 new but has depreciated over the past 2 years to a value of $67.

It became clear that if something has a potential value ceiling, such as 100 points (no wine can actually score 101 points), then the process of evaluation is comparative and deductive. It then stands to reason that the use of a 100-point scale is actually a depreciative process: comparing a wine against an imaginary 100-point scale and deducting points for any failure to measure up. Some may argue (you know who you are) that the way wines are scored on the 100 point scale is by adding up the appropriate points for the color, smell and flavor of the wines but the expression of the points is clearly depreciative. An 87 point wine is 13 points below the 100 point target of value, just like the equipment deprecated by $13 from the original value of $100.

Eureka – we have wine depreciation, not appreciation! Thus was born the Guild of Wine Depreciators or GOWD for short.

Wine depreciation has been practiced for a long time using various point scales or representative symbols. Over time these scales have increased in scale. I learned wine rating starting with a 9 point scale popular in the 1970s. Later I was introduced to the 20-point system. Finally I moved up to the 100 point scale introduced way back in the 1930s but popularized and refined in the 1980s. You can also depreciate wine using medals, puffs, stars – all the same in that a goal of gold or five stars as set and wines are measured and depreciated against the benchmark.

The focus today is mostly on the one hundred point scale (or OHPS) popularized by Robert Parker and employed by *Wine Spectator* and practically everyone else. The process is nearly the same for each: A perfect wine is envisioned and then other wines are depreciated (points are deducted) for failure to meet the standards of the perfect wine. Not enough complexity? Deduct. Too much oak? Deduct. Alcohol not high enough? Deduct. Not enough new French oak? We "insiders" all know the depreciation drill.

An inherent problem with the OHPS is that it is really only a 50-point scale. No wine can score less than 50 points by this method. I know of no wine ever depreciated to less than 50 points by the prevailing OHPS critics. I guess a wine gets 50 points for just showing up.

What would it take to depreciate a wine to a score of 42 points? What about if it killed someone? This brings in the omnipresent conversation of subjectivity. Some people might give a wine bonus points depending on who it killed: "No thanks I don't want any of the wine for myself, but I am giving the wine kudos for knocking off Freddie the Jerk!"

The point is that the OHPS used today allows 50 points go to waste. GOWD is not pleased by this. If we have 100 GOWD-given points to depreciate wine, then we need to use them all!

The conversion from the OHPS 100-point system to the GOWD system is quite easy. There are two sections for the GOWD 100-point scale:

- 50 points are available for depreciating the wine
- 50 points are available for depreciating the experience with the wine.

Simply put, a wine that scored 83 points on the OHPS would be equal to 33 points (83 minus the 50 points for showing up). The extra 50 points are then used to depreciate the experience you had while consuming the wine. What fun! It could be that you had a mediocre wine but a really great time drinking it. The answer to the question, "How was that wine you had the other night?" might go something along the lines of, "The wine was OK and there was lots of it -- we watched the entire Lord of the Rings series non-stop on Blue-ray with a killer sound system and had a blast. I would give the wine a score of 91 by GOWD!" If you hate the Lord of the Rings series, were bored by the people or disliked the wine, the score might have been a 60.

Consider some of these factors and then depreciate the wine you are evaluating accordingly. Also keep in mind Vinotypic plasticity and how environment and mood can affect your perception:

- Who picked up the check? Really expensive wine is always vastly more enjoyable, smoother, and delicious to me when someone else is paying the bill.
- Did you like the people you were with? Criticizing and depreciating people is even more popular than criticizing wine for some – learn to be more appreciative for cryin' out loud.
- Did you have it by yourself and not like yourself at that particular time? Maybe you were sad about the fact that you were alone with your wonderful bottle? Deduct, deduct, deduct. And go back to the bullet on appreciating people, you geek.
- How was the food? Was there enough food? Was the food the right color and size for the wine? Did the wine stand up to the food?
- Was the music the right choice? My good friend and fellow whacko Clarke Smith had done some remarkable work on how different music affects wine perception:
  http://www.sfgate.com/wine/article/Music-to-drink-wine-by-Vintner-insists-music-can-3235602.php
- Were you in the wine country secreted away in the vineyards, naked and pouring locally grown, virgin olive oil over you and your lover while swigging wine from the bottle…never mind.

Now you can begin to see how much more useful the GOWD system is. Here are some notes from my personal experiences to help you familiarize yourself with the format. This is an example using one of the most exalted wines in the world of wine connoisseurs, collectors and geeks: 1945 Chateau Mouton Rothschild.

Wine Evaluated: 1945 Mouton Rothschild -- 50 points
Total score: 50 total points by GOWD system (50 for wine, 0 for experience)

Wine notes: (50 points)
I had the opportunity to taste the legendary 1945 Chateau Mouton Rothschild. The wine itself was almost a religious experience;; full, deep, perfect state of maturity. Concentrated, powerful and exotic. WOW! This wine was simply as good as it gets for my Tolerant, geeky Vinotype.

Experience: (0 points)
Tasted at Chez ChiChi Restaurant in New York. I had to take a client there and could have sworn this guy was Freddie the Jerk's evil twin. He said that if I ordered the most expensive wine on the list it was likely he would send his business my way. I tried to recommend the $25 Syrah but he insisted and hinted that I might have my kneecaps damaged if I refused to order the Mouton. Jeez. The saddest part was that since I was selling and he was buying, I was stuck with the bill. A really big bill. I really would have preferred being home with my family or having a draft beer, eating an order of chicken wings and watch the game on the big screen. The food was great but this was New York - did I mention the really big bill, not to mention the person I was with was a jerk?

OK – so you get the picture. Great wine; lousy experience. Here is another example that is mostly (somewhat) true:

Wine Evaluated: Beringer White Zinfandel – 100 points
Score: 100 points by the GOWD system (35 points for the wine, 50 points for the experience, 15 bonus points 'cause I say so and you will see why later).

Wine notes: 35 points
Frankly I did not try the wine but I give it 35 points for getting the job done (which was making my date happy) so who the hell cares what it tasted like! I remember that my date LOVED it. It was lightly pink and so was I from the bubbling hot tub we were sitting in at the time.

Experience: 50 points plus 15 bonus points
Tasted in my hot tub after band practice when I lived in a little house in the vineyards in Rutherford, California in the heart of the Napa Valley. The singer in the band agreed to come over to my place for a relaxing hot tub and told me, "I just love White Zinfandel and drinking it makes me do crazy things." We are now married and have two great kids. She remains the love of my life and I adore her. She later evolved to a Hypersensitive Vinotype enjoyer genre who loves Pinot Noir – mostly due to peer and social pressure for marrying a wine geek.

What would qualify as a perfect 100 rating on the GOWD system? Maybe if Kate had brought along a bottle of 1945 Mouton Rothschild and said, "Someone gave me this wine and I hate red wines – they taste awful. You can drink this all by yourself and I will have some of that yummy White Zinfandel that somehow makes you look very attractive" That is the word of GOWD.

The take-home messages for the wine industry

No one wine suits all people all the time, but we can improve how to segment the market, target wines to reach specific segments, and in many cases, remove stigmas or arcane wine and food messages that drive consumers to other beverage choices. This means returning sweet wine to a place it has occupied for centuries: the table. It also means allowing people who love big, red wines to feel completely at ease enjoying a glass of the wine they love the most with their sushi or shrimp cocktail — a combination they may savor with relish.

We have distinguished four primary flavor categories of wine that map to the flavor preference and language each consumer group is predisposed to favor. Each segment, Sweet, Hypersensitive, Sensitive, and Tolerant, has its own boundaries for flavor preferences in wine and its feelings about the overall experience of wine that influence their purchase and consumption of wine.

Words that best describe desirable wine flavors for different Vinotypes.
Values at 25 percent or above are colored more darkly;
values between 20percent and 24percent are colored more lightly.

Word	Sweet	Hyper-sensitive	Sensitive	Tolerant
Sweet	79	24	12	10
Fruity	50	14	15	18
Light	37	14	9	4
Fragrant	16	24	19	12
Smooth	51	55	48	47
Balanced	23	41	30	36
Full-bodied	12	40	41	49
Rich	9	23	21	28
Dry	3	34	41	39
Complex	4	29	34	39
Earthy	3	15	17	20
Bold	3	16	13	20
"Big Red"	1	17	16	31

Taste sensitivity is a deeply personal quality and it is not "better" to be one or another, just different. Taste sensitivity is also tied to flavor preferences, personality traits and consumer behaviors. An appreciation and understanding of these differences are fundamental to finely tuning your wines and message to potential consumers. If you learn to target your marketing and to sell your wines according to consumer physiology and psychology, you will increase your chances of pleasing your consumers, and by pleasing them, you will increase your chances of success.

Keep in mind that there are many mitigating psychological factors involved that play an equally important role in the development of our ever-changing personal preferences. The more natural or unbiased a person's wine preferences are, the more useful this categorization of wine styles becomes for looking at your products against the market opportunities. Applications for this means of grouping wines by words that are meaningful to consumers are in the next generation of Progressive Wine lists in restaurants and flavor-based wine sections that provide a safety zone for consumers who do not relate to the confusing, metaphorical descriptive terms favored by the industry and more aspirational wine consumers.

Sweet wines

This is the most easily defined flavor category of all: The wines are sweet. The second and third most important descriptors the Sweet types look for are "smooth" and "fruity." White Zinfandel is the benchmark and Moscato is the wine that is showing explosive growth from a small base. Sangria, Lambrusco and sweet red wines all fit into this category, but there is a lot of room to offer higher priced wine with marketing focused on developing cachet and appropriateness at the table.

Our research confirms the people who prefer sweet wines unabashedly declare that they want wine that is sweet, not just off-dry or slightly sweet, and the reticence of the wine industry to employ the word sweet as a descriptor to this segment is unfounded. This flavor category is for wines that range from about 1.5 percent residual sugar (15 grams per liter) to a "sweet spot" in the range of 3 percent residual sugar (30 grams per liter) and then up to the neighborhood of 8 percent residual sugar (80 grams per liter) or even more. Alcohol levels should be kept very low; typically in the 10 percent alcohol by volume range or less. Bitter elements, reductive aromatic characteristics and high acidity are experienced at exaggerated intensities and sulfites must be closely kept in check.

The wine industry's misguided efforts to "move them up" to dry wine results in their migration to cocktails or other sweet beverages and contributes to the disenfranchisement that we have erroneously created for sweet wine consumers. They also want to enjoy these wines with steak, chicken and fish so be careful of creating wine and food pairings that virtually eliminate the wines from consideration for everyday enjoyment with the meals the Sweet Vinotypes really prepare and enjoy.

Given the proper products and messaging, Sweet tasters can be sold much more expensive products than conventional wisdom dictates. Properly understanding what these very sensitive tasters want, rather than relying on pervasive misinformation and false assumptions, could pay huge dividends for the wine industry as a whole new way to engage and cultivate reticent but willing consumers.

The Sweet market segment is large and under leveraged. If the wine industry continues to stigmatize sweet wine, they will continue to opt for cocktails and opt out of the wine category. Indeed Sweet phenotypes drink wine significantly less often than the other segments, and have the least confidence in choosing wines.

Sweet consumers have no use for the point system for judging wines except to warn them away from these wines. The wines that garner the highest points are most often dry and high in oak, bitterness and astringency. Just the kind of flavors the Sweet and Hypersensitive Vinotypes hate the most.

The direction to take for Sweet consumers is towards wines with 3 to 6 percent residual sugar, impeccably made, and towards promoting these wines with the foods that they eat on a regular basis; and do not forget to give them confidence in their good taste when they choose sweet wines! An even bigger opportunity exists in restaurants and bars where these consumers usually migrate to beer and cocktails rather than wines — give them the opportunity to feel secure and proud in their wine choice, and they may migrate back!

Delicate wines

Pinot Grigio made in a low intensity, lower alcohol and traditional manner, hits this segment smack on the head. Attempts to make barrel-aged, high alcohol and more "serious" styles of Pinot Grigio may steal away or may capture a few Chardonnay drinkers. But the Hypersensitive crowd, those responsible for the explosive growth of Pinot Grigio, wants their wine light, smooth, low in alcohol and fruity. Riesling stands as a great fit for this segment but confusion about sweetness levels and aromatics tend to keep the potential growth in check.

Delicate wines are mostly dry or may be up to about 1.5 percent (15 grams per liter) of residual sugar, and the popularity of wines, such as Chardonnay and many Sauvignon Blancs, with traces of residual sugar, is best explained from the point of view of the Hypersensitive taster. They are by far the group that "talks dry and drinks sweet" but at a level of sweetness significantly lower than the clearly-defined Sweet wine consumers. There is little doubt that many of the most successful brands today, especially wines not traditionally considered as sweet like Chardonnay, have more than a little residual sugar.

Consumers inclined to prefer delicate wines also favorably respond to the word "fragrant." Care must be taken in managing the aromatics for this highly sensitive segment so that the intensity of aromas does not become like being stuck in an elevator with someone doused in cologne! Again, bitter elements, reductive aromatic characteristics and high acidity are experienced at exaggerated intensities and sulfites must be closely kept in check in your delicate wines. Many modern wineries decide a "more intense, riper, higher alcohol and oak-aged" version of a wine like Pinot Grigio will be "better." Not to the intended audience. The wine may appeal more to a Chardonnay lover but they usually know they don't want a Pinot Grigio so it becomes a tough sell.

Smooth wines

"Smooth" is far and away the most often cited positive descriptor across all of the segments in our research, and this aligns with results from many other studies. The word "smooth" as a flavor category resonates as a primary category descriptor with the Sensitive type and is inherently associated with a wine that is dry, full-bodied, richly fruity and complex. This category runs the widest gamut of regions and grape varieties from Alsatian whites, Chardonnay, richer-style Pinot Noir, Rhone wines and all sorts of white and red blends.

Smooth wines can be well concentrated, higher in alcohol and, to demonstrate the benefit of residual sugar in suppressing bitterness, have up to and a bit over 1 percent (10 grams per liter) of residual sugar. Wines in this category are usually made with modern techniques: whites benefit from the smoothness associated with malo-lactic fementation and reds need to be deeply extracted with minimum harsh bitter or astringent characteristics.

Intense wines

Defining "intense" as a flavor category is relatively simple. More color (almost invariably red), more flavor, more alcohol, more oak, more tannin and you are in! The frustrating thing for many in the industry is the dominance of this style of wine and the accompanying 100 point system that is custom built for assessing this style of wines. It resonates with the psyche of the Tolerant types who love intense wines.

There is an interesting opportunity unfolding as we deepen our focus on the wine and food dilemma of the Sweet wine consumer. The common message is that sweet wine doesn't pair with mainstream foods, yet that is what this segment prefers. As well, people who love intense wines also often want these wines from beginning to end in their meals, and it's equally important to ensure that they feel completely at ease ordering the wine they love with seafood, chicken, vegetables or anything else they fancy. The Tolerant phenotype is not subject to the metallic, bitter clash more sensitive people experience so let's remove the limitations!

Consumer studies conducted by wine companies, universities and independent research organizations find that consumers are not confident when it comes to choosing wines for themselves or others. Sweet and Hypersensitive Vinotypes are not only less confident, they consume wine far less often.

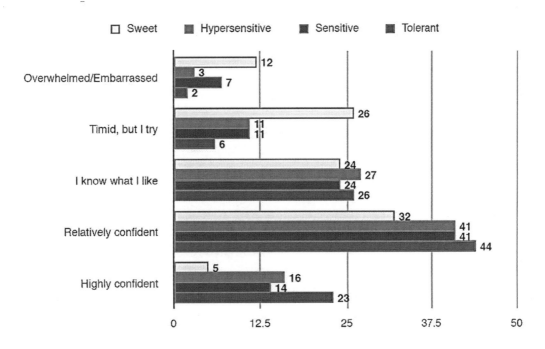

Source: Consumer Wine preferences, Attitudes and Behaviors – see Appendix 2

FREQUENCY OF WINE CONSUMPTION

Percent of respondents consuming wine at each frequency for each taste group.

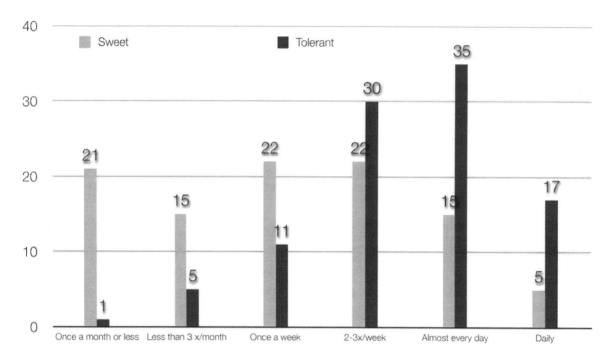

Respondents *in the* **Sweet** *group* drink wine **far less often** *than do* **Tolerants**.

How do we encourage 'sweet' consumers to drink wine more often?

Source: Consumer Wine Preferences, Attitudes and Behaviors – see Appendix 2

Chapter 4 Q&A

Question: Don't sweet wine drinkers just drink cheap wines?

Answer: That is more of a self-fulfilling prophecy than anything else. Fifty years ago a good quality Mosel Riesling was as expensive and classified growth Bordeaux wines. As we alienated sweet wine consumers they simply turn to cocktails when they want to spend more money. This is a huge opportunity for the wine business to make high quality sweet wines and market them as aggressively as we market dry wines. A Sweet or Hypersensitive Vinotype will gladly pay a high premium for an ultra-smooth vodka!

Question: Hasn't the wine industry made great strides in expanding the popularity of wine, particularly in the US?

Answer: By all means, wine is more popular than ever in the US and certainly growing in countries like China. But remember wine consumption has been plummeting in France, Italy and Spain. Here is an interesting take on the wine industry efforts to market more effectively and take even more advantage of the opportunities at hand.

"Years of missed opportunity?"

"The fragmented, historically insular (wine) industry generally seems resigned to accepting the wine consumer pool as is rather than aggressively pursuing new markets... the next decade could easily be referred to by future wine historians as the "years of missed opportunity."
Brand Week, May 1, 2000

10 Years After

So what does the wine landscape look like 10 years after Brand Week's prediction that "the next decade could easily be referred to as the 'years of missed opportunity'"?

"The wine industry is guilty of going out of its way to confuse the consumer, and must urgently come up with 'a new big idea', according to a British advertising heavyweight...'The wine industry is the most fragmented market I've seen. Fragmented, confusing, impenetrable.'

"The [wine] industry fails hopelessly on accessibility. This is market that goes out of its way to confuse the consumer," he said in his keynote speech, titled "The wine business viewed from the outside."

Hegarty's solution was to redress wine's image as an accompaniment to food - which he suggested was a drawback - instead promoting it to stand alone with the slogan "wine flavours our life."
Sir John Hegarty, June 28, 2010, Masters of Wine International Symposium, Bordeaux, France as reported by Monday 28 June 2010 by John Abbott in Bordeaux

Notes: _____

_____

_____

_____

_____

_____

_____

_____

_____

_____

_____

_____

_____

_____

_____

_____

_____

Chapter 5: Sense and Sense-ability

Dr. Linda Bartoshuk: "The truth is, we live in different taste worlds. To try to say that one wine is better than another is just not sensible."

"We've known for a long time that people don't all live in the same taste world. Supertasters (hypersensitive tasters) live in a neon taste world - everything is bright and vibrant. For non-tasters, everything is pastel. Nothing is ever really intense." John Hayes, Ph.D., an assistant professor of food science at the Penn State College of Agricultural Sciences.

In the last chapter we saw how your unique sensory configuration, capacities and capabilities determines how the universe occurs for you. The reasons and roots of why we human beings like what we like, and dislike the things we dislike, boils down to two factors. One factor is physiological, encompassing our genetically determined, anatomical sensory features. The second factor is the programming and on-going reprogramming that occurs in the human processing unit we call our brain.

The first factor, sensory physiology, determines our individual capacity to perceive any given sensory stimulus and the intensity to which you perceive it. It is easy to think of this in terms of sight (color blindness, light sensitivity) and hearing (some people have incredibly acute hearing, like my wife when I say something I don't want her to hear) but this is also the case in taste and smell.

The second factor, sensory psychology or neurology, is how we are programmed to respond to sensory stimuli. This programming comes in two basic forms: Pre-programmed (instinctive) responses including the required commands that keep our heart beating and our lungs breathing and also the commands for responses to things that may be dangerous or provide pleasure. Then there are responses to life experiences that we store as memories. These are how we respond to sensory stimuli over time by observation and learning. An instinctive response can be overwritten by an experience. Over time we add more positive or negative associations, which modifying the meaning or context to the different sensory stimuli we experience. Acquiring a taste for coffee is a good example. As we observe the grownups drinking the vile-tasting beverage we want to be considered grownup ourselves. We associate coffee with waking up to "smell the coffee." Over time we decide if we like it at all and if we do acquire the taste, we get to determine how want it to taste. We may even become passionate and learn to speak according to the new coffee groupthink and vernacular. "Could I have a *venti*, flat, skinny latte with a hazelnut shot, please?"

The analogy of hardware and software helps explain how these two factors work. Sensory physiology is the genetically-determined "hardware" that determines the range and intensity of sensations you are capable of experiencing. Your sensory software determines how those sensations are processed.

Sensory hardware provides the means to convert sensory stimuli (taste and aroma molecules, sound waves, light waves, heat or cold, etc.) into a transmission to our brains for processing by our sensory software. The intensity of sensations sent to the brain can differ radically from one person to the next. While most people have an awareness of these differences, few have any idea of how our individual perception capacities show up in everyday disagreements about things like thermostat settings, the volume for the stereo, or the need for extra salt. It certainly affects our wine preferences.

Discovering how very differently people respond to sensory stimulation goes far, far beyond learning more about wine preferences.

Sensory and Perceptual Sensitivity

A sensation involves the physical process of receiving stimuli which connect with our sensory organs and receptors, and then converting that into signals that are relayed to the appropriate area of the brain for processing.

- *The wine tasted sweet.*
- *I saw the wine was red.*

Perception occurs when our brain interprets these signals and ascribes meaning to them. Perception is how the brain evaluates and measures the sensory information that is relayed.

- *The wine was not sweet enough for me.*
- *The wine was too sweet for me.*

Sensory sensitivity (or sensory acuity) is the actual physical ability of the sensory organs to receive input or stimulation and determines the types of stimulation, threshold of detection, and intensity of sensory information sent to the brain.

- *Tags in my clothes are so annoying I have to cut them out.*
- *I don't find this wine bitter but others do.*

Perceptual sensitivity can be defined as a psychological or environmentally influenced change in sensitivity. The changes will be proportional to your sensory sensitivity influenced by focus, attention, distraction, awareness, movement – even by mood, temperature or the color of a room!

- *I learned to focus and pay much more attention to the smell of wines.*
- *Wines taste really different to me when I am in an airplane.*

Revising the "Supertaster" paradigm

The notion that certain people are "supertasters" has gained a lot of attention and is an area in dire need of some clarification. Like so many delusions there is a popular idea that wine experts are somehow specially endowed with super powers or sensory superiority. In fact, the most super-sensitive people often find modern dry wines repulsive.

In the late 1990s I discovered the research of Dr. Linda Bartoshuk, an experimental psychologist at the University of Florida. Based on her research at the Yale School of Medicine in the early 1990s, she had concluded that some people had elevated taste perception of certain compounds. People, she concluded, cannot share one another's sensory experiences and in fact, "live in completely different sensory worlds."

Eureka! This could explain a lot in terms of the dissonance and disagreement I was observing between wine experts and wine consumers. Linda was later interviewed by Stacy Finz for a San Francisco Chronicle article and was kind enough to provide encouragement and support for my expansion on her work:

Unconventional wine expert says the number of taste buds determines your wine preferences

Tim Hanni's unconventional wisdom says that you owe your wine preferences to the number of taste buds on your tongue.
San Francisco Chronicle, Stacy Finz, Chronicle Staff Writer
Friday, March 7, 2008

"Linda Bartoshuk, a professor of taste and smell at the University of Florida in Gainesville who coined the term supertaster and is a leading authority on the subject, praises the way Hanni has applied the research to wine appreciation "I think Tim is a real hero," says Bartoshuk. "What he's doing is applying sensible science. The truth is, we live in different taste worlds. To try to say that one wine is better than another is just not sensible."

To go back a bit further, in 1931, A.L. Fox, a DuPont chemist, was working in a laboratory when chemical compound called phenylthiocarbamide (PTC) was spilled. Some people in the lab complained of a horribly bitter sensation from inhaling the PTC while others seemed to be oblivious to sensation. This led to the idea that there was a significant difference in our individual sensory perception abilities.

At a meeting of the American Association for the Advancement of Science that year, Fox collaborated with geneticist named Albert Blakeslee to have attendees taste PTC: 65 percent found it bitter, 28 percent found it tasteless and 6 percent described other taste qualities.

Subsequent work revealed that the ability to taste PTC was genetic in nature. In the 1960s, Roland Fischer was the first to link the ability to taste PTC, and the related compound propylthiouracil (PROP, a prescription thyroid medication), to food preference and body type. (PTC today is considered a health hazard and not often used in trials or demonstrations.)

Bartoshuk and her colleagues built on this work to discover that people could be put into one of three PROP sensitivity groups:

- "Non-tasters" who report no bitter taste whatsoever.
- "Tasters" who found it somewhat bitter and unpleasant, but not that bad, or at least not at first; the unpleasant sensation often increased over time.
- "Supertasters" who immediately found the compound tastes horribly and intensely bitter.

Most estimates suggest 25 percent of the population are non-tasters, 50 percent are medium tasters and 25 percent are supertasters. Here was the origin of the term "supertaster," which in the wine world suggested a superior sense of taste.

Supertaster, however, is an unfortunate term – misleading at best. In the wonderful work of Dr. Bartoshuk the term "supertaster" referred to people with a specific to sensitivity to a relatively narrow group of compounds; PTC, PROP and other forms of thiourea. The bitter taste receptor gene TAS2R38 has been associated with the ability to taste PROP and PTC but it cannot completely explain the "supertaster" phenomenon. People with a hyper-sensitivity to these compounds, tend to have general sensory hypersensitivity (smell, touch, hearing and sight) but it is quite possible to be highly sensitive to bitterness in general and not taste PROP. But you can be sensitive to PROP and not bitter sensitive in general.

The term "supertaster" led to the erroneous idea in the wine media and wine community that wine experts are specially equipped and must be supertasters. An article in the Glove and Mail in Canada ran a March 20, 2012 headline, *Wine experts more likely to be supertaster,* in response to a study of PROP sensitivity between professional sommeliers and consumers at Brock University in Ontario, Canada. The methodology employed really pointed more to the self-fulfilling prophecy that the sommelier training and wine tasting practices favor a narrow range of

Genetics and cilantro

Talk about different perception and viewpoints! Just try to convince some people that cilantro is delicious and they should learn to like it. Back to our "shoe analogy," this would make about as much sense as telling someone with size 11 feet that they should "learn" to like stuffing their feet in size 8 shoes.

To most people cilantro is a fragrant, tolerably bitter herb most frequently associated with Mexican cuisine.

To a select few people, maybe 4-5 percent of the population, cilantro elicits a horrible and bitter sensation that is often described as "soapy." According to Dr. Charles Wysocki, sensory researcher at Monnell Chemical Senses Center, this is a genetic condition and identical twins will have the same perception of cilantro. He surmises that this is due to a mutated or missing gene or receptor.

So what wine pairs with cilantro? I guess that may have something to do with your personal preferences.

Vinotypes, thus is it is relatively predictable they will tend to be in the hypersensitive end of the sensitivity spectrum. To the contrary of the results of the Brock study I know many world class wine experts at both ends of the sensitivity spectrum.

Being a supertaster or non-taster represents normal variation in the human population like eye or hair color and should not be construed as making someone a better or lesser wine expert. As we have seen, people with extreme taste sensitivity often have trouble enjoying wine, or any alcoholic beverage at all, due to the intensity of burning and bitterness they experience. The probability is that people who like things sweet indeed seem to have the utmost taste sensitivity of all.

Linda's work was an important stimulus for me in deepening the understanding of how physiological, genetically related traits impact our sensory perception and how dramatically this can vary from one person to the next.

My intention is to clarify the understanding of the phenomenon and remove the "super" and exchange it with a less superior-sounding word. Everyone at first glance would want to be a "super" taster so we created the distinction hypersensitive taster. This helps improve our understanding of consumers and getting the right wines to the right people without the inappropriate, negative and cynical attitude wine people have towards sweet wines or the false premise that a wine expert needs to have super powers of perception.

In creating Vinotypes, we looked at more sensitivity factors than a single compound reaction; thus we are replacing term "supertaster" with Hypersensitive. Our estimates are somewhat similar with 50 percent at higher sensitivity (Sweet and Hypersensitive Vinotypes), 35 percent Sensitive Vinotypes and about 15 percent Tolerant Vinotypes from a genetic, physiological standpoint.

Keep in mind that there are many variables involved in the range and intensity of taste sensations you experience, such as the number and type of taste receptors on each taste bud and the intensity of the transmission of the taste stimulus to your brain. In a general sense, however, the number of taste buds you have indicates your overall taste sensitivity.

Are people with more sensitive palates generally better able to describe wine characteristics? Here's what's funny — well, maybe not funny but interesting. People who are at the highest level of sensitivity seem to have the hardest time picking out sensations to describe because of the cacophony of sensations they experience.

Sweet and Hypersensitive Vinotypes also get mental fatigue much more quickly when they taste because they are processing so many different things. The Tolerant tasters tend to be very decisive, much more accurate in replicating their scores and results, because they are dealing with a lesser amount of total sensory input.

Do we want to encourage the Tolerant taster? We want to encourage everybody. But we want to free people from the prevailing dominance of the tolerant taster. In judging or writing about wines, there needs to be different systems for different people. A great system is available for the Tolerant taster: The Parker or Wine Spectator 100 point system. But the evaluations and scores are often directly in opposition to the preferences of Sweet and many Hypersensitive Vinotypes, like Dr. Virginia Utermohlen and Joanne, my mother-in-law. They both know the more points a wine scores, the more they'll dislike the wine, so it's actually a valuable system but in the inverse.

How (or if) you wear underwear may provide insight to wine preferences

Individual sensory sensitivity is manifested in strange ways. As Dr. Utermohlen and I were reviewing data collected from wine consumers, our discussion was focused on the ways heightened taste sensitivity is manifested in many other behaviors related to sensory sensitivity — ranging from finding the right thermostat settings to the need to cut tags out of clothing because they are so irritating. She asked me, "Have you ever asked people if they wear their underwear inside out?"

"Dear God," I replied, "what on earth for?"

Virginia went on to explain that a common behavior of ultra-hypersensitive people is to invert their undies due to the irritation from the seams against their skin. Or, she said, they oftentimes just abandon wearing undergarments altogether.

Inquiring minds want to know, so I decided to try asking this question at the next event where I conducted our Sensitivity assessment – the questions about salt, coffee, sweeteners and the like. At a tasting in San Francisco, I asked the questions of a gentleman who hit all of the other questions for a Sweet taster dead-on: He can't stand coffee (too bitter), loves salt (a sign of more taste buds, not fewer), and experiences a horrible, bitter, metallic taste from artificial sweeteners. And yes, he loved sweet wines and could not stand the horrible taste of dry wines.

I proceeded to make assertion after assertion on things like his need to cut tags out of his clothes, and how loud restaurants completely ruin even the most delicious food. I suggested that his mother had experienced severe morning sickness with him. He was amazed.

Feeling this was the perfect chance, I asked, "Do you ever wear your underwear inside out?"

He almost fell over. His friends were quite amused. The red-faced and flummoxed man cried, "How the hell did you know THAT?" Another connection to the term "blush wine"? Just kidding.

And boy, this assertion is going to get my detractors' panties in a wad. That is, if they wear any.

Paint your tongue blue: a do-it-yourself sensitivity test

The easiest way to test your selective sensitivity to PROP is to get some thiourea strips that available from several online biological supply houses. Put the strip on your tongue and wet it. If it is repulsively, horribly bitter you are a supertaster TO THIS COMPOUND. If it is bitter but no big deal, or it builds up over time – you are sensitive or a "taster." People with non-sensitivity or tolerance to the compound will shrug and just mumble, "Tastes like wet paper." You are (gasp) a non-taster.

This experiment is best done with a group of people so you can see how wildly the reactions vary!

Here is another way to find out more about your general taste sensitivity without the strips.

Here are the materials you will need:

- Some thick paper (3×5 note card or construction paper)
- A hole punch or (easiest) a binder-ring hole reinforcement sticker
- Blue food coloring
- Mirror - a lighted and magnified makeup mirror works best
- Magnifying glass, even if you have the magnified mirror
- Cotton swab or paper towel to apply food color

Step 1:
Swab your tongue with blue food color using a cotton swab, paper towel or your finger. Swab off the excess food color, dabbing your tongue with a paper towel. The tongue should be a pretty light blue color. You will notice under the magnifying glass that the food coloring will tend to show up on most of your tongue, but the papillae, or taste buds, will show up as little, pink bumps on your tongue.

Step 3:
Place the hole on the paper or reinforcement ring over the part of your tongue toward the tip and just to the left or right of center

Step 4:
Use the magnifying glass and a mirror to count how many papillae you see on your tongue through the hole in the paper. The papillae should appear like tiny pink dots surrounded by blue food coloring. If you count 35 or more, you are probably hypersensitive. If you counted between 15 or more up to around 35 you are a sensitive taster. If you counted less than 15, you are probably tolerant. The more papillae you counted the more you are toward the hypersensitive end of the scale.

Caveats

I find it really hard to distinguish between the papillae and other parts of the tongue. Also, there are many factors, such as the number of actual receptors on each taste bud and the intensity of transmission of the sensation to the brain, that probably have a very important role in determining your true sensitivity. I have looked at and photographed hundreds of tongues and here are some examples.

To the right we have four pictures:
1. Sweet
2. Hypersensitive
3. Sensitive
4. Tolerant

Physiological and psychological factors influence all sort of preferences and behaviors far beyond just the wines you like or dislike. Including possibly how you wear your underwear.

A very good friend of mine, John Stallcup, works part time in a prestigious, Napa Valley tasting room. He recently started taking a medication that has rendered him a very hypersensitive Vinotype. Recently he told me, "I can now relate to how really sensitive tasters experience dry wines – they taste just awful!"

For the most part our sensory hardware is relatively fixed. Sensitivity changes over time are usually gradual and subtle. Plus don't forget that psychological changes play a very important role in our wine preference changes. There are key exceptions, like medications mentioned above and physical or neurological injuries, which can have a profound and immediate effect on your perceptive capacities.

Your sensory software comes somewhat pre-programmed at birth, providing instinctive responses to stimuli.

It's important, however, to keep in mind that psychology plays an important role in determining final wine preferences and the part of your preference system that is most changeable over time.

Sensations are illusions

Did you know there is actually no color in the universe? It only occurs in the way your brain reacts to, and interprets, light wavelengths. And don't forget about Olga and her sister who did not discover, until late in life, what they were experiencing was not the norm and that our perceptive differences can be very minor or radically different.

Just as you brain needs only the first and last letters to be in place to figure out the words below, people "trained" to match wine and food just need a few ingredients and wine descriptors to come up with a wine and food match. The imagination of descriptors for the type of a wine mixed, compared with a list of ingredients, preparation and seasonings for a food dish, and *voilà;* a wine and food match!

Here is a fun illusion of how the brain takes the first and last letters of words and then sorts out the rest of the letter that have been mixed up in between:

Rsreaceh swohs taht the mnid wkors in couruis wyas. If I wirte auobt wneis, lkie Cohannrdy, Cbrenaet Svaigunon or Wihte Zfdaneil and hvae the ltetres mexid up yuor biran wlil be albe to frgiue out the wdros cerorctly. Jsut gvie the bairn a few pomrpts and it wlil flil in the bnlkas. Wtih pcatrie you can raed this amslot as fsat as nmraol txet.

The trained mind will almost immediately match the appropriate descriptive words for the wine. Ask about wine and food matching and their brain will then match the descriptive attributes of the food, or vice-versa. Keep in mind that it is all in your head. Humans just love describing the things they experience, even if they are just illusions and metaphors. See if you can figure out what the words below are actually describing. This is a real description.

(89) …medium to full body, low acidity, often deeply pungent or bittersweet, with an aromatic complexity that may range from floral and fruit notes … through the more typical cedar, papaya fruit and dark chocolate notes. …with just the barest hint of musty ferment. Enough to introduce some hearty cedar-toned richness and a dark chocolate twist to the fruit, but mild enough to allow some of the classic floral and fruit top notes to bloom.

How many of you guessed a cup of coffee? The point is that humans love to describe things and often get carried away. Notice also the employment of a depreciative point score. Coffee and even beer are starting to go down the dark hallway of overcomplicating things and even matching coffee and beer to food. Note to the coffee and beer industries – knock it off!

Chapter 5 Q&A

Question: Don't our taste buds wear out or get burnt out by eating things like really hot, spicy foods?

Answer: The prevailing Conventional Wisdom (and you know how I feel about Conventional Wisdoms by now) is that our "palates" change over time. There is some truth to this but most our changes in preferences are neurological, not physiological.

An example is, "his taste buds were burned out by eating too much spicy foods." As we started to learn more about the really sensitive Vinotypes we were surprised to see the people who crave really hot foods tended to be really sensitive – and this greater sensitivity means the chemesthetic (touch/irritation sensations triggered by the capsaicin and other hot compounds) has their brain release euphoric chemicals into the blood stream. For the lucky people this hot, burning sensation "hurts really good!" Just like sadomasochism and runners' high. Their taste buds are not burning out. They are just having a private, *Harry Met Sally* moment. And let them have their strong, high alcohol wine if that is what they love! The unpleasant burn it causes for you makes their experience that much better.

The other thing that came from further investigation into the phenomenon of changing tastes is that we get an entirely new set of taste buds every 24 hours! Yes, taste buds can be injured or damaged to the point of dysfunction but that is relatively rare.

> Taste buds and olfactory receptor cells are the fastest growing and most rapidly regenerating cells in the body. Taste buds regenerate completely in a 24-hour period. The entire bud is replaced by new cells on a daily basis.
>
> Growth of Taste and Smell Receptors, the Taste and Smell Clinic:
> http://www.tasteandsmell.com/nov07.htm

Question: What do towels, sheets and pillowcases have to do with wine preferences?

Answer: People with general perceptual hypersensitivity tend to be very, very picky about the softness of towels and demand specific thread counts and texture for their sheets and pillowcases. This hyper-acuity to touch also contributes to the perception of food textures and often contributes to their food pickiness. All of this relates to wine preferences, especially how they perceive alcohol levels (hot and burning), bitterness (exaggerated) and thus plays a key role in their wine flavor preferences.

Question: Do people with more taste buds make better wine tasters?

Answer: Sweet and Hypersensitive Vinotypes are not better or worse tasters – just different. Dr. Gary Pickering, a professor of oenology at Brock University in Canada, asked whether hypertasters are at an advantage when it comes to wine tasting, is quoted as saying, "I would speculate that supertasters (hypersensative tasters) probably enjoy wine less than the rest of us. They experience astringency, acidity, bitterness, and heat (from alcohol) more intensely, and this combination may make wine – or some wine styles – relatively unappealing."

Question: I frequently hear that women make better wine tasters and winemakers.

Answer: Not better, just different. The chart at the right shows the percentage of each Vinotype by gender from a study we conducted. Women make up about 70 percent of the most sensitive tasters but that still leaves 30 percent men. The number of Hypersensitive Vinotypes is nearly equal! In fact, if you can find a winery with a winemaker that is your same Vinotype sensitivity, genre or interests and shares your passion for making the types of wine you love, you would be amazed how great you will find their products. That goes for ALL Vinotypes and covers the gamut of wine styles and regions.

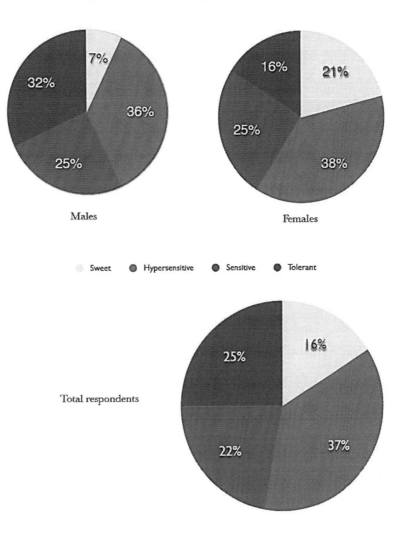

Notes: _____

_____

_____

_____

_____

_____

_____

_____

_____

_____

_____

_____

_____

_____

_____

_____

_____

_____

Chapter 6: It's All in Your Head

Vinotypes are defined by a combination of their sensitivity quotient (Sw, Hs, Se, and To), their genre (enjoyer, enthusiast, wonk, etc.) and by the types and styles of wines they enjoy most on a regular basis. By the way, "but I love every type of wine and style" is a completely acceptable answer to the question: "What wines do you enjoy most on a regular basis?" It can be completely wide open or very specific. It is well known that many people change their wine preferences over time. What is misunderstood are the dynamics and factors that contribute to our preference changes.

The reason we refer to Vinotype "genres" is that different people can be grouped by their aesthetic interests, level of expertise, basic wine preferences, learning and other factors. In my grand scheme of things this will provide an important dimension for connecting people with similar interests, values and aspirations.

This provides a way to sort people into groups and helps knowledgeable wine professionals understand much more about a person before launching into new wine recommendations. Your genre is determined by your level of interest in observing, learning and evaluating wine.

Thus your wine preference changes are "all in your head." It is your genre (learning, aesthetics, environment), not your palate per se, that is much more likely to be responsible for changes in your personal preferences over time.

Keep in mind is that your personal perception is based on illusions of tastes, smells, colors and the like. These illusions are created in our brain and then we determine what we experience is reality. As a quick reminder that the human perceptive

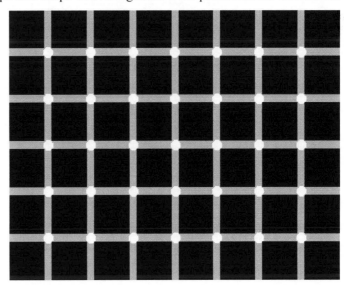

As you move your eyes around the illustration the white dots in the line intersections will seem to change from white to black or disappear. The dots don't change, you do - it all happens in your head.

system is not that reliable look at the illustration on this page.

As you move your eyes across the picture the dots will seem to change from black to white. Note to self: The dots are not changing. YOU are changing. More precisely, your brain is changing the way you perceive the dots. Always remember that even the simplest of changes in environment or the slightest distraction can affect your perception.

This means that all too often when we experience a perceptive change we immediately jump to the conclusion that external factors are responsible. Rarely do we consider that perhaps it was an internal, positional or even neurological shift responsible for our change in perception. Examples include, "Wow, this wine really changed when tried it after we first opened it and then again after we left it open for an hour." Another biggie is, "This wine is completely different from when we tried it in Italy on that beautiful day when we were making love on the river bank."

Your genre may change one moment to the next or slowly over time. There is also a special category for what we call a "conflicted" Vinotype. This is not so much a genre in and of itself. There is nothing inherently wrong with being a conflicted Vinotype. A conflicted Vinotype is simply someone with a high degree of Vinotypic plasticity (ability to adapt and change) who has adopted wine preferences, attitudes and behaviors that go far beyond the normal boundaries of their natural proclivities and predispositions. A conflicted Vinotype can usually go back in his or her mind to the defining life experience and discovering exactly where, when and how they made their decision to radically change their preferences, attitudes and behaviors. Here is my favorite conflicted Vinotype story.

Definition of a genre

1: A category of artistic, musical, or literary composition characterized by a particular style, form, or content.
2: Kind, sort

Definition of a Vinotype genre

The definition of a Vinotype genre is the category or categories that best describes where a person stands in terms of enjoyment, aesthetics, learning or expertise.

If your "tastes" in wine change, it is in an aesthetic sense, like your "tastes" in music. This is a neurological phenomenon and not particularly in your perceptive sensitivities.

People's tastes, in an aesthetic sense, change over time. Thus our tastes in music, fashion and movies shift. One can say that our tastes also change in terms of genres, from rock to jazz, from action pictures to classic movies.

We may simply choose a certain genre as more appropriate for a certain occasion. This might look like, "I'm in the mood for (your genre here) tonight." Some people are capable of wild swings in genre shifts – say from rap or the Rolling Stones in one period of their life to Tchaikovsky the next.

I used to like sweet wines

Vinotypic evolution is completely natural. Sometimes the changes are slight, other times the changes can be quite radical

Having dinner in Istanbul, Turkey, I was seated next to a wonderful young lady who was the CEO of her family winery operations. She was interested in learning about her Vinotype so I asked her a series of questions from the sensitivity assessment. I drew a line on the back of the menu with Sweet, Hypersensitive, Sensitive and Tolerant plotted along a continuum.

After the first round of questions I put an x at about the cusp of Sweet/Hypersensitive. Then she disclosed that she loved single malt Scotch so I scratched out that x and made one toward the Tolerant end. After few more questions, I scratched that x out, put a big x in the middle of the line and circled it.

"What does that mean?" she asked.

I said, "You are a conflicted Hypersensitive Vinotype, that is, a wine professional who has come to love intensely flavored, highly oaked and high alcohol wines."

"Why in the world do you say I am conflicted?" she asked.

I explained that many people feel torn or pulled in different directions in life by environmental or cultural factors. This can lead them away from their natural predispositions. I asked her how many older brothers she had. Not if, but how many. Her answer was two. "How did you know I had

The Spinning Lady

There is a perceptive illusion, known simply as the "spinning lady," which demonstrates just how differently things may appear to people and also how quickly what we perceive can change. A link to the fully-functional version of the illusion and a blog explaining the phenomenon by Dr. Steven Novella, an academic clinical neurologist at Yale University School of Medicine, is available on my website at www.timhanni.com/book.

The long and short of it is that three people can view the illusion at the same time and see her spinning in completely different ways: clockwise, counterclockwise or first one way and then seemingly switching direction. If she appears to switch she did not change – you did. Your brain has decided to switch the processing hemisphere and this creates the illusion of the direction change.

When I show this illusion in my live presentations people find it hard to believe when the person near them sees her turn in an opposite direction. Those who see her "change" will often shout out, "There, she just changed direction again." They are oblivious that "she" did not change – their perception changed.

The illusion is best viewed with several people so that you can argue about which way she appears to be spinning!

older brothers?" she asked. That was simple — at some point, something happened and she made the conscious decision, "Screw them, I can compete with men and beat them at their own game." Sure enough, she told me about her brothers ganging up and picking on her when she was 4 years old. This was her defining moment. Her competitive spirit, particularly toward men, has been fierce ever since.

I asked, "What were your dreams, passion and expectations when you went to college and what kind of degree did you graduate with?"

Her answer was, "I entered college to study dance, my passion, and dreamed of becoming a world-famous dancer. I ended up with a degree in finance and an MBA."

Bingo. There's nothing wrong with this in any way, but certainly here was a smart, beautiful example of how Vinotypes adapt and change to environmental influences!

"How did you predict the difference in what I entered university to achieve and where I ended up?" she asked.

I told her that, during our discussion, I had observed her gesturing with her hand, clenched in a loose fist, firmly hitting the table in a series of linear steps away from her as she punctuated a particular point she was making.

Dr. Utermohlen had once told me this particular gesture was associated with the Tolerant, usually male, Vinotypes who also tend to be linear thinkers. In this case it was the learned, not intuitive, gesticulation of a Hypersensitive Vinotype who had made the decision to compete in the linear-thinking, male-dominated Turkish business environment. Along with that came the need to learn to love Scotch, to demand intensely flavored red wines and beat those bastards at their own game. Not only that, she learned to succeed and thrive in this environment and love it immensely.

So, she is a Hypersensitive who loves intense red wine, Scotch and getting back at her brothers by being super successful in business. Now I knew all kinds of wines to recommend for her.

She was absolutely cracking up during this whole conversation. This was, indeed, the story of her life.

The phenomenon of changing preferences

My Turkish dinner is a story that comes to mind when someone says to me something like, "Hey, you got me wrong – you pegged me as a Hypersensitive but I love rich red wines." Or when people ask, "Don't our wine tastes evolve over time?"

Yes, indeed — our "tastes" change over time but not in the way that the most people tend to think. The word "taste" for the conversation "my tastes is music have changed" is more consistent with another definitions - our tastes in fashion or aesthetics - than from our perception of taste sensations. As humans we acquire and dispose of our preferences on a regular basis. This is a natural and normal neurological function. What is important is to realize that these changes occur in our brain as a part of the phenomena of neural plasticity. Just like the "spinning lady" seems to change, so does our perception of many things in our fields of perception.

Just as we may adapt to enjoy a style of art we at first found hideous, grow fond of an animal we once feared or learn to enjoy eat raw oysters, we may choose to adapt ad migrate to dry and/or more intense wines over time. This is primarily due to the psychological factors that influence our preferences and are largely responsible for our ever changing "tastes" for different styles, such as dry versus sweet, or types of wines as we explore and try new things. Peer or social pressure plays a big part in our decisions and wine fashions, like any other, come and go.

An "acquired taste" is the neural process of re-associating a sensation that you instinctively find unpleasant with aspirations or aesthetics that provide a new positive memory, an accomplishment or positive reinforcement. Conversely you can dispose of a "taste" via negative association or reinforcement over time. For example, some people lose their taste for salt or sugar because they believe these are bad for their health. Disposing of a taste for sweet wines has mistakenly become symbolic of becoming sophisticated and educated about wine.

Applied to wine, I call these adaptations of acquiring and disposing of tastes Vinotype plasticity – the ability of a Vinotype to adapt and change to his or her environment. Your level of sensory sensitivity or tolerance has a direct effect on your Vinotype plasticity; it often explains how far people are willing or able to go. This, in part, is why some people find it easy to give up salt or sugar, whereas others find giving this challenging if not impossible. Many people have acute textural sensitivity to foods and raw oysters are beyond the range of adaptational plasticity.

Why do it? The woman I described earlier in the Mondavi tasting room was working at losing her taste for sweet wines because she had been told dry wines were "better" and more sophisticated. My Turkish friend had added a taste for Scotch to hold her own in a male-dominated world. Aside from issues of fashion, many people work at changing their taste because of the role wine plays in their lives. I call this their genre, and it has a powerful effect on the wines you like and why you like them.

Vinotype genres

There is a Vinotype genre for everyone. You may have grown up in a culture where wine was an everyday part of most meals or in a culture where wine was considered sacrilegious. You may convene with peers who love beer or cocktails or belong to a social or peer group that takes wine seriously, even to the extreme. Your environment, enthusiasm, aspiration, learning and values relating to wine constitute your Vinotype genre.

After years of studying wine drinkers, I've come up with seven basic genres that include enjoyers, enthusiasts, connoisseurs, wonks, experts, professionals and geeks. The list can certainly be expanded and whatever you might want to call yourself, from anti-snob to zealot, penny-pincher to collector, is fine.

Your genre may also be expressed as a group or organization you align with or belong to: the Anything-But –Chardonnay (ABC) movement, Women for Wine Sense or Zinfandel Advocates and Producers (ZAP).

You may discover that you are a complex blend of genres, or that your genre changes from day to day or by occasion. You may be an enjoyer with your family, turn into a connoisseur at a business dinner, then newly return to becoming an enthusiast all over again on a trip to the wine country and then hit your geek stride when you are boring the bejeezus out of people telling them about your wine country trip and the things you learned about malo-lactic fermentation and extended macerateion. Remember: Genres are changeable and flexible.

Others may have a different point of view of your genre. If you are wondering about your genre you may ask a friend, a spouse, significant other, or someone you convene with when you drink wine. You may be surprised to find out that you think you are a witty wine afficianado while others around you think you are an over-bearing geek.

Another example of differeing points of view.

There are also a number of condescending designations I am asking be retired from the wine vernacular. These include beginner, naïve, uneducated and unsophisticated. If you enjoy wine, any wine, you are a wine drinker. If do not care to get caught up in the ritual, protocol and ceremonies associated with wine, you are a wine enjoyer.

Vinotype Genres

Following are definitions for Vinotype genres, in order of ascension, from people who have a simple enjoyment of wine to those who are perhaps guilty of going a bit overboard with their zeal:

Enjoyer: Someone who takes pleasure in wine.

Enthusiast: A person who is filled with interest and enthusiasm for wine and/or some wine-related pursuit.

Connoisseur: A wine aficionado, a person with informed and discriminating taste (real or imagined) pertaining to wine.

Wonk: One who studies wine thoroughly or even excessively.

Expert: A person who has special skill or knowledge in some particular wine-related field; a wine specialist or authority.

Professional: A person engaged or qualified in a wine-related profession or field.

I like everything and you can't put me in a box: This is a self-explanatory genre.

Geek: A person who others consider single-minded in wine pursuits to the point of being over-bearing or even socially inept.

An assemblage of geeks, like some wine events, is referred to as a "gaggle of geeks." If there are several or more onboard an airplane in flight or otherwise off the ground they are considered a "flock of geeks."

If you have been taught that Americans are the only ones who like sweet wines take a wine course that does not also believe the world is flat. Sweet wines have been enjoyed and prized more than dry wines for centuries. If you were to create a timeline comparing sweet wine versus dry wine preferences over the thousands of years that wine has been consumed dry wine pales in comparison. And during these thousands of years wine was sweetned with anything from honey, lead (probably causing the dementia and downfall of the Roman Empire), sugar, other fruit juices and unfermented grape juice to wine to make it taste better. It was appropriate to add herbs, spices, oak and even pine resin to flavor wine. It used to be that wine was allowed to be enjoyed on the sheer basis of personal and cultural preferences.

The *enjoyer* genre is the largest market segment of all. It includes most people who simply take pleasure in a glass of wine. Their own method of rating a wine is "Yum-Yuk." They like a wine or they don't and very frankly wonder why people get so danged fired up about wine. They may or may not become more interested in learning more, trying new wines or expanding their horizons – but it should be their choice. Not the will of wine zealots that they *should* evolve. They are just fine in their genre, thank you very much. My hope is that this is the genre of consumers who will gain the most from this book and when their choice of wine is met by the sneer, smirk or snicker of a wine-deluded member of the Conventional Wisdoms wine crowd they will fill them in on the new knowledge that is available and that the world is not flat.

The other genres are relatively easy to understand. They range from people who are really enthusiastic about wine, individuals who love to study and learn about wine, wine experts and all the way up to the full-blown socially inept wine geeks. My own career has gone through all of the phases. It began as an enjoyer thinking, "Wow, this is good stuff." Then I became enthusiastic, filled with interest and wanting to know more. As I acquired more and more knowledge and started hanging around with people who had large cellars and drinking rare and great vintages. I became regarded as a connoisseur known for my discriminating taste (real or imagined). After achieving the Master of Wine credential I was finally acknowledged as an "expert." For almost my entire career, I was also the "professional" making my living in the wine industry. And yes, I was a geek of geeks. Just ask my first wife. For fans of the *big Bang Theory* sitcom about physics geeks, I was the Sheldon Cooper of wine.

The future I envision is simply being free to unabashedly declare what kind of wine you like. From there you can easily explain where you might like to go. You may just want to stick with what you know. On other occasions you might be in the mood for discovering something new and different. You do have the inalienable right to expect to receive professional courtesy and help getting there. Lincoln said, "We are not enemies, but friends. We must not be enemies. Though passion may have strained it must not break our bonds of affection." Don't let your wine passions strain your affection for people.

Understanding the diversity of Vinotype genres is an important piece of the wine recommendation puzzle for all consumers who enjoy wine. It also offers the opportunity to restore the art of hospitality for the experts and professionals who write about, teach, recommend and sell wine.

Life experiences and memories influence our perception

It's difficult to rewire our sensory hardware, unless there is some sort of physical injury, metabolism shift or pharmaceutical interaction, but we can be constantly rewriting our software to incorporate our aspirations and experiences. An article titled "The Intimate Sense of Smell" in the September 1986 issue of National Geographic magazine noted that "Depending on one's early exposure to horses, the aroma of a stable might delight one person, frighten another and sadden a third." The thought of a horse, a smell associated with horses or stables or a depiction in a magazine or movie, may illicit memories and unconsciously evoke the emotions you associate with horses."

Many things happening at once determine how your brain interprets a singular sensation. Nothing happens in a vacuum and memories, either conscious or unconscious, may alter the way your brain interprets a sensation. Why you like what you like is determined by the coalescence of immediate sensations, preprogrammed intuitive responses to sensory stimuli and memories from our life experiences all coming together for processing in our brain.

If I say the words "Sauvignon Blanc," those of you familiar with the aromatic metaphors used to describe this wine will imagine grassy and your brains process grassy thoughts or memories. If you smell the grass and hear the lawn mower, it will evoke certain meanings. It might remind you of happy, relaxed summer days — or of being the kid who had to mow the lawn while everyone else was out playing and having fun without you. You might have been one of the kids playing baseball and liked the smell of grass until the day you struck out and were blamed for losing the game while the lawn was being mowed, and from then on, the smell was horrible for you. Or you might have grass allergies and the smell of grass triggers a subconscious signal that this is not good.

We're finding that a lot of people who hate Sauvignon Blanc have grass allergies or unpleasant memories of summer or experiences with lawns or lawn-mowing incidents. If you are allergic to grass, for example, your subconscious may be telling you, "Whatever this is it will make you sneeze and swell up. Get away – this is bad."

For many people the smell of fresh cut grass and the sound of a lawn mower can elicit a very strong memory of summer from when we were young. The smell of fresh cut grass can also trigger allergies.

When you are pouring Sauvignon Blanc, install this into your education and allow people to hate it. Because their brain is telling them they hate it.

Framing, metaphors and the language of wine

Describing and evaluating what we perceive is a natural and important human trait. Our complex sensory system, made up of receptors, pathways, routing, memory and recall, allows us to identify things in the present, remember things from the past, and even seemingly "predict the future" by creating expectations out of our past experiences.

Is this person family, friend or foe? Which baby is mine? How do I find my way home? Is this food safe to eat? Why is this purse $3,000? What was that sound? I know if I flip this switch the light will come on. Should I run after this animal to eat it or run away because it wants to eat me? Why does peanut butter go with jelly? What is the meaning of life? Is that a whiff of lavender I am getting from this wine?

Framing and metaphors play key roles in how we think and communicate. They are particularly useful for decision-making and problem-solving. They are required for basic tasks such as recognizing danger and the identifying and evaluating situations, objects and people. It is easy to see how these come into play for describing wines or when creating and communicating wine and food pairings — and how they are misconstrued as reality. Then we are entering the dimension of collective delusions.

A few years ago I discovered the fascinating work of Dr. George Lakoff, a linguistics professor at the University of California, Berkeley most known for his work on political neurology and decision-making. He is a specialist in "framing:" the way that language shapes how we think. Although his work primarily deals with political discourse, his ideas on how the brain processes information seem to explain a lot of how people think of wine, and wine with food, in the natural evolutions of Vinotype genres. He is the author of the book "Don't Think of an Elephant." The point of the title is that if you are asked not to think of an elephant, it is impossible to do. Go ahead – don't think of an elephant. You can also find many of George Lakoff's talks, in whole or in part, on YouTube and other video sharing sites. If you get hooked into these concepts as I have, I urge you to go online and learn more.

Lakoff's work also provides insight into the psychological aspects of preferences. His investigations of framing and metaphors show the extent to which we are able — or unable — to perceptually experience anything from a political view, a glass of wine or a night at the opera. In *Metaphors We Live By*, he writes:

"Metaphor is a fundamental mechanism of mind, one that allows us to use what we know about our physical and social experience to provide understanding of countless other subjects. Because such metaphors structure our most basic understandings of our experience, they are 'metaphors we live by'— metaphors that can shape our perceptions and actions without our ever noticing them.

"Our brains take their input from the rest of our bodies. What our bodies are like and how they function in the world thus structures the very concepts we can use to think. We cannot think just anything – only what our embodied brains permit."

Dr. George Lakoff

Wine descriptions and explaining wine and food

fra·ming *v.*

The cognitive process of creating a "picture" in our mind and filling it with elements (objects), subjects (people) and roles (activities the subjects are performing) corresponding our thoughts and imagination .

met·a·phor ln.

1. A figure of speech in which a term or phrase is applied to something to which it is not literally applicable in order to suggest a resemblance, as in "this is a picnic wine."
2. Something used to represent something else; "it was a serious and brooding wine."

a·nal·o·gy n.

1. A similarity between like features of two things, on which a comparison may be based: "The wine has an herbal aromatic quality."
2. In logic, an analogy is a form of reasoning in which one thing is inferred to be similar to another thing in a certain respect, on the basis of the known similarity between the things in other respects. "A wine with herbal aromatic features is best paired with a dish that is prepared with herbs."

sim·i·le n.

1. A figure of speech in which two unlike things are explicitly compared, as in "the wine was as fresh as a summer's day."

Essentially, Lakoff and other researchers describe the brain as constantly creating frames for associating and managing occurring sensory information and memories. For example, you see a closed door and someone tells you it leads to the laundry room. Your brain most likely will begin to fill in this mental frame with the expectations of finding a washing machine, dryer, ironing board, laundry basket, soap and so forth, in the room behind the door. You may also fill the frame with images of people and their roles associated with this frame, such as your mother doing the laundry. If, however, you open the door and discover that, in fact, this particular laundry room contains a sofa or a refrigerator, it will in essence "break" that frame, as it is not consistent with the expectations your mind created. Expressions associated with broken frames are words and phrases like surprising, startling, unforeseen, unexpected, no way, not what I thought, astonishing, wtf? and unreal.

Here are some of the key points Dr. Lakoff makes, followed by my speculation of how they relate to wine perception.

Simple Framing

by George Lakoff
Carry out the following directive: Don't think of an elephant!

It is, of course, a directive that cannot be carried out — and that is the point. In order to purposefully not think of an elephant, you have to think of an elephant. There are four morals.

Moral 1. Every word evokes a frame.
A frame is a conceptual structure used in thinking. The word elephant evokes a frame with an image of an elephant and certain knowledge: An elephant is a large animal (a mammal) with large floppy ears, a trunk that functions like both a nose and a hand, large stump-like legs and so on.

Moral 2: Words defined within a frame evoke the frame.
The word "trunk" as in the sentence "Sam picked up the peanut with his trunk" evokes the Elephant Frame and suggests that "Sam" is the name of an elephant.

Moral 3: Negating a frame evokes the frame.

Moral 4: Evoking a frame reinforces that frame.
Every frame is realized in the brain by neural circuitry. Every time a neural circuit is activated, it is strengthened.

Three blind men, the elephant and descriptive frames

Do you remember the old Sufi parable about the three blind men and the elephant? The first blind man reached out and grasped the elephant's trunk and described a serpent; the second felt its tree-like leg, the third its rope-like tail. When the blind men each tried to describe the elephant an argument ensued. Each drew on his experience, yet they could not agree on what the elephant looked like.

Which metaphor best describes the elephant: rope, snake or tree trunk?
It all depends on your perspective and personal experience.

This is often how different our perceptions and opinions might be for the same wine or combination of wine with food. Each of the blind men possessed an "objective truth" from their own personal experience but that "truth" was limited to their own experience and interpretation. In many ways, experiencing, interpreting and describing wine, and wine with food, is analogous to this parable, making the topic of wine unnecessarily complicated.

Here is how I apply the concept of framing to how people think about wine as we gain more wine-related experiences and learning. It is an on-going process of collecting more wine-related metaphors and memories to fill our vinous mental frames that we then use for wine and food matching recommendations. See if my logic doesn't make at least a little sense:

> The aromatics of wine often remind us of foods such as fruits, herbs, spices and butter. You can create a good match by including ingredients in a dish that echo—and therefore emphasize—the aromas and flavors in a wine

> For a Cabernet, for example, currants in a dish may bring out the wine's characteristic dark fruit flavors, while a pinch of sage could highlight hints of herbs

Source: How to Match Wine with Food - 6 simple tips for successful pairings
Wine Spectator staff Posted: September 23, 2011

Quick – what's wrong with this picture?

Matching wine and food in today's paradigm

Don't think of a Pinot Grigio (just kidding). Here are word clouds with typical descriptive words that might be associated with a Pinot Grigio and an appropriate wine match. Remember that this is a very normal way that humans organize information in relation to thoughts and concepts.

It becomes pretty obvious how one might associated the following recipes below to the descriptive frames of the wine examples above. Now compare the descriptive frames for a Merlot and relatively predictable matching duck dish:

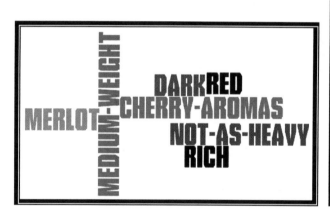 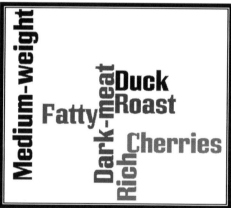

It is not hard to see how we come up with wine and food combinations by simply comparing the metaphorical descriptions of a food recipe and then conjuring up a food that has similar frame elements.

The "dark, red and rich merlot with cherry fruit aromas will perfectly compliment the rich flavors of the roast duck with cherry sauce. You need a medium-weight wine as a Cabernet Sauvignon might be too heavy and overpower the dish."

"The simply-prepared halibut with lemon begs for a light, white, delicate and acidic wine to pair with."

My favorite metaphor is the "marriage" of wine and food. Let me see: If my memory serves me correctly that means the wine and food get together, argue, get angry and call each other names. They end up in litigation over who gets the silverware and custody of the garnishes. That about sums up my first marriage!

Instructions for old-school wine and food matching

Here is everything you need to know about matching wine and food in today's collective delusion of wine and food pairing:

Match wine to food: Learn and memorize the appropriate descriptive lexicon for a lot of wines and match it to a food dish that has compatible ingredients and metaphorical descriptions. The longer your list of wine descriptors and metaphors, the more expert you will appear. When in doubt use obscure spices or specific varieties of fruits so that no one has a clue what you are talking about. Fenugreek, cardamom, Tellicherry peppercorns, aijwan and golpar are good ones. For fruits, use things like pomegranate, ackee, Arlet apple (not just plain-old apple), gooseberry, Olalla berries, etc. If you know some wine terms like buttery, minerality, etc. you can throw them in for good measure. Make sure the color or character of the fruit correlates to the color of the wine (more to come on this in the Color of Odors section.)

Match food to wine: Reverse process above; match the ingredients and descriptive metaphors of the dish to the wine that has the best descriptive compatibility, e.g. "This mahi-mahi with a pineapple curry salsa would be perfect with a rich Viognier from a cool regions that can stand up to the heaviness of the fish, yet has the acidity and the tropical fruit flavors and a touch of spiciness to match the pineapple salsa."

Go ahead – look at all of the wine and food matching explanations and see if this is not true. I dare you!

You can bet there will be an outcry from the practitioners of the metaphorical wine and food framing community on this one! Don't forget this piece from Chapter 1: "There is always an 'old guard' that will fight against change and if necessary persecute the agents of change in order to hold on to the familiar (or to the personal advantages they derive from the existing frame)." You may notice that the collective delusion or current paradigm is even referred to as "the existing frame."

This gives me an idea! Let me see if I can frame out the backlash from the wine and food matching crowd. I will put certain roles and descriptors and see if chatter on the Internet corresponds to my prediction about the results.

Anticipated responses to Tim Hanni's wine and food pairing paradigm challenge:

What about tasting wines "blind"?

Blind tasting (a tasting where the identity of the wine is unknown by the taster) helps to eliminate many prompts that profoundly influence our perception. This also introduces new influences as well. Remember if you break one frame, you simply create a new frame to replace it. Thus, knowing that you are participating in a blind tasting has an enormous effect on your Vinotypic state of mind and your perception will be affected. If you were to tell someone that the wine in glass #1 is a two-dollar creation, it's likely they'll be ready to dismiss it as cheap and uninteresting. But if you were to say, "Oops, my mistake, that's the $300 a bottle of super-premium Napa cab that no one can get their hands on," it's amazing how quickly that wine will open up. Now, it's great!

Does Price Affect Taste?

My wife hates it when I tell this story. A good friend brought a wildly expensive (literally worth *thousands* of dollars) to our house for a dinner party. It was a lovely wine. The next day Kate confronted me and demanded, "Why didn't you tell me that wine was so expensive!" Like any insensitive and relatively stupid husband I asked, "What would that have mattered? It's not like someone is going to smell the wine and declare, 'WOW – this must be worth thousands of dollars!'"

Her response was, "If I had known it was that special I would have paid more attention and enjoyed it more." She is, of course, right." I hope she reads this part – it is kinda hard for me to acknowledge she was right and I was wrong. Here is a study that supports Kate's position on knowing the value of a wine how that affects perception.

The following synopsis of a study about the effect of the price of a wine on the perception of wine quality appeared in an article by Lisa Trei on the Stanford Graduate School of Business website dated Tuesday, January 1, 2008 (go to http://www.gsb.stanford.edu/news/research/baba_wine.html for the full article).

Tuesday, January 1, 2008

Does a Wine's Pricetag Affect Its Taste?

Lisa Trei, http://www.gsb.stanford.edu/news/research/baba_wine.html

According to researchers at the Stanford Graduate School of Business and the California Institute of Technology, if a person is told he or she is tasting two different wines—and that one costs $5 and the other $45 when they are, in fact, the same wine—the part of the brain that experiences pleasure will become more active when the drinker thinks he or she is enjoying the more expensive vintage.

"What we document is that price is not just about inferences of quality, but it can actually affect real quality," said Baba Shiv, of Sanwa Bank, Limited, Professor of Marketing who co-authored the paper. "So, in essence, [price] is changing people's experiences with a product and, therefore, the outcomes from consuming this product."

The study

The researchers recruited 11 male Caltech graduate students who said they liked and occasionally drank red wine. The subjects were told that they would be trying five different Cabernet Sauvignons, identified by price, to study the effect of sampling time on flavor. In fact, only three wines were used—two were given twice. The first wine was identified by its real bottle price of $5 and by a fake $45 price tag. The second wine was marked with its actual $90 price and by a fictitious $10 tag. The third wine, which was used to distract the participants, was marked with its correct $35 price. A tasteless water was also given in between wine samples to rinse the subjects' mouths. The wines were given in random order, and the students were asked to focus on flavor and how much they enjoyed each sample.

The results

The participants said they could taste five different wines, even though there were only three, and added that the wines identified as more expensive tasted better. The researchers found that an increase in the perceived price of a wine did lead to increased activity in the mOFC (medial orbitofrontal cortex) because of an associated increase in taste expectation. Shiv said he expects enophiles will challenge the results, since his subjects were not professional connoisseurs. "Will these findings replicate among experts?" he asked. "We don't know, but my speculation is that, yes, they will. I expect that the oenophiles will show more of these effects, because they really care about it."

According to Shiv, the emotional and hedonic areas of the brain could be fundamental to making good decisions because they serve as a navigational device. "The brain is super-efficient," he said. "There seems to be this perfect overlap in one part of the brain between what happens in real time and what happens when people anticipate something. It's almost acting as a GPS system. This seems to be the navigational device that helps us learn what is the right thing to do the next time around."

Our frames and metaphors are the inescapable way our minds work. Knowing that this is how our brain works can at least lead you to keep an open mind not only about what you are tasting but about others' preferences.

Say "White Zinfandel." What fills in the frame in your mind?

Hey, I experienced it – it must be real!

I don't know of anyone who would disagree that our minds play tricks on us. That being said, it is amazing how adamant people can be in terms of their perception of the illusions of wine and wine with food. You will hear people say, "Of course, this is a great combination, I tried it myself!" Or: "You should be able to smell the crushed Olalla berries, I do, and it is as clear as the nose on the spinning lady's face!"

We all have different sensory and perceptual capacities and we all have different life experiences. Thus we all have different, and equally valid, points of view.

At the risk of being repetitious, there are many ways of describing, judging or scoring wine allows us to acknowledge and honor everyone's point of view. There should be no more wondering "What is wrong with them?" for employing points or puffs or stars or words. Whatever value system you find works for you is valid. We should eliminate the inference that what works for you will or should work for everyone or anyone else. It is possible and constructive to embrace and respect the many differing points of view that have become standards for appreciating wine and put an end to the petty bickering about who is right or who is wrong.

While a wine quality or characteristic may seem clear as a bell for you at a given place or time, it is very likely that things we perceive are greatly distorted by other elements like subconscious memories. It can also be a setting or environmental factors of which we are oblivious that completely distort our perception. You may be drinking a glass of wine that for all intents is pleasant but later you are asked how you liked it and respond, "It was nice but I wasn't really all that thrilled with the flavor." It could quite literally be the colors of the walls in the room you are in were evoking an uncomfortable and subconscious memory that made you feel uneasy without ever recognizing it. Perhaps you were embarrassed in class or sent to your room for punishment and the walls were similarly colored. Thus, something was "off" about your state of mind and the wine tasted less pleasant as a result.

It is hard for people to believe something is an illusion and their minds are only playing tricks on them so I am including an illustration to demonstrate how environmental factors can distort you perceptions. This is the old tabletop trick and you may have seen it before. It seems so clear one of the tables is longer and narrow and the other is wider and shorter. When I show this illusion to groups I have to let someone come up and measure the dimensions to prove they are really, the same length and width. Get out a ruler or something to measure them.

The table on the left looks clearly longer and narrower in relationship to the shorter, wider illustration on the right. Most people would bet money that these two tabletops are not the exact same length and width. Maybe they have the same surface area, but surely not the same exact dimensions of length and width!

Tabletop area illusion - could they possibly be the same dimensions?

Sorry, your brain is not working quite right. But don't worry. It is a universal mental programming error that distorts reality due to external factors. In this case the position of the legs of the table creates the illusion. It is a malfunction in all models of humans and there is no known fix for this neurological error.

Taste, smell and memories

Did you know that you can taste everything you are capable of tasting when you have a cold? If your nose is plugged you cannot smell your wine or food, but the two sensations are in reality completely independent. For anyone interested in a deeper conversation about individual sensations and definitions you can find more information in Appendix 2: Redefining Critical Wine Terms.

Consider for now:
- **Taste:** a primary sense comprised of the basic sensations of sweet, sour, bitter, salty and umami.
- **Smell:** our sense of olfaction.
- **Flavor:** a combination of any and all sensations that may provide us with gustatory perception and evaluation – taste, smell, touch, sight and sound.

Thus when you have a cold you can technically taste everything. In fact you have greater perceptive awareness of taste when you can't smell so it is plausible you taste things more acutely when you have a cold or condition that incapacitates your sense of olfaction. Without the smell you lose a very important component of flavor and this greatly obstructs your perceptive abilities.

This is a demonstration that helps explain how taste and smell are in fact independent yet imperative to realize the full gustatory experience of flavor.

What you will need for this demonstration:
1. Cinnamon powder
2. Cumin
3. Chinese 5-spice powder
4. Vignon seasoning (www.napaseasoning.com) or other seasoned salt (Lawry's, McCormick, etc.)

Put a little pinch of each of these spices on a plate in the order in the illustration. Pinch your nose shut then wet your fingertip and stick it into the cinnamon. Continue holding your nose tightly and lick your finger. You will probably get almost no taste whatsoever, but you will be able to feel the powder.

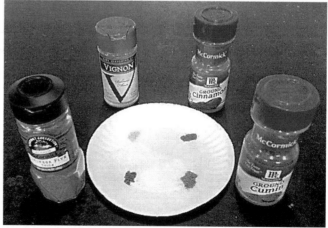

From top-right clockwise: cinnamon, cumin, 5-spice powder, seasoned salt

Release your nose and breathe through it. WOW! Cinnamon. It cannot be identified by taste alone; you need the smell. You can taste what you can taste with a cold; you simply have lost your sense of olfaction and it seems like you cannot taste. More specifically, you now get the full flavor of the cinnamon, which technically has no taste.

The next step is to think of what the sensation of cinnamon reminds you of. What memories come to mind? Certain foods like pumpkin or apple pie or the holiday seasons? If I insert the idea of "airport" while you are smelling the cinnamon you may think of the dastardly wonderful, pillowy, gooey pastries from the Cinnabon shops (sensory marketing at its finest!). When I conducted this demonstration in Istanbul, Turkey, many of the participants associated the smell with lamb. Cinnamon is commonly used there in savory preparations and they do not usually celebrate the same holidays as Americans, thus they have no association to our memories.

Now try the cumin, powder #2 – same drill. Hold nose, taste cumin and there is again almost nothing with the exception of some graininess. Let go of your nose, inhale then exhale and voila – cumin. You probably won't think of sticky buns and pie but are likely to be reminded of Mexican food or possibly curry. You will relate the sensations to your personal past experiences. In large groups there is a likelihood that many people will not immediately identify the smell as cumin – it is a little less common in our culture than cinnamon.

Now onto powder #3! Clinch nose, lick finger and taste. Still nothing. Let go and…wait for it – this is complex! An aroma can be defined as a singular smell, like cinnamon, cumin, raspberry, oak, and a bouquet is best defined as a collection of smells. 5-spice powder usually has star anise, cloves, Sichuan pepper and fennel but there are many variations. It is harder to distinguish the individual elements or aromas due to the complexity of many aromas or what can be called an aromatic bouquet.

For the wine wonks, these definitions are much more useful than the current definitions for distinguishing aroma (secondary smell of the grape) and bouquet (primary and tertiary smells associated with fermentation and aging of the wine) you will find in wine books or wine education classes. The New Wine Fundamentals use of the word bouquet is much closer to the true definition of a "bouquet," or collection of something like flowers. Etymology for "bouquet" takes us back to a word for thicket or shrub. Again, there are more definition details in Appendix 2: Critically redefining wine terms.

OK – let's get back to our plate of seasonings! Hold your nose and try some of the seasoning salt. You will clearly and immediately taste the difference! Salt is a primary taste and that will be most evident, even when holding your nose. You may even get a little sweetness depending on which seasoning salt you use, plus the more hypersensitive may get bitterness. If you are trying the Vignon seasoning you will get salty, umami and sourness (from spray-dried lemon juice). Now again let go of your nose and the complexity of smells come into play. You get the full flavor of the seasoning you are using: the tastes, aromas and bouquet of smells.

There are a couple of points to take away from this demonstration.

1. In more formal or technical terms, smell and taste are completely separate and independent sensations.

2. In reality, we perceive flavor, both taste and smell simultaneously and utilize other sensations that influence our perceptions, in order to gain a more definitive identification and evaluation of gustatory experiences.

3. Your memories define what you can and cannot identify. Your experiences and even emotions contribute to the identification process. You associate with the sensations YOU perceive.

4. Your mind uses sensory prompts, especially smell, sight and hearing, to create an expectation for experiences to come. When you walk into someone's home and smell cinnamon, you don't expect a pizza in the oven. When you are told certain things about the cost or ratings of a wine it WILL change your perception.

5. What you perceive is personal and cannot be replicated by another person.

An AROMA can be defined as a single smell while a BOUQUET is a collection of aromas. Wine aromas may faint or intense, identifiable or indistinguishable.

Wine bouquets can be simple and made up of relatively few aromas. Other wines have highly complex bouquets, gushing with a cacophony of aromas.

Many people can look at a flower stand or bouquet and identify each and every type of flower: Peonies, honeysuckle, iris, solidaster, delphina, freesia, tulips and even specific variations of roses or camellias. I am not one of these flower aficionados. I had to Google flower names just to come up with this list! Flower people have learned to identify flowers through learning and observation and wine is no different. Does a flower expert appreciate a field of wildflowers any more than someone who cannot rattle off the names? Not necessarily. In fact, someone with a lot of expert knowledge may become so wrapped up in trying to identify all of the varieties, while trying to impress others with their flower knowledge, they may enjoy the experience of the field of flowers even less! This is where I get to say that maybe it is time for wine people to stop and smell the roses. Or the rosés. Whatever.

Here are some wine terms to memorize and throw out at a party or tasting: corpulent, creosote, sweaty socks, ethereal, grippy, laser-like, lush, wet dog, monolithic, opulent, stony, torrefactious, unctuous and cat's pee. I did not make these up. Now brush up on your spices and flowers and you are in!

Learning and observation

Another area to consider is how learning, general observation and critical focus or acute attention changes our perceptual experiences. Learning and observation do not change your sensory physiology. These change how sensory information is processed and evaluated along with our descriptive capacities, filling our heads will all sorts of new framing data for wine. Conventional Wine wisdoms dictate that the "palate" of a trained expert is in some ways superior and that expert opinions are superior to evaluation and opinions by simple wine enjoyers. Humbug, I say! The learning, training and experience simply changes the perceptive focus and adds more and more metaphors and frames to work from. I assert, with conditions, that the evaluations and recommendations, unless matched to people who share similar sensitivities and preferences, are *less,* not more, meaningful.

But, wait, isn't there such thing as a *sophisticated palate?* Sure – but what does that really mean? It is now time to share one of my favorite forays into etymology:

Sophisticated, adj.
- Deceptive; misleading.
- Of, for, or reflecting educated taste, knowledgeable use, etc.: *People are drinking more sophisticated wines now.*

Sophisticate, verb (used with object)
- To make less natural, simple, or ingenuous; make worldly-wise.
- To alter; pervert: *to sophisticate a meaning beyond recognition.*

Hmmm. Deceptive, misleading, perverted. Who feels more *sophisticated* already? Raise your hands, you know who you are. I chuckle inside every time I hear or read the word in the context of sophisticated wine drinkers. Perverted and corrupt, indeed.

The serious side of this is that as we experience new things, our focus, attention and points of view change. If one thinks that this new facility with wine knowledge and expanded wine lexicon makes them superior to others, they fit the definition of arrogant,: "having or showing an exaggerated opinion of one's own importance, merit, ability, etc; conceited; overbearingly proud: *an arrogant wine expert, enthusiast, wonk connoisseur, professional, etc.*" One may also have an arrogant assumption that certain wines, or wine opinions, have greater importance or merit: *"Their view was that any wines from this region/variety/style/producer are inferior or poor quality."*

A personal opinion or preference is not arrogant unless it is "an exaggerated opinion" of one's self or of their personal point of view.

- "I hate sweet wines," (or Cabernet, or French wines, or whatever) is an opinion.
- "People who drink (any wine name here) are naïve/uneducated/beginners/not wine drinkers," is arrogant. Let's cut this out and not stand for it, people!

To reiterate: the brains of different Vinotype genres work differently. Not better, not worse, just different. The following points are taken from a wonderful study conducted comparing how the perceptive activity of a wine enjoyer differs from the perceptive neural activities of a professionally trained sommelier.

Following is the abstract and I urge anyone with a greater interest in the neuroscience of sensations to obtain a complete copy of this and similar works pertaining to sensory perception. The point is that people taught to focus and pay attention to flaws and collectively-generated benchmarks, who are often slurping and aerating, spitting and deep in thought about wine characteristics, are *not* experiencing wine in the same way a normal person would.

The appreciation of wine by sommeliers: a functional magnetic resonance study of sensory integration

Alessandro Castriota-Scanderbeg *et al*,

NeuroImage, Volume 25, Issue 2, 1 April 2005, Pages 570-578
http://www.sciencedirect.com/science/article/pii/S1053811904007062

The researchers were looking to investigate the differences in brain activity and processing between trained wine experts and everyday wine consumers. The hypothesis was that there are different neural recognition "strategies" employed by the trained expert. The association of previous sensory experiences and focused training provides the ability to correctly identify wines under "blind" tasting conditions.

They used advanced imaging techniques to observe differences in the brain activities between the sommeliers and consumers. The results provided expected results that "trained" brain processes wine sensory information much differently from the "untrained" brain.

> "The preliminary data of this study highlights the fact that the processing of gustatory stimuli (i.e. taste and olfaction) essentially occurs according to different strategies that are determined by previous experience of wine tasting. Particularly, the specific competence (expertise) of the sommeliers may be associated with the activations in the prefrontal cortex and in the left amygdala-hippocampal complex, both brain areas where different sensory modalities converge and are integrated with previous cognitive, mnemonic, and emotional experiences of the individual. Such integration may lead to the conscious construction of a unitary perceptive experience, and therefore to the recognition of a complex beverage like wine."

The net-net? The brains of professionally-trained Vinotypes work differently from normal people. Not better (unless you are aspiring to become a highly trained enthusiast, connoisseur, wonk or expert) just different. Just as the brain of a trained florist works differently from a person who limply likes to look at the pretty flowers. And don't forget that the more different you become, the more important it is to remember this when communicating with others.

The color of odors and the power of suggestion

Another work that opened my eyes to the power of suggestion, and later reinforced the concepts of framing the influence of environment, came from a study conducted at the University of Bordeaux in France, which I found about ten years ago. Later, when I started learning more about Dr. Lakoff and his work on metaphors and framing, I merged the two ideas together and (slap on the forehead) *voilá* – this makes even more sense when I combine the two concepts! The English translation of the study can be accessed at:

http://www.stanford.edu/class/linguist62n/morrot01colorofodors.pdf

I am now in touch with Frederic Brochet, one of the authors of this study, and we are comparing notes to begin to collaborate on our studies on consumer preferences, behaviors and attitudes. We met formally via Skype just a few days before I wrote this section of the book and we are as excited as a couple of kids to start sharing ideas.

I want to make it completely clear that the intention of the authors of this study, as well as my own intentions, are to demonstrate the phenomena of human brain function. There are other credible studies that demonstrate the ability of novices and professionals to differentiate between red, white and rosé wines when the examples are distinctly diverse in character, such as Sauvignon Blanc, heavily oaked red wines, etc. The point of the Color of Odors was to demonstrate that we are just human and that external factors, such as simply seeing the color of a wine, can have an impact on our perceptive abilities.

When this study hit the news wires, the over-sensationalized headlines read, "Wine Experts Cannot Tell White from Red Wines" or "Wine Experts Proven to be Frauds." This study provides important insights into framing and the power of suggestion, all part of being human. While the Stanford study looked at the power of price suggestion with consumers, this one demonstrates how the brain processes odor stimuli after receiving a visual prompt of color even if you are an expert. This fits into the earlier discussion in this book of sensory adaptation and Vinotype and neural plasticity – changes that are brought about by additional environmental sensory information.

The study by Morrot and Brochet took place at the University of Bordeaux in France, and involved 54 wine experts. They were given two glasses of wine, a white and a red, and asked to describe the aromatic qualities of each. The fun part of this experiment is that the wines were identical white Bordeaux wines and that the "red" wine had been colored red. (You can find a more complete synopsis on the research in Appendix 7.)

Below you will see how the results of the experiment were plotted out and it becomes apparent how the "framing" concepts were consistent with the visual prompts of a white or red wine.

The lists on the left side of the chart (labeled White wine descriptors on the upper left and Red wine descriptors on the lower left) identify the primary descriptive terms employed by the tasters. These are abbreviated and in French with the translations directly below: FIG 2.) The tasters were not limited in the use of the descriptive terms and allowed to use any of the descriptors for either wine.

Quite predictably, the descriptors employed correlated to the color of each wine with a few variations in each case.

- White wine descriptors included words like lychee, floral, citrus, apple, honey, passion fruit, pear, banana, peach, butter, acacia, etc.
- Red wine descriptors included spice, wood, cherries, cassis, pepper, strawberries, anise, vanilla and prunes.

Below you will find the actual chart with the distribution and frequency of terms applied to each wine. The two "frames" on the upper and lower quadrants on the left plot the frequency of the descriptors used for white wine (W). The top left frame, words from the white wine lexicon, is densely populated descriptors associated to the white wine lexicon. The frame below, descriptors from the red wine lexicon, does indeed show very few, but some, of the red wine descriptors were applied to the white wine; primarily spice, wood, cassis, pepper and vanilla.

I reiterate, the 54 participants were served the exact same wines – a white wine and the same wine colored with odorless, tasteless coloring. The frames on the upper and lower quadrants on the right (RW), for the *same wine* as above colored red, show clearly the descriptions shift to the red fruits and red wine terms in the bottom right frame: spice, wood, cassis, cherries, pepper, anise, prunes raspberries. And again there are a few white descriptors that show up in the top right; floral or citrus with an occasional peach, apple, butter or banana thrown in for good measure.

		Descriptors used for wine W	Descriptors used for wine RW
White wine descriptors	LIT		
	FLO		
	MIE		
	AGR		
	FRU		
	POM		
	BAN		
	BON		
	POI		
	ANA		
	PAM		
	ACA		
	PEC		
	BEU		
Red wine descriptors	EPI		
	BOI		
	CAS		
	FRA		
	CER		
	PRU		
	FRS		
	VAN		
	CAN		
	POV		
	ANI		
	REG		

FIG. 2. Distribution of the odor descriptors used by at least 3 different subjects during the second session of the wine comparison test for the description of W and RW by 54 subjects. Labels "White wine descriptors" and "Red wine descriptors" contain the terms used for describing the W and the R wines during the first session, respectively.
White wine descriptors: LIT = litchi (lychee); FLO = floral (floral); MIE = miel (honey); AGR = agrume (citrus fruit); FRU = fruit de la passion (passion fruit); POM = pomme (apple); BAN = banane (banana); BON = bonbon (candy); POI = poire (pear); ANA = ananas (pineapple); PAM = pamplemousse (grapefruit); ACA = acacia (acacia); PEC = pêche (peach); BEU = beurre (butter). Red wine descriptors: EPI = épice (spice); BOI = boisé (wooded); CAS = cassis (blackcurrant); FRA = framboise (raspberry); CER = cerise (cherry); PRU = pruneau (prune); FRS = fraise (strawberry); VAN = vanille (vanilla); POV = poivre (pepper); ANI = animal (animal); REG = réglisse (liquorice).

How many of the 54 participants said, "Wait a minute – these are the exact same wines?"

Zero. O. Nada. Zip. None. To reiterate – the purpose of this is to show how the mind works. Not that experts are frauds, stupid or unreliable. The study applies to Vinotypes of all genres, genders, age and expertise. We are ALL influenced by external factors not only for wine but everything we perceive.

I recently receive a follow up e-mail from Frederic Brochet about new work he is conducting. "I am experimenting with wine professionals coming to Bordeaux University for upgrading their levels but of course in less precise conditions and except that now the experiment is being known {by most professionals], only people who are not drinking wine at all do usually say 'but these glasses smell the same!' These people are not 'framed' [the wine lexicon] and can then somehow judge more clearly," he has observed. This means people with less formal training have less or a predisposition to fill the red or white wine "frames" with words intended to correspond to the color of the wine.

As a counterpoint to the Color of Odors investigation an excellent study was also conducted in 2009 by researchers Jordi Ballester & Hervé Abdi & Jennifer Langlois & Dominique Peyron & Dominique Valentin. It is well worth a look for anyone interested in looking more deeply this topic of wine descriptions and learning. This research also indicated that un-trained wine drinkers were nearly as adept at identifying red versus white or rosé wine as trained experts: *The Odor of Colors: Can Wine Experts and Novices Distinguish the Odors of White, Red, and Rosé Wines?*

http://www.utdallas.edu/~herve/abdi-balpv2010-inpress.pdf

The cartoon to the left illustrates how quickly our behaviors can change in response to learning that something is more valuable than first thought. Keep in mind that this is a simple and frequent human response. Learning that the wine scored 96 points creates a new frame and immediately affects the behavior of the individual.

Obviously the original intention of the illustration, and how I initially interpreted the scenario, is to show the shallow nature of wine consumers who use the 100 point rating system. "The wine sucks – oh, it got 96 points? Give me a case!" But the more I have studied the incredible influence that environment, value systems and our memories of life experiences can have on our preferences and behaviors, the more I simply see human nature at work.

Just imagine picking up a figurine in someone's house and he says, "Be careful, that is from the 17th century and worth tens of thousands of dollars." Your

The power of suggestion and expert recommendations can have a profound influence on how we make decisions — Vinotypic plasticity and wine value! Credit: Bob Johnson

behavior and perception of the figurine will change in a nano-second as you gingerly put the figurine back and even step farther away from it. Plus you will probably wonder what kind of idiot would put something so valuable out where someone could break it? And how can he afford something so valuable living in this kind of house –where does his money comes from? All we need is a little prompt, and our imagination will run with it from there.

Even when experts taste wine "blind," meaning they do not know what the wine is, the fact that they are in a blind tasting environment and surrounded by a flock of geeks like ourselves changes their perceptive focus and sensitivities. It is common for wine judges to sit at the same table during wine evaluations and a smirk, smile, sneer or frown can have other judges reconsidering their own scores.

Of course, seeing the label of the wine, the price tag or a rating can profoundly influence opinion. This happens at the end of blind tastings when everyone tries to rationalize their scores that are completely out of step with the other judges – or even at odds with what they profess to be their most prized wine preferences.

What is identical among human beings is that sensations provide us with the information to try to process, understand, evaluate and predict both the beginning of life and also the future. Our sensory equipment is different. We are not all getting the same information sent to our brains and yet we find that hard to imagine. Certainly our value systems, our religions, cultures, races, genders and languages are limited to our own experiences yet we try to convince others that "MY perspective is right, MY opinion should be shared by others, e.g. "My religion, my political party and even my wine cellar is better than yours!" This is called self-righteousness, and why human beings end up killing each other and going to war. But I digress.

Here is what I would like you to take from this chapter: It's just wine fer cryin' out loud. Some people like wine; others do not. Some people study wine; others do not. Some people revere and collect wines; others do not. Some people look for intense, high-scoring wines and some people love sweet, light pink wine.

As I mentioned earlier, wine is just grape juice that has not finished going bad…yet. I thought it was a quote I read but began to wonder that maybe I had made it up. I turned to the source of all truth and knowledge in our modern world – the Internet.

⚠No results found for quote: "Wine is just grape juice that has not finished going bad"

It is hard to come up with "⚠No results found" for just about anything on the Internet. Then I thought, "Wow, look how far things have come considering the Internet did not even exist not long ago – now wasn't THAT a disruptive innovation?"

Then that made me think, "If it is not on the Internet, does it exist?" Maybe I made up the quote after all.

Chapter 6 Q&A

Question: Don't our wine tastes evolve over time?

Answer: Yes, indeed – our tastes as defined in the context of fashion or aesthetic "tastes," and not our ability to perceive taste sensations. It is important to recognize is that these changes occur in our brain and are a natural part of the phenomena of neural plasticity, cognitive psychology and the evolution of a Vinotype. More important is recognizing that many people simply reject certain dogmatic attitudes about wine quality, especially where sweet wine and matching wine with food are concerned.

Question: Is anything really objective or is everything subjective?

Answer: We like to think we have the capacity to be objective, but this brings up a very interesting philosophical question: "If sensations are indeed only illusions of energy that can be interpreted by individuals differently due to varying sensory capacities, perception and interpretation, does that mean that a human being has no capacity for objectivity? Is the object itself only objective and any attempt to describe, quantify or rationalize it therefore subjective?" Sorry – I don't have the absolute answer to that question, only a point of view. My point of view is that everything a human being experiences is subjective and the only thing that is objective is the object itself. Don't get me started…

Chapter 7: Match the Wine to the Diner, Not the Dinner

Revising the tenets of wine and food

Now that you have permission to love the wines you love, the next step is to debunk the myths and misconceptions that encompass the collective delusions of wine and food pairing. Deciding which wines to serve with meals has evolved into a complex and often bewildering art. The points of view are often intense and emotionally charged, and for every expert recommendation to serve this wine with this food, there is a counter opinion advising to never serve that wine with that food. Nowhere is there a better example of how confusing and complicated the experts have rendered the world of wine than in the arena of food pairings.

Advice, attitudes and opinions on the subject of how wine is enjoyed and what to do when wine and food are served together cover an almost limitless gamut of options. Positions range from a simple, laissez-faire attitude of "drink and eat what you like" to intense and emotionally charged, wine-based micro-cultures replete with their own language, rituals, protocol and propriety.

The vivid imagination of wine wonks

Here are some examples of the confusing and contradictory points of view that I gathered from various wine and food web sites. Each of these represents an opinion of a different wine enthusiast trying hard to help consumers make the right choice when it comes to serving wine with food.

- To avoid the always possible awkwardness of an error of judgment, observe these few classic rules [implying it would be inept to not follow the rules]. One of the best known rules is to pair red wine with meat; white with fish.
- The first rule of food and wine pairing is there are no rules.

- Learn the rules.
- Forget the rules.
- The combination of Cabernet Sauvignon and chocolate is better than sex.
- One of the worst combinations ever is Cabernet Sauvignon and chocolate.
- Enjoy the wines you love with any food you feel is appropriate.
- Aromatic molecules in certain wines and foods act as sensory bridges.

Well, who should you believe?

Almost all wine and food matching occurs in the fertile imagination of usually well-meaning and earnest wine and food enthusiasts and professionals. I know that this will elicit howls from the wine-and-food-matching-is-my-life genre. If you are one of these, please refer back to Chapter 4 for a refresher on sensory illusions. I know — you have experienced good and bad matches. I know you think it is an imperative to select the "right wine with the right dish."

From determining "bridge" ingredients between foods and wines to mind-boggling analysis of comparing the molecular structures of the wine and foods, things are completely out of control. The misinformation, false premises and misunderstandings are at an all-time high.

Understanding Vinotypes and reigniting respect for personal preferences is the first step to returning wine enjoyment back to the individual. The next step is to get past all of the BS, or fertilizer as I will call it, to restore wine in its rightful place at the dinner table.

Updating wine and food history

Before the mid-20th century, pairings of food and wines were more coincidental and rarely intentional. It is clear from early texts that wines served during formal meals followed an order of propriety and no strict tenets of wine and food matching. Red wine was certainly served with red meat, but sweet or dry white wines were offered as well. Did you know that the French drink more Port wine than any other country and that it is most often served as an aperitif?

An excerpt from the 1961 edition of *Larousse Gastronomique*, originally published in 1938, demonstrates that the guest at a great meal was offered a choice of either fine, dry red or sweet white wine: "With the *entrements*, the Bordeaux-Lafite, the delicious Romanée, the Hermitage, the Côte Rôtie, **or if the guest prefers, the white wine of Bordeaux, the Sauternes, the St. Péray, etc. should be served.**" The directive is to match the wine to the diner.

the sc... or Graves. The passage of these wines is rapid. Margaux, or Graves. The passage of these wines is rapid. 'As soon as the third service has succeeded the roast, with the *entremets*, the vegetables, the elegant pastries, the Bordeaux-Lafite, the delicious Romanée, the Hermitage, the Côte Rôti , or, if the guests prefer, the white wine of Bordeaux, the Sauternes, the Saint-Péray, etc. should be served. But dessert soon follows the third service; then all the delicious wines of Spain or Greece make their appearance, the old port, the sweet Malvoisie, the Royal-Jurançon, the Malaga and the Muscat, the Rota and the wine of Cyprus. Tokay wine is poured into very small glasses. Finally, to crown the feast, champagne froths into crystal, and gaiety, which has already spread

In the European wine cultures, local wines were served with local food. More likely than not your family would have the same wine every day – with your beef, lamb, fish or cheese. At formal dinners a variety of wines were served but always with the guest in mind when determining which wine was appropriate for the occasion.

As wine became more popular in the U.S., basic rules were invented for consumers to promote the enjoyment (and really the sales) of wine and food: "red wine with red meat," "light wine with light dishes" or "complex wines with complex recipes." It became almost impossible to envision a table in an Italian restaurant with the clichéd checkered tablecloth and *fiasco* of Chianti. In the 1980s, however, things really went off the tracks as these simple rules evolved into increasingly convoluted and contradictory dictates as to what to pair and why. Pairing food and wine started to become a new art form, and eventually a forbidding minefield of potential disasters that can befall poor, unsuspecting consumers or hosts if they make a mistake and order or serve the wrong wine with the wrong food.

It's time to get rid of the myths of food and wine pairings and return to the inclusive and hospitable basic premise: "If the guest prefers …"

You do not have to five up the idea of looking for the perfect match. Just remember, different people are going to perceive the wines — and therefore the matches — differently anyway. Combinations that some will thoroughly enjoy, others will quietly, or not so quietly, suffer through. In fact, the exact combination you have one day can taste completely different the next.

Does this mean put any wines with any foods — that there are no rules? No, not really. The difference is you get to make your own rules. What I am going to introduce are "principles" for replicable flavor interactions. Then you can decide if certain combinations are a rule or not. Hate red wine, even with steak? Rule it out. Love red wine with steak? Rule it in. Hate White Zinfandel? Rule it out with everything. Love White Zinfandel? Rule it in with everything. Think you have to have a delicate Riesling to match the delicacy of the sushi? Rule it in! You get to decide and make up the rules that work for you.

The basic premise of the New Wine Fundamentals is that you should be able to drink your favorite wines with any meal. Rather than matching ingredients, success in serving wine and food is a question of balancing flavors. This can be done easily — in fact, you will see, it's a basic culinary practice in the cuisines that have evolved in wine cultures, like Italy and France.

Meet Sarah Scott

My guide and companion in challenging the tenets of wine and food matching is Sarah Scott, one of the Napa Valley's most respected chefs. Sarah got her start cooking when she won the Betty Crocker Homemaker of Tomorrow Award at Henry Grady High School in Atlanta, Georgia. After studying journalism in college, Sarah headed to Napa intending to become a writer.

The 1980s was a dynamic time in the Napa Valley, when interest in food was growing along with the revived wine industry. The valley's vintners and chefs were just beginning to discover the complexities of matching wines with food. Finding herself being drawn into the world of food, Sarah worked at the Wine and Culinary Center and Napa Valley Cooking School alongside renowned chefs like Jeremiah Tower, Marion Cunningham and Michel Richard. She was the one who introduced me to Chef Michel Trama, who I mentioned earlier in the book.

She went on to become part of Madeleine Kamman's first class at Beringer Winery's School for American Chefs, and in 1991 Robert Mondavi asked her to join the culinary team at his winery, where. as Executive Chef in the Mondavi Winery's Great Chefs program she cooked with Thomas Keller, Julia Child, Jacques Pepin, Alice Waters and Daniel Boulud.

When I got to know Sarah at Beringer, it was a meeting of the minds — we were both beginning to see the pitfalls of food and wine pairing. Sarah has since gone on to become one of the foremost proponents of Flavor Balancing, a growing movement whose tenets have been adopted by the prestigious Wine & Spirit Educational Trust (WSET).

Today she is in demand as one of the Napa Valley's most talented chefs, and those who enjoy her meals marvel at the successful "pairings" she creates to showcase wines and wow guests. Yet she will tell you her secret comes down to two primary balancing elements: acidity and salt.

She has generously written a piece for this book to tell about what her view was before we joined forces challenging the Conventional Wisdoms of wine and food. What happened during our period of exploration and discovery, and how she implements Flavor Balancing in her professional culinary career today, can be found in **Appendix 1: How my cooking changed.**

Wine and food basics

The sensory impact of food on wine is almost entirely determined by the balance of primary tastes in the food: sweet, sour, salty, bitter and umami. The way these elements interact with wines is perceived as an increase or decrease in the intensity of the wine's flavors. If the interaction is agreeable it is a good match. If it is unpleasant, it is a poor match. Beyond this is a world of vivid imagination, collective delusions, metaphors and the personal experiences of the individual.

When sweet and umami tastes dominate in a dish, a wine will become more thin, bitter, sour and unpleasant. Acid — like lemon — and salt decrease bitterness, acidity, astringency, chemesthesis (burn) and increase richness and smoothness of wine for all but a small percentage of people. They are integral to Flavor Balancing.

Umami is a natural savory or ripe flavor. If you are unfamiliar with umami, taste a raw mushroom and then one that has been cooked, without any seasoning or oil, for 30 seconds in a microwave oven. The latter one will give you the taste of umami. Meats, soft cheeses, mushrooms, tomatoes and asparagus are all high in umami.

Sweetness in food is the number one culprit for creating unpleasant wine and food interactions. In classical French cuisine, you will rarely find any sweetness in the food with the exception of dessert. This is why, when serving wine with dessert, it's important to make sure the wine is sweeter than the dessert or the wine will become relatively dry and unpleasant for most people.

Bitterness in food increases bitterness in wine, but the perception of bitterness varies dramatically from one person to the next depending on their personal sensitivity. What one person finds horribly bitter another may be incapable of sensing. Hypersensitive tasters will constantly complain about unpleasant bitterness while a more tolerant taster will be oblivious to the interaction.

Chemesthesis, the hot, burning effect, such as chili heat in the food, will increase bitterness and astringency in wines, in direct correlation to alcohol level of a wine and an individual's sensitivity. Hypersensitive Vinotypes will experience an increase in burn while, curiously, Tolerant tasters perceive a sweetness from the same combination. It's interesting to note that for many people this heat can cause a pleasurable release of chemicals into the bloodstream. What is a burning and unpleasant experience for one person may be providing sensations related to runner's high and orgasm (seriously!) for another.

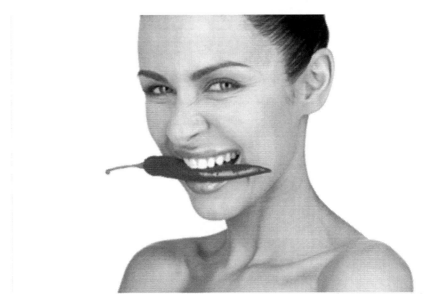

Many people get a euphoric, almost orgasmic, sensation from extremely hot foods — especially Sweet and Hypersensitive Vinotypes.

Sensory Adaptation

OK – it's imagination time! Imagine jumping into a swimming pool. It is usually chilly but with a little time and exertions you become accustomed to the temperature and it is not nearly as bad as it seemed at first. Now go run and play in the sprinklers. WOW! That's cold! Brrrr. Quick, jump back into the pool. What happens? Most of you know that it will seem warm in comparison to how it felt before and certainly in comparison to when you first plunged into the pool. The temperature did not change, your perception did.

Another example is thinking about a route that you frequently take when you drive. It is quite common to quit noticing things along the way with repeated exposure. Day after the day you go by the same buildings, signs, trees and elements of the landscape. You do, however, notice if something is amiss or changed. I vividly remember learning about this phenomenon from Dr. Michael O'Mahony, a professor at the University of California at Davis. He was one of my earliest sensory mentors and performs research on the senses and brain processing and how they relate to sensory and consumer testing.

As a side note, Michael was one of the first people to help me on my quest to understand the umami taste phenomenon in the late 1980s, along with his colleague Dr. Rie Ishii. He also introduced me to the realm of psycho-sensory phenomena of how our minds work with our sensory apparatus in processing the information sent by receptors. Especially fascinating to me was an area of research for the different ways in which our perception of sensations varies, sometimes dramatically, under certain conditions.

This is known as sensory or neural adaptation and accounts for changes the brain makes in the way it responds to repeated or constant stimulus. Sensory adaptation affects all of our senses. It can involve physical changes, such as our pupils adjusting to the level of ambient light to help us see as light grows dim, or the loosening or tightening of our eardrums to protect us from damage from the volume at a rock concert.

Sensory adaptation can also involve the way in which sensory information is processed. It seems

Try this NOW!
Tim's Tequila Trick

This simple sensory adaptation demonstration goes a long way to change conventional wisdom about pairing wine and food. Coupled with some other principles I'll get to later in this book, it means that you are no longer conditioned to drink certain types of wines with certain types of foods. All you need is a glass of wine (an intense red wine like Cabernet Sauvignon works best), a wedge of lemon or lime and a salt shaker.

Put some salt and lime juice on the back of your hand (or on the neck or body part of a consenting partner). Try a sip of the wine and pay attention to the balance of flavors. Then take a lick of the salt and lime, followed by another sip of the wine. Voila! The wine will become smoother, more rich in flavor and most likely much more delicious.

This is a quick introduction to Flavor Balancing. I do not suggest that you lick lime juice and salt off your hand every time you have a glass of wine, but acidity and salt, in much smaller quantities incorporated into food, can soften wines to the point that they are "just right" for the food. And you can do this sitting at a restaurant or at home to make the wine you really want to drink taste delicious with the food you really want to eat. Swear to god.

This balancing of acidity and salt is an integral part of every classical cuisine in Europe where wine plays a fundamental role at the table. The slightest addition of the acidity and salt will often make your food more delicious and the wine you love smooth and wonderful.

our brain often receives far too much sensory information to process and tends to tune things our to mitigate some of the sensations to prevent overload.

When we eat and drink, our brain is constantly changing the way it processes information sent from sensory receptors and quite possibly causing changes in the receptors themselves. The "cause and effect" of wine and food is based on an understanding of the amplification and diminishment of sensations we may perceive from a confluence of sensations.

Here are some common examples of sensory experiences:
- Visit a new mother with screaming children and see how she may be able to tune out the racket.
- Brush your teeth and then drink orange juice. The orange juice, once sweet and pleasant is now horribly bitter and sour. (If you don't know what I mean about the toothpaste and orange juice you are part of a very small minority of people who have never tried the combination. But try it: Go brush your teeth and drink some orange juice.)
- One example I can relate to is roller skating on a rough asphalt surface and then transition to smooth concrete – aaah, that feels so smooth in comparison to skating on the asphalt!
- You cook some fish at home, go out to run and errand and when you walk back into the house the smell of the cooked fish smacks you in the face, metaphorically speaking.

Consuming wine and food together creates an ongoing series of adaptations. If a message to the brain is constantly repeated, such as the taste of sourness, it will suppress our sensitivity to the source of stimulation, making the wine that is being consumed concurrently taste less sour in comparison. If the food is sweet it will magnify the intensity of the acidity. Whether it is a good match or bad match will depend on the intensity of the change and whether you like or dislike the change you experience. Your evaluation, in turn, is dependent on your personal sensitivity and expectations for how you want the wine to taste.

One of the other things I've learned is that a sensation may be suppressed until another sensation "wakes up" your brain. Put your foot into hot water in a bathtub and hold it still. After a short time your brain will acclimate to the temperature. Move your foot and the water seems to get "hot" again. Your sense of touch is suppressed by the constant stimulation from the hot water. When you move your foot, the change of pressure against your skin is felt and this new source of stimulation will enervate your sensitivity to the heat of the water, making the water feel hot again. Likewise, hold a mild solution of salt and water motionless in your mouth for a few moments and you will find the salty taste becomes less pronounced or disappears. Move your tongue around and you will find the salty sensation returns as you reintroduce the touch sensation from swishing it around.

Taste is also influenced by other physical adaptations made by our body during different times of day or due to physical or psychological conditioning. Each of us has a different rate at which we produce saliva. When fatigued or under stress, our bodies also tend to produce less saliva. Our saliva contains sodium chloride and potassium chloride as well as protein. These compounds have a buffering effect on many things we taste, but we do not taste these compounds in our saliva due to sensory adaptation. When we have less saliva, we are more sensitive to sourness, bitterness and astringency in the wine and food we taste. The pH of our body is also in a state of constant flux. When our body acidity becomes higher, we are more sensitive as well.

Sensory adaptation is at the root of what happens when wine and food are consumed together. There are basic elements that dictate the primary taste interactions and later you will find instructions for setting up a demonstration of the primary adaptations between wine and food flavors. Learning the simple principles of Flavor Balancing and understanding the dynamics of sensory adaptation opens up a whole new world for a sensible and personalized approach to enjoying wine and food. This is what is meant when I say we should forget the "rules" of wine pairing but recognize there are certain principles to help everyone enjoy wine with food on their own terms.

The first principle is to recognize that certain combinations of wine with food will intensify or suppress primary tastes in the wine: sweet, sour, bitter and umami (there is really little or no saltiness in wine).

Secondly, and most arguably, the primary effect for most people is how the wine reacts with the food. Some individuals may experience differences in the food flavors after the wine and certainly this is dependent on the balance of the food and intensity of flavors of the wine. I will add here that the idea that a "big red wine will kill the taste of a delicate dish" or a piece of red meat or strong food will overwhelm a wine, is largely metaphorical and simply not true. This is sure to set off something similar to the village taking up arms against Dr. Frankenstein from the delusional collective, but I stand by my assertion. There is more to this story such as umami-laden foods suppressing umami and sweet tastes in the wine, rendering them weak and watery. Just follow the techniques in the following section, and balance and harmony will be restored in the wine. See, isn't that simple?

Flavor Balancing

Flavor Balancing means that food flavor intensifying (sweet and umami) and suppressing (salt and acidity) ingredients are added in correct proportion in preparations. This is accomplished by using common condiments that are natural ingredients that can be added to any recipe. Salt, lemon, mustard and vinegar are often already on the table. This assures that the food served is delicious with the diner's preferred choice of wine.

Oh no! Sacrifice the recipe, bastardize the food – are you crazy? The culinarians and foodies now get to howl and join the screaming mob of wine enthusiasts demanding that I be burned at the stake!

> This does not imply that you should drink a wine you do not like or not match
> wine and food if that is something you love to do!

Before you break down the gate, consider that many great chefs have taken the time to consider this proposal, question the premises and thoroughly understand the principles, only to come to the same conclusion. Flavor Balancing makes sense from the standpoint of making delicious food. Examples of

Flavor Balancing can be seen in classical recipes and regional practices in any region where wine is an essential part of the cuisine and allows people to savor both the food and the wine. Want an intensely-flavored red wine with your meat? Do it!

Feel you just gotta have a crisp, dry white wine with your oysters? I think you should too! Just don't think that you should infringe on anyone else's choice to have a wine they love. If you go back to the customs of 100 years ago, a sweet Sauternes was considered an appropriate choice of wine with oysters as well as the dry wines we think of today.

Flavor Balancing is not new. It is a simple culinary technique that is the basis for classical French and Italian cookery and found incorporated into the recipes in almost every country where wine has evolved with the cuisine. Steak, for example, is extremely high in umami. What is most frequently recommended to go with a big thick steak? An intense red wine, of course. The delicious, satisfying umami taste is further intensified by an aging process that breaks down proteins into umami-synergizing nucleotides. By

aging higher quality cuts of meat you are intensifying the umami taste that makes beef so delicious to most of us carnivores, yet is actually the culprit that will most likely make a wine taste thin and bitter – provided there is bitter-suppressing salt added in the cooking or at the table,

Try cooking a really high quality cut of beef, *without any salt*, and try a Cabernet Sauvignon or other strong red wine, then the unsalted beef, then the wine again. Most people will find the reverse of what is promised by the conventional wisdom that the proteins and fat of the meat will render the wine smoother and more pleasant. In fact, the wine becomes more astringent and bitter for most people.

In Italy, *Bistecca alla Fiorentina*, the wonderful porterhouse-like steak of Tuscany, is traditionally served with lemon. The acid from the lemon and a little salt bring the steak into harmony with a glass of Chianti. That's Flavor Balancing. Try it with your unseasoned steak and you will find that the addition of the salt and lemon make the steak much more delicious and your wine will become smooth and wonderful. The illusion of red wine and red meat being a "perfect" combination has little or nothing to do with the meat and everything to do with the bitter suppressing factor of the salt we put on the steak. Try the same experiment with a piece of lamb, poultry, pork, fish or vegetables and you will get the same results.

Another food high in umami is asparagus, which is often considered "unfriendly" to wine. Adding lemon to asparagus makes it completely "friendly." The use of verjus, mustard and wine reductions in Burgundy, the vinegar in Alsace and the final squeeze of lemon juice for Mushrooms à la Bordelaise in Bordeaux are other examples of Flavor Balancing where increasing the acid makes the food and wine work together in creating a more predictably good combination of flavors.

Just for those who did not try this earlier, here are the instructions for Tim's Tequila Trick. This one is a slightly expanded version this is a version of what you I introduced earlier in the book and includes a demonstration of how sweetness in food can have a negative effect on a wine. You need grapes, a piece of lemon or lime and a glass of wine you like. Taste the wine, eat a grape and then taste the wine again. What's happened to it? Not so great? Now put just a touch of lemon and salt on your hand or a friend's body part. Lick your hand, or the body part, and sip the wine again. Did the salt and lemon/lime combination make the wine taste soft and mild again? That is positive sensory adaptation at its best!

At extreme levels, too much acid may render a balanced wine flat-tasting, although it often restores balance to highly acidic wines — it is the mignonette made with vinegar that made oysters and acidic white wines so popular, not the oyster.

Flavor Balancing is when you get to that point where you've got the proper amount of umami and sweetness; you've got the right amount of salt and acidity for your personal preferences, and food is in balance. Adjusting the balance of acid and salt ensures delicious, well balanced food that is wonderful with virtually any wine "if the guest prefers."

FLAVOR BALANCING
UN-pairing Wine and Food

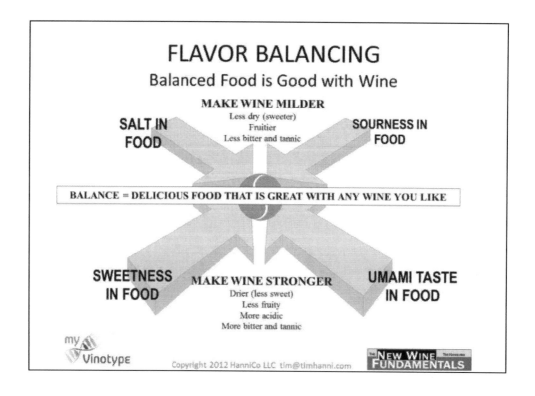

Learning to experience the experience

Some people will absolutely love a Moscato with a steak while other people will only believe it could be good with a red wine. Within this realm of wine and food matching often metaphors and expectations are so dominant that experts are not even experiencing the experience.

A few years ago I was in Spain to attend a wine event, and at a grand dinner I found myself sitting next to Steven Spurrier. He is the British wine expert who, in 1976, put together the Judgment of Paris tasting where a Napa Valley Chardonnay and Cabernet Sauvignon took top rankings over French wines. It's the event that catapulted California wines onto the global stage.

Steven told me he had heard of my flavor-balancing ideas, although he couldn't make heads or tails of what I was talking about.

On the dinner menu that night was roast lamb, and it was being served with a robust Spanish red wine. It was, by current standards, a classic pairing.

I asked him what he thought of the pairing. "Excellent," he said.

Then I asked him to really pay attention to it: What did he really think?

He took a sip of wine, tasted the meat and tasted the wine again. "Good god," he said. "It's awful."

I asked the server for some lemon and salt, which we lightly applied to the meat. Steve tasted it again. He got it.

Match the wine to the diner, not to the dinner

What would happened if we changed the wine and food matching game from the daunting task of trying to find the elusive (and imaginary) "perfect match" for wine and food to a more intimate and personal mission of providing immense pleasure to everyone? What if the intention became how to match the diner to the best wine recommendation, not the best wine for the dinner or dish? Keep in mind that this also accommodates anyone who cares to play the wine and food "matching" game. This is a win-win.

When people come to my house for lunch or dinner and I get the question, "What wine should I bring?" I describe the meal I'm planning and tell them to bring a wine that will **not** go with the dish. The wine should be something they like but would be considered a disaster with the food.

For example I love to serve a delicate fish dish, like *Filet of Sole à la Bonne Femme* — *paupiettes* of sole rolled up and poached in white wine and fish fumet with tarragon and mushrooms. The wines guests bring range from intense Lodi Petite Sirah to Napa cabs, the intense reds that are so *de riguer* these days. I mean really intense and dark red wines: the kind of red wine that should metaphorically overwhelm, overpower and even kill the taste of a delicate dish. Not one of the hundreds of people I've cooked for over the years has ever tried a delicate piece of fish with an intense red wine to see what would happen — ever.

The results of a flavor balanced sole dish and red wine? Yummy food, wonderful wine. The sole is delicious. The wine does not overpower the food nor does the food do anything other than make the wine more rich and delectable. The wine and food "disaster" is all in our heads for the most part.

The same goes for steak and Riesling or lamb and Pinot Grigio. If the food is green and vegetal the conditioned response is Sauvignon Blanc. Oysters and Syrah? Ask winemaker Ken Brown. We spent an afternoon at Edna Valley Winery many years ago with a whole group of people slurping down fresh oyster and sucking down Syrah, Cabernet — anything that was supposed to "not go with" oysters. If a slight metallic or bitter edge

Spaghetti with Tomato Sauce and "Fusion" Cuisine

"Fusion cuisine" can be defined as a cuisine that results from combining the traditions, techniques and/or ingredients from different regions or cultures. I propose that all cuisine qualifies, in some respect or at some point in time, as fusion cuisine. The fun thing for me is to look back and decipher the movement of ingredients and cultures then develop a much better understanding and appreciation for the myriad cuisines in our modern world.

Raymond Sokolov's book; **Why We Eat What We Eat** given to me by writer and food Wonder Woman Jeanne Bauer around 1990 (thank you, Jeanne!), had a profound effect on my critical rethinking of wine with food.

If there were no cucumbers, sweet peppers and tomatoes before the discovery and distribution of these foods from the New World, what the heck DID go into gazpacho? It was usually not much more than the bread and water or at most weak broth. The word *soup* seems to share its roots with the word "sop" – as in sopping up your soup with some bread.

What about Italian cuisine and the clichéd bowl of pasta and marinara sauce?

The tomatoes were first brought back from the Americas as poisonous, yellow fruit on an ornamental shrub in circa 1550. Red tomatoes did not show up for another 200 years it seems.

Who would think that eating tomatoes in Italy would stand as shining examples of both fusion cuisine and disruptive innovation? Or French fried potatoes. More about this on the next page.

arose, the tiniest bit of fresh lemon juice brought the wine back into wonderful balance. There were a lot of quizzical looks — not one person in the large group of expert wine people had ever tried the combination.

Put it to the test yourself! Go ahead and try the wrong wine with your food, or vice versa. You will be surprised at the success you will have finding delicious matches you never imagined. This is your permission to play with your food!

Italian tomato dishes and other fusion cuisine and wine

Here's another popular myth: Serve a red wine with pasta that has a red sauce. It seems simple enough. After all, pasta with a marinara sauce and Chianti are a natural, classical pairing, right? Think again.

The story of pasta alone is one of continuous evolution. The current thinking is that early forms of pasta were known to the Etruscans, and that Marco Polo introduced how to make pasta in new forms such as noodles and dumplings, which later became the Italian ravioli.

And what about the tomatoes? They must go back in Italian history forever? Nope. Tomatoes, along with eggplant, peppers and cucumbers came from the New World. Some sources actually point to the year 1544 as the year there was first hard evidence that tomatoes came to Italy. Tomatoes were first thought to be poisonous because they are members of the nightshade family. This assumption was apparently fueled by the fact that a lot of dinnerware was pewter and the lead from the pewter was leached by the acid in the tomatoes resulting in lead poisoning. Most early tomatoes were used as ornamental shrubs.

The Italian name for tomato, *pomodoro*, means the "yellow apple." The red ones did not show up until the mid-eighteenth century, 200 years later. There is little evidence of any sauce using red tomatoes before the year 1800. And, even today the tomato is much more part of the culture of southern Italy, not Tuscany, which is in the north and the home of Chianti

Many wine and food experts maintain that tomatoes and red wine "do not go together" in the first place. An equal number seem to disagree thinking they are perfect together. Red wines become less fruity, bitter and even metallic tasting for many people. The false assumption here is that it is the acidity of the tomato that causes this effect.

My sensory and umami research has shown that the real culprit here is twofold. Firstly, many people, due to biological individualism, experience no such "bad match." Secondly, if acidity in food makes wine taste smoother and milder, how can it turn around and have the opposite effect in a tomato? To top off the misinformation, a touch of lemon juice on the tomato or in the dish, i.e., more acidity, will restore the balance to most any wine. Just another prime example of the polarity that exists between wine and food actualities versus wine and food myths.

The ripe taste of tomatoes and many other fruits and vegetables, however, relies on umami taste, which can cause any wine to seem to go haywire to the tasters sensitive to this phenomenon.

Try it yourself. Taste a pasta sauce and the wine you really want to have. If the wine tastes thin and unpleasant, add a touch of balsamic vinegar or lemon juice and a touch of salt if the dish needs it. Your wine will become instantly delicious.

Oysters and red wine

Unless you are a Sweet or Hypersensitive Vinotype, try oysters and red wine. First try the wine, then an oyster and the wine again. The more sensitive you are the more likely you will find the wine gets bitter and metallic. This is relatively predictable because oysters are high in umami. Now, do as the French do: Dip the oyster in a little vinegar or give it a little spritz of lemon and a tiny touch of salt. Try it again and try your wine, and I swear to you you'll see a change — and the red wine is no problem.

Here's a more detailed account of my favorite red wine and fresh, raw oysters episode that I alluded to earlier in the book. It took place at Paradigm Vineyards in San Luis Obispo during a wine and trade event. They had platters of wonderful, freshly shucked oysters there for the taking. I boldly sashayed up to the oysters, glass of dark, red Syrah in hand, and started slurping away. A couple of people commented, "How can you stand that – isn't the combination horrible?"

I asked if they had ever tried red wine with oysters and everyone admitted that no, they had only heard it was a horrible match. Collective delusion time!! If you would like verification of this story ask Ken Brown, then winemaker at Byron Winery and now of Ken Brown Wines. It is fun to watch the face of someone experiencing a disruptive realization. People started coming over to the part of the room in droves to see why everyone was laughing.

And, to top it off, what was on the trays that is ubiquitous with fresh seafood in general? Fresh lemons. In France they have learned to serve mignonette sauce, simply vinegar with shallots and sometimes a bit of herbs and/or spices, with fresh oysters. This is the same Flavor Balancing application just in a more classic and traditional context. And by the way, sweet wines with oysters are also just fine in France.

A great, briny oyster with a few drops of lemon juice can be wonderful with even the most intense red wines imaginable. Not for everyone, mind you. Many more Sweet and Hypersensitive Vinotypes will find the metallic, unpleasant reaction cannot be mitigated. But the people who get an unpleasant reaction are the very same people who would want a lighter intensity wine in the first place – and more likely to be fine with a light, delicate white wine. Love oysters and a traditional Muscadet, Chablis or other crisp white wine? Have at it. Do you love big, intense or sweet wines? Give them a try. Does a certain combination taste horrible to you? Don't do it again. For the wine wonks reading this you may be amazed with the results and find many wines that you would have never dreamed are delicious with oysters. Ken and I reminisce about the oyster story every time we see each other.

Salmon, Pinot Noir and Metaphors

The collective delusion of Pinot Noir wines being the "perfect match" for salmon corresponds with the rise in popularity in Pinot Noir wines in general. This "classic pairing" is a hoot for a couple of reasons. People in the Northwest U.S and southwest Canada are particularly staunch defenders of the salmon and Pinot Noir combination, and almost any Pinot Noir aficionado will tell you that there is a natural affinity for this combination. The main reason is that the Northwest has become a great producer of delicious Pinot Noirs, and salmon are native and abundant.

I have had some horrible run-ins involving salmon and Pinot Noir. Salmon is notoriously high in umami taste but this can be easily taken care of with a spritz of lemon juice and a tad of salt to taste. Problem solved. I was conducting a wine and culinary workshop with a wonderful and well known seafood restaurant in Vancouver, British Columbia. Their signature dish was a salmon filet with a light maple syrup glaze and cooked on a plank of wood. I asked what wine was the "house" recommendation and it was, predictably, Pinot Noir. We all tried the dish with one of their best-selling Pinot Noirs and it sucked! The chef adjusted the recipe adding a bit more lemon, some lime and salt to the glaze; the Pinot, and every other wine on the list, smoothed right out.

If you canvas wine and food experts and ask what fish goes best with Cabernet Sauvignon you will find the answer is most frequently tuna. Here is my hypothesis on how this analogous combination, based on comparisons of relative size and flesh color, came about:

- Tuna fish are big fish. A tuna is the closest a fish can be in comparison to a cow in our imagination. Cabernet Sauvignons are often described as big wines. "Big" wines go with "big" foods.
- Tuna fish are heavy, and Cabernet Sauvignons are often described as heavy wines. Heavy wines go with heavy foods.
- Tuna flesh can be a dark red color, and Cabernet Sauvignon is most often a dark, red color. Red wines go with red meat.
- Tuna flesh is cut into steaks and is often grilled. Cabernet Sauvignon goes with grilled steak.

Voila! A wine and food match is made.

Now, let's do analogical deconstruction of the salmon and Pinot Noir match:
- Salmon are not typically as big as tunas. Pinot Noir is not typically as "big" a wine as Cabernet Sauvignon.
- Salmon are not typically as heavy as tunas. Pinot Noir is not typically as not as "heavy" a wine as Cabernet Sauvignon.
- Salmon is not as dark red as most tuna and Pinot Noir is typically not as dark red as a Cabernet Sauvignon.
- Delicate wines go better with fish, and Pinot Noir is a more delicate wine than a "stronger" Cabernet Sauvignon.

I honestly think that this is the deductive process of how we created this match of salmon and Pinot Noir. Here is what I can prove from countless trials: Order or prepare salmon in a delicious way, and have the Pinot Noir or Cabernet Sauvignon or Chardonnay or Riesling or other wine that you really want to have. If the umami in the salmon makes your wine a bit bitter and unpleasant, find a source of some acidity and add a bit of salt if you wish and your Pinot Noir, or any other wine, will be delicious.

A Wine and Food Adventure in Turkey

The collective delusion of wine experts in Turkey is that Turkish food does not go with wine. How limiting, how disenfranchising could be this possibly be? I was invited to conduct a wine and food pairing dinner during a consulting visit in 2012. The host for the event made the comment. "Of course, Turkish food does not pair well with tine." HA! We changed the venue from a hip but non-traditional restaurant to one that was run by a Turkish family and specialized in really traditional Turkish cusine.

At a wonderful Istanbul restaurant, called Maria's Garden, we set out to test the theory that Turkish cuisine "did not pair with wine" and also to demonstrate how Flavor Balancing could restore harmony to any combination. The Turks have salt and lemon on virtually every table! We served a flavor spectrum of six wines; a sweet, late harvest Alsatian; a dry Pinot Blanc; an oaky, Australian Chardonnay; a light red Beaujolais; an intense Vega Secilia from Spain and a high-alcohol Amarone from Italy.

We set up the wines from mild to strong and then we had plate after plate of food, trying the steamed fish with Amarone, a rich, dry wine, and it was fantastic. We had dishes with yoghurt, hummus and olives. If it got a little bitter a touch of lemon juice and salt made the fish better and the wine came completely into balance. By the end of the meal, we had completely busted the myth. Turkish food, Greek food, Mexican food - you name it - can all be delicious with wine.

The family who owned the restaurant was fabulous and the host, Dr. Yunus Emre Kocabasoglu and his partner Burcak Descombre, a sommelier and enthusiastic wine professional, were all completely amazed. By the way, if anyone wants to promote wine in any given country the last thing you might want to do is insinuate that wine does not go with the national cuisine!

Wine with Asian food

This brings us to the foods of Asia. The varied and popular foods form countries as diverse as China, Japan, Thailand, Malaysia, Korea – you name it - are often considered "wine unfriendly." Yet wine and food matchers march forward, conjuring up all sorts of metaphorical rational to match the Asian dishes to wines.

There are grounds for some of the "wine unfriendliness" attitudes about many Asian dishes. This generalization is especially applicable when there are dishes that have a high level of sweetness combined with lots of umami taste or are very spicy and you do not get the orgasmic euphoria of the chosen few.

The rationale provided for the wine and cuisine unfriendliness is often unjustified and similar to the tomato and wine myth where the "culprit" is actually the solution. Soy sauce is often singled out as the source of the incompatibility when a modicum of soy sauce is the cure! The saltiness of soy sauce quickly tones down the tannin and bitterness in wine. Try it – taste a wine, try a touch of soy sauce, taste wine again. Smooth.

Just for some giggles I have compiled a collection of wine recommendations for Peking Duck from a single, online comment thread from a recent expert discussion: What wine goes best with Peking Duck? Here are the recommendations provided from the web:

> Reisling, Sauvignon Blanc, Chateauneuf-du-Pape, Oregon Pinot Noir, 100 percent Pinot Meunier Champagne, Alsace blends, a big ol' Pride Cabernet, Dolcetto, ripe vintages of Rosso di Montalcino, Sangiovese, Australian Sparkling Cabernet, Gewurztraminer, Grenache, Dry rosé, especially ones based upon Rhone red varieties, a good Portuguese wine from Douro...the list continues.

Holy moly. who should I believe?

Basically everyone just conjures up the dish and then goes to the mental rolodex of wines they love in their heads and comes up with a match. The process is not based on any reality — just our fertile imagination and personal wine favorites. There is nothing wrong with this but just what is a poor consumer supposed to do with this information?

You can bet that the contributors on the "Peking Duck and wine" thread would defend their choices. You could also bet that if the wine you serve is a wine you love, it will be great with the Peking Duck. If it turns out that it is not a great match, a dash of soy sauce or a light addition of the vinegar typically on the table will set the dish right with any of the wines recommended. Just as long as it is a style of wine you like in the first place.

Dishes served at a banquet in Hangzhou, China: tripe, pork, seafood, beef and more.

If you took list of the internet wine recommendations to your retailer, you'd end up saying something like "I'm looking for a big, delicate, fruity and spicy late harvest sparkling nouveau white Cabernet-Pinot Noir-Grenache-Sangiovese rosé from Portugal made by an Australian winemaker with lots of new-oak owned by an Italian family to go with Peking Duck..."

Ok – so what wine goes with the dishes all served simultaneously and pictured in the Chinese banquet photo? You have salted preserved carp, jellied tripe, crocked salted pork belly, braised lamb, pickled seaweed, steamed greens, BBQ beef buns and, just to top things off, a fish broth with clams, shrimp and vegetables.. By the way, the little 2-section dish to the top right of the plate? Vinegar and soy sauce. Problem solved – serve a wine you love.

Try the "wrong" combinations!

If you are a cynical wine and food matcher I recommend trying the wrong wine and food pairings for a week or two. Try to order the things that shouldn't go well. Make sure you have selected a wine you like. Don't think some combination is going to magically make you like White Zinfandel if you hate it. Honestly do your homework and try it out.

There are principles and there is predictability. Another principle is the more hypersensitive you are, the more you are going to notice changes in the reactivity of wine and food. But if you know why and know the solution is a little salt, lime, lemon, vinegar or other form of acidity, little wine and food problems disappear.

The more tolerant, the less you will notice these changes and the easier it is for you to have your Cabernet with your oysters or shrimp cocktail. Because that's what you love.

The New Wine Fundamentals even apply to the order of eating a dinner for food or wine. Typically the general order is to go from delicate to strong. A meal starts with the white fish and progresses to the red meat. But actually you don't have to have a certain order in the wine and food; there is no right or wrong. If you love Muscat and Cabernet, try them both with a dish.

You can eat a meal and drink the wines in any order that makes sense to you. If you start with a big steak, it's not going to change how your delicate fish or oysters taste afterwards. Try the steak with some salt and lemon and a big red wine, a Muscat, Muscadet, Chardonnay or whatever wine you like, and then go to the oysters — as long as you understand that salt and lemon is imperative; the acidity the brininess of the oyster with the lemon or the mignonette sauce is what actually has influenced the ideas that oysters go or do not go with different wines.

Although many people may more likely agree on how the wine is changed by their food, different people may experience very different changes and, finally, opinions may vary on whether they like the change or not. Our opinions are derived from life experiences, cultural and social mores and learning. Thus, one person's defining moment of a magical wine and food match may clash with another person's memories, mental associations or ideals.

Replacing wine and food rules with simple principles

1. The wine should be in a flavor or style category you have some capacity to like. If you hate high alcohol Zinfandel, White Zinfandel, Pinot Grigio or whatever, it will taste terrible with or without your food.

2. The more emotionally you are tied to wine and food matching, the more likely it is the imaginary wine and food matches you conjure up will work together. This is a psychological phenomenon and self-fulfilling prophecy of wine and food matching, not an experiential reality.

3. The more sensitive you are — that is, if your Vinotype is Sweet or Hypersensitive — you'll instinctively avoid the big, red wines that experts love and you'll stick with what you prefer. You are more likely get a bitter reaction from strong wines (high extract, higher alcohol) with foods with lots of umami. As you will see, a tiny addition of lemon and salt will cure most negative reactions but you don't tend to favor huge reds or oaky whites in the first place Stick to the wines you love the most.

4. Those with Tolerant palates won't usually want a delicate Riesling, even with sushi. They, too, should stick with what they like. If you like matching heavy wines with heavy foods or light wines with light foods, stay with it.

Wine and food is an important part of many people's lives. Truth be told, most people could care less. Sorry to be so brutal, but this is the truth. But the people who don't care about wine or food aren't likely to be reading this book, now, are they?

For those of us who do care, whether you are in the hotel or restaurant business, a wine distributor, a retailer or a host preparing dinner at home, you will find the combination of learning about Vinotyping and the principles of Flavor Balancing are a game-changer for anyone interested in getting more enjoyment out of every opportunity to share wine and food. Organize wine and food dinners by putting out a spectrum of carefully selected wines. Conduct a tasting with the wines letting everyone determine their wine flavor comfort point. Explain the concept of Vinotypes and include a Vinotyping exercise as a part of all wine tastings. Then serve all of the wines through the meal and let everyone try different wines with different combinations or simply stick with the wine they love the most. Anyone who wants to match certain wines to different dishes is encouraged to do just that!

All of a sudden winery hospitality and special events are completely different. You will notice a whole new dynamic. The hospitality is limitless because you are saying, "What kind of wine can I open?" "Who's here?" "What Vinotypes do we have?"

Drink wines you like with the foods you enjoy and learn to understand and celebrate our differences. I guarantee you will be absolutely blown away by how excited the hardest to excite people become when you keep in mind that flexibility and working within the personal preferences of your guests is more important than any hard, fast wine and food pairing rule. Pleasing your guests, after all, is the most immutable and time-honored of all principles of true hospitality and connoisseurship.

Once again in my life it turns out that the more I learn, the more amazed I am at how much remains to be discovered. But for me today, I have renounced my once-adamant stance that there are irrefutable wine and food combinations. I am now convinced we need to return to the true spirit of hospitality and encourage all wine lovers to feel completely at ease enjoying the wines they love the most with the foods they desire.

It all goes back to the principle so clearly stated, but something I overlooked in 40 years of reading in *Larousse Gastronomique.* The choice between red or white, dry or sweet wine, should always be left to the preference of the guest. Offer choices with every course, feel free to concoct the "perfect pairing" but make sure that our ideals of wine and food pairings are put aside "if the guest prefers."

Here are the principles of great French wine and food and more importantly how wine, and wine with food, should be best approached:

- Be proud of your history, land and culture.
- Grow food and grapes with great care; then prepare your cuisine and make your wine with passion.
- Ensure your love of family and community are always held in greater importance than propriety and any sort of false rules of wine and food matching.
- Eat the foods and drink the wines that you love the most.

When you share wine with others, offer your guests a choice of wines and do not presume everyone is going to like the intense dry red or high-acidity dry white wines, regardless of our own personal passions or convictions.

My unabashed passion for French cuisine and French wines has never diminished and the love affair continues to this day. When I am entertaining I still love to cook really classic French foods and love to immerse myself and others in the rich diversity of French wines and greatness of the cuisine. But you can bet I do not impose my idealistic wine and food pairing folly on my guests. When you come to my house, you can have white wine with the lamb, red with your oysters, and you will probably be thunderstruck at how wonderful the wrong wines can be with most dishes. I will serve the wines I love but am always delighted to open another bottle of something different, if my guests prefer.

Here are some examples of how Flavor Balancing is applied in classic dishes in France and Italy:

- The pervasive use of vinegar, lemon juice, *verjus* (very acidic juice from unripe grapes) and wine reductions.

- Lemon, vinegar and mustard used as condiments and on the table.

- Foods that are salted and brined including olives and pickles (the Italian word *insalata,* now meaning salad, was actually used to describe any food preserved in salt).

- Cooking techniques like blanching asparagus or artichokes in acidulated, salted water thereby reducing their reactivity with wine.

- The role of sauerkraut, especially when combined with the salted, preserved meats, in the cuisine of Alsace had a powerful effect tempering what used to be very acidic wines of the regions.

- Oysters served with vinegar-based *mignonette* or lemon. In the Arcachon region of Bordeaux you would get lemon or *mignonette* and salty little lamb sausages – and a glass of nice red wine would be just fine with this combination.

- Different compound butters and sauces incorporating lemon juice, vinegar, verjus or wine reductions from *á la Bordelaise* (sauces and the famous *Cépes* mushrooms), Sauce *Hollandaise* or *Béarnaise, Maitre d'Hotel* butter…the list goes on and on.

Many years ago I had the honor of proposing and demonstrating the concepts of Flavor Balancing to Michel Trama, the renowned and decorated Chef and Proprietor of Les Loges de l'Aubergade in Puymirol, France. He completely agreed with the principles and went to far as to declare that reintroducing Flavor Balancing to modern culinary programs would help restore fundamental culinary traditions that have been lost in French cuisine over the course of the past few decades.

Try this! The cause and effect of wine and food

Get some friends together, buy some wine, prepare these bites of food and discover how primary food flavors effect the flavor of wine and how easy it is to use Flavor Balancing to correct any possible flavor conflicts.

Here is what you will need and a picture of how to set up the place settings for each guest.

Wines should be set up from left to right in the order below. You can conduct this entire demonstration with just the strong red wine – it demonstrates the flavor interactions most clearly. A really good wine consultant at a good store should be able to help you find great examples of each of these wines if you want to conduct the full Monty.

Wines:
1. Sweet white (a White Zinfandel, Riesling or Moscato with 2.5 to 5 percent residual sugar. For reference a White Zinfandel is typically about 3 percent residual sugar)
2. Light, dry white (Pinot Grigio, Sauvignon Blanc, un-oaked Chardonnay)
3. Rich Chardonnay, Pinot Noir or very smooth, lighter style Syrah, or Merlot
4. Cabernet Sauvignon or any other strong, tannic red

Setting:
- Fork
- Napkin
- Water glass/water

Food:

- Asparagus, with and without Vignon Flavor Balancing Seasoning
- Cherry tomato cut in half, both halves on each plate
- Lemon wedge
- Individual salt packet OR ¼ tsp salt on plate OR salt shaker available
- Red seedless grape
- Medium-size white mushrooms; raw and cooked with one-half or a bite-size piece RAW, the other half or another bite-size piece COOKED until soft with NO seasoning (60 seconds or so in a container in the microwave)

Option: If you want to simultaneously conduct the "taste, smell and memories" exercise in Chapter 6, along with the Cause and Effect tasting, you can put the spices along the edge of each plate. can refer back to that section for the instructions.

Another addition is cooking any combination of meats, chicken, seafood – with NO SEASONING. Grill, sauté, poach or bake anything and you will find that they almost all have mostly negative effect on the wines. After going through the basic Cause and Effect steps below, play around with all of the different proteins and check it out. Especially a rare, unseasoned piece of quality steak grilled rare and try it with your favorite red wine.

Instructions (take small sips, you will go back and forth between the food and wine several times):

1. Everyone participating in the tasting should take the Vinotype assessment in the book or at www.myvinotype.com. This will help you understand why the opinions may vary on the sensations each of you experience.

2. Instruct everyone to hold off on trying any of the food until the instructions dictate.
    *   Start with the optional smell, taste and memory demonstration with the spices from Chapter 5 if you choose that option.

3. Taste through the wines from left to right – not like a professional wine evaluation but more just taking a small sip as you would with dinner or just having a glass of wine.

4. Determine which wine you personally prefer, discuss with your guests to see if there are any differences in preferences. Talk about other people you know who like wine and which wines might appeal to them – friends, family, associates and the like. This is not an exercise to determine if one wine is "better" than another. It is simply a demonstration of styles and discussion of who likes which, and why? And if you, or even none of you, like one or more of the wines, do you know others who might?

5. Take a sip of the strong red wine, eat your grape, and try the wine again. For most people it will be similar to the experience of brushing your teeth and drinking orange juice. It is, in fact, the same perceptive adaptation in both cases.

    > **Principle 1:** Sweet food makes wine taste stronger. Starting with the stronger wine in the first place will create a more intense reaction than trying a sweet food with a delicate dry wine or sweet wine.

6. Take a lick of the lemon and a little salt (the tequila trick). Not too much, just a little bit!

    > **Principle 2:** Salt and acidity make wine taste milder. Acidity and salt, added to food in very moderate quantities, has a near-magical effect on the taste of a wine that follows a bite of food. The additions can be made in the recipe or at the table using common condiments, namely a salt shaker and wedge of lemon. Care must be taken as sometimes acidic condiments like the vinegar at a sushi restaurant or on a Chinese table

may have been heavily sweetened thus negating the wine-softening effect.

7. Umami demonstration: The best way to learn to identify this subtle and delicious sensation is to take a bite of the uncooked mushroom, which is high in natural glutamic acid and for all intent and purpose tastes pretty plain. Now try the microwaved mushroom – it is softer but also something about the taste is more yummy, maybe broth-like and definitely more delicious. The cooking converted the non-umami-tasting glutamic acid into the glutamate, the natural umami taste compound. Umami taste is found in all sorts of vegetables, fruits, meats cheeses and, as you remember from earlier in the book, human breast milk.

Food that is high in umami taste tends to render the wine you are drinking less rich or fruity and more bitter, sour and astringent – very similar to the reaction of wine with sweet foods. This is why asparagus and many foods high in umami taste are considered "wine enemies" and brings us to the next demonstration.

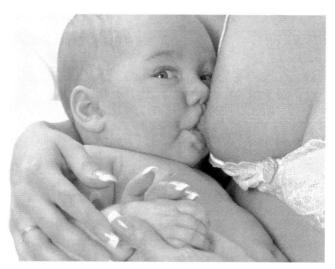

Breast milk has 10 times more glutamate, natural umami taste, than cow's milk. Oooh, mommy!

8. Try a bite of asparagus (which is high in umami taste) and try the wine you liked the most. You may find complete disagreement over the reaction between the asparagus and the wine. It seems the Sweet and Hypersensitive Vinotypes tend to have adverse reactions. Sensitive Vinotypes are less likely to perceive the reaction and Tolerant Vinotypes rarely encounter a problem. The more people you have when you conduct this tasting the more varied the results will be.

9. Put a little squeeze of lemon and a tiny pinch of salt on the asparagus and try the same combination. The wines will be restored back to their original balance. Not only is the wine reaction problem solved but you will notice that the asparagus tastes better with the lemon and salt whether you serve wine or not.

10. The taste of ripeness in a tomato is from the development of umami taste in the ripening process. The demonstration is identical to the asparagus demonstration but have everyone try this with the strong red wine. Take a sip of wine, a bite of tomato and then discuss what happens. We find this

combination is split almost evenly between 1. An unpleasant, bitter reaction. 2. No problem or 3. The wine gets smoother and tastes better.

11. Now season the other piece of tomato with a little salt and drop of lemon juice and you will find near-unanimous agreement that the tomato tastes better and the wine is smoother, and usually better-tasting, for everyone.

Wine and food miscellany

Following are some bits and pieces from some of the more popular wine and food disagreements and also some helpful wine and food hints.

Tomatoes, wine and differing opinions

I covered tomatoes in depth in another section of the book and want to use the question, "What wine goes, or does not go, with tomatoes" as a wonderful study in contrasts of perception and opinion. There is a valid point of view and rationale provided by the "anti" tomato and wine faction that tomatoes are notoriously difficult to pair with wine. For many people, especially hypersensitive Vinotypes, this seems the case. The delusion comes in when you find expert's finger pointing to the high acidity of a tomato as the cause of the flavor dis-harmony.

In reality, tomatoes are considered relatively low-acid fruit. The real culprit for the mismatch, typically experienced at an increased level by more sensitive Vinotypes, is the umami taste that is part of the yumminess of a ripe tomato and NOT the acidity. In fact, more acidity is the solution to making your wine more delicious! Try a bite of one of the pieces of tomato and try the wine you like most.

In a large group only about a third will find the wine unpleasant. Add a little salt and lemon to the second piece of tomato and two things happen. First, Flavor Balancing makes the tomato taste better. Second, **all** of the wines will taste smoother – less harsh, less acidic. You will clearly see that the answer to the tomato and wine dilemma, if you even encounter a dilemma in the first place, is adding **more** acidity to the dish. As usual, take it with a grain of salt, quite literally.

The following insight and advice comes from PickYourOwn.org: "Are tomatoes low acid or high acid (acidic)? In short, they are borderline (note: about the same as a fig), and whether they are acidic or not, for the purposes of home canning, depends upon the variety. In practice, it is a moot point: as long as you add a small amount of lemon juice (it won't affect the taste) to each jar, it will always be acidic enough to be safe!"

And notice the solution to the wine pairing dilemma is solved in the advice to make your canned tomatoes safer: lemon juice!

Most tomato lovers will agree a fresh, ripe tomato with a light sprinkle of salt and a few drops of fresh citrus juice or Balsamic vinegar is nirvana. The good news is that the same light seasonings that make the tomato more delicious are your ticket to Flavor Balancing so you can enjoy your favorite wine: sweet or dry, red or white. You decide.

What to do when you are dining out

Applying the principles of Cause and Effect dining out is simple. Order the wine you really like the most and the food that looks most appetizing. If you love to match wine and food then just do it -- order the wine that you think will best complement the dish or meal you choose. If you want the service professional or sommelier to take you to Paris go for it! Do not forget that I am not saying to stop matching or pairing wine and food if you love to play the game – just understand the realities and do not impose your will and preferences on others unless they ask or give you permission. If the service professionals of sommeliers sneer or smirk about your choice of wine with food tell them to get with the program. They are using outmoded wine and food technology and need to upgrade to the newest version.

What do you do if you know that the dish you are having is relatively sweet? If you hate the sweet food and dry wine reaction, order a more delicate, or even off-dry, wine with your sweet food. This is why experts often recommend more delicate or off-dry wines like Rieslings or light reds with Asian cuisine or other dishes that might be sweet. This one is not a myth! But if you love big reds, oaky chardonnays or anything else then damn the torpedoes and go for it.

Stick to the wines you love! If there is an unpleasant reaction just take a break between sips. Or order a little lemon and salt.

As a final note – a restaurant that does not put salt on the table, or even worse refuses to provide salt, is demonstrating the epitome of sensory and gastronomic ignorance. Tell them so or just tip accordingly.

Desserts

If you are serving sweet wines, and would like them to remain sweet, make sure the wine is sweeter than the dish. This goes for main dishes (usually not much of a problem) and especially with dessert. This is well known and not a myth.

If you are serving a really rich and luxurious sweet wine, try the salty, acidic Roquefort or other fine bleu cheeses (a classic pairing that does really work for many people) or a lemon or citrus-based dessert. Arguments over chocolate and wine and other things are just arguments. If you love the idea of chocolate and wine have it with whatever floats your boat. If you don't care for chocolate and wine, fine and dandy.

The more experience I have sharing the concepts of Vinotypes and giving people permission to freely express their wine preferences, the more resolute I become that we really need this change in the gastronomic paradigm of wine and food matching. Dinners are so much more fun and engaging. Wine and conversation flow freely and it offers much more opportunity to everyone to explore and discover new and different wines.

Cheese and wine

Many dishes, such as cheese, are served by with little intervention from the kitchen. Flavor Balancing is therefore inherent in the cheese itself. Here are the guidelines:

- Wines high in umami (usually more ripened or aged) will tend to bring out a bitter and unpleasant taste. Try a young brie and older, aged brie with the same wine (red works best) and you may notice the flavor interaction. Do this with others and you will see people get different reactions.

- More highly sensitive Vinotypes are much more likely to get bitter, even metallic reactions from some combinations, such as red wine and Bleu cheeses, where other find the same combination smooth and harmonious. Recommendation: if it sucks, quit doing it. Besides, the Sweet and Hypersensitive Vinotypes tend to like wines that will react less with the cheese in the first place – less bitter, less astringent, less alcohol.

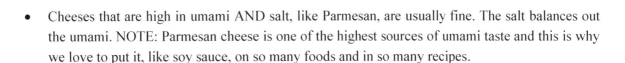

- Roquefort and most any fine bleu cheese is wonderful with sweet wines – and any wine for most people. Salty, acidic and high in umami so see the caution above for really sensitive Vinotypes.

- Cheeses that are high in umami AND salt, like Parmesan, are usually fine. The salt balances out the umami. NOTE: Parmesan cheese is one of the highest sources of umami taste and this is why we love to put it, like soy sauce, on so many foods and in so many recipes.

- QUIT SERVING FRUIT WITH YOUR CHEESE IF YOU ARE SERVING DRY WINES! Sorry for yelling, my editors asked me not use capital letters. In this case I am yelling. The idea of the fruit (brush teeth, drink orange juice) being served with the wine is just a crazy, delusional Conventional Wisdom.

- Serve salty, acidic olives or even little dill pickles (cornichons) with your cheese. A nice little salad with olive oil, lemon juice or Balsamic vinegar and salt is wonderful to offset any unpleasant interactions.

Never lose sight that people who love to exercise their imaginations and passionately envision the perfect pairings are still respected and encouraged to follow their desire. Never let this passion infringe on someone else who simply wants to enjoy a glass of wine they know they will like. This is restoring traditions and hospitality in the truest sense of the word.

Lose the fruit with your cheese plate! Cheeses high in umami may make your wine bitter and metallic, salty cheese will be less reactive. Serve some nice olives, salty crackers and maybe even a small salad dressed with Balsamic vinegar or a squeeze of lemon juice, olive oil and lightly salted.

Chapter 7 Q&A

Question: What do you do if you have a dish that is perfect the way it is or you don't care to add lemon or salt?

Answer: You have a couple of options. First, simply order the wine you really want. If there is a reaction it will not be the end of the world. Two – if the recipe indicates the dish might be sweet or particularly rich in umami with no indication of citrus or acidity, select a wine that is down a notch or two in intensity. The "wine and food disasters" are primarily created by Vinotypes with really specific expectations for their wine experience – far beyond simple enjoyment.

Question: What about chocolate and red wine?

Answer: Talk about a perceptive confluence of sensitivities, preferences, emotions and experiences! If you love it, do it. Many people try the combination and it is horrible – back to the "brush teeth drink orange juice" phenomenon. Others swear it is heaven. You decide and everyone quit arguing about it!

True story - Digression warning!

I was presenting my wine, food and sensory sensitivity seminar in Hong Kong about 1995. Seated in the front row was a young, successful-looking Chinese man in a designer suit and his very lovely wife. Someone asked, "What do you think about matching red wine and chocolate?" I queried the 120 or so people asking who liked the combination and who did not. As usual it was a split decision somewhat in favor of "not." When the topic came up I noticed the young man in the front row leaned forward and his wife folded her arms and leaned back in her chair.

I then asked, "Who really, really loves red wine and chocolate?" The young man waved his hand enthusiastically. I directed a question to him, "May I be so bold as to suggest you particularly love Merlot with chocolate?"

"Yes," he replied, "how did you know?"

I then said, "Actually, I would even go so far as to predict your favorite wine with chocolate is Newton Vineyards Napa Valley Merlot."

He was stunned. He cried, "Oh my god – it is like you are psychic. That IS my favorite wine with chocolate. That exact wine! How did you know?"

"I was watching how enthusiastic you became but your wife seemed to become a bit upset, and folded her arms," I explained. "The more you talked about the subject the deeper back in her chair she receded. Her face clearly showed more displeasure. My guess is that you both attended a Newton Vineyards wine tasting, or wine dinner, and Dr. Sue Hua Newton (a scientist, fabulous wine emissary and strikingly beautiful Chinese woman who frequently was in the Hong Kong market and who co-founded the winery with her husband Peter Newton), shared with you how wonderful the combination of their fabulous Merlot and chocolate can be – 'almost better than sex!' You were in, and your wife was out! It was evident from the different body language you both exhibited to the same combination but came away with different opinions."

Question: Doesn't the protein and fat in a good steak or cheese make wine smoother? I hear it coats the taste buds or that fat makes wine, especially astringent red wines, smoother by providing lubrication lost when drinking astringent wines.

Answer: That was my story for a long time. I have not been able to find the studies that corroborate this but have been counseled (actually admonished) by two sensory specialists in the area of "lubricity." Another delusion! Pour a glass of tannic wine and try it with olive oil, beef suet, lard or unsalted butter. The wine becomes MORE astringent almost every time. Another collective delusion dashed on the rocks in a raging sea on a flat earth!

Chapter 8: What the Future Holds

Here is an example of the kind of thinking that permeates the wine industry and suppresses the potential for expanding the enjoyment of wine world wide:

"As Long As Night Follows Day, Consumers Continue The Journey Of Sweet to Dry AND Value to Mainstream to Premium As They Become More Sophisticated AND More Affluent." — Wine industry executive presenting at a conference in Vienna, Austria

What I see in the future for wine is the possibility that all wine consumers, from enjoyers to enthusiasts to wonks and even geeks, feel free and confident to openly share their wine preferences. Gone would be the stammering, "Well, I don't really like wine" from the people who love sweet wines. Gone as well would be the look of disapproval from those who have been programmed to think that dry wines are good wines and sweet wines, and the people who love them, are inherently unsophisticated.

Conversely, anyone who loves intense, tannic red wines can celebrate and enjoy the wines of their choice where and when they care to; as an aperitif, on a picnic in the summer or with their shrimp cocktail.

And don't forget that in this new future there will be entirely new opportunities for the wine wonks and professionals. This new future throws the doors wide open! The studying, selling and producing of wines will have a much larger and diverse consumer base, contributing to the need of an equally wider range of wines - many of which stand on the verge of extinction.

Sweet Vinotype comes out of the closet...after 45 years

Harvey Posert is one of wine gurus and preeminent wine public relations professionals in the Napa Valley. A former newspaperman, he worked in public relations in Chicago and New York before he came on board with the Wine Institute. From 1965 to 1980, he supervised Wine Institute's award-winning program to educate Americans about California wines. In 1980, he took over public relations for the

Robert Mondavi Winery and was instrumental working with Bob to bring world-class Napa Valley wines to the attention of the rest of the world. Since 1997, he has been a public relations consultant for a number of the valley's most prominent wineries. You might say he's a guy who knows about wine.

In 2010 I was attending a holiday wine bash on Nob Hill in San Francisco. Invited to this annual gathering were the usual suspects from the wine industry and really great wines — that is, great wines by the standards of conventional wisdom standards, meaning intense, dry wines only.

In the midst of all this eating, drinking and hobnobbing, I saw Harvey coming across the room toward me. In his wonderful, baritone Memphis drawl, he said, "I read the report you and the doctor at Cornell University published and it has changed my life."

"Is that a good thing?" I asked.

He explained that in his 45 year career in the wine industry, he had never been able to stand "those horrible wines that everyone else oohs and aahs over" — including the famed, intense big reds of the Napa Valley.

Harvey, it turns out, is a Sweet Vinotype. Because of his high level of sensitivity, the intense, dry red and white wines considered apropos by the wine industry are extremely bitter and unpleasant. Apparently he never got the memo that he was supposed to like Chardonnay and Cabernet Sauvignon if he wanted to become "more sophisticated and affluent."

"I have been told that I have no taste buds by people who are experts and should know," he said, "but it turns out they don't know squat. Now I find out that I actually have the most taste buds – and this explains why I can't stand those wines. I have always been embarrassed about my wine preferences and you are saying that I don't have to be."

The more I've talked about my research, the more stories I've heard from people who've been led to apologize for their taste for sweet wines but Harvey's stands out as a sterling example of smart, sophisticated and savvy people, who just happen to like sweet wines. Dr. Utermolen is another. So is my mother-in-law, Joanne.

Since the 1980s when someone wants to learn more about wine, we've been trying to whisk them off to Paris, metaphorically speaking, without first learning where they really want to go.

We as a wine industry can get smarter about the recommendations and information we provide to people in tasting rooms, retail stores, restaurants and in published information, online, in magazines — or even books.

Wine competitions

I have no complaint with any wine competition, evaluation process or rating system. What is missing is a way to ensure that wine consumers can get to wine recommendations that are relevant for their Vinotype.

Anyone who participates can appreciate the chaos and arguments that ensue when you put opposite Vinotypes on the same judging panel. Quite literally one highly qualified, expert judge may claim a wine to be commercially unacceptable while another is pushing to have it awarded as Best of Show!

The Consumer Wine Awards

Imagine a wine competition where everyday wine enjoyers were asked to taste and evaluate wines that were limited only to the category or wine styles they love the most? The Consumer Wine Awards, held annually in Lodi, California, is the first international wine competition to recognize and celebrate the fact that every person has unique physiological and sensory differences that profoundly affect wine and food preferences. Thus, the people evaluating each wine category are the very consumers who are most inclined to buy and enjoy those wines. This creates a new way for other consumers, who share similar tastes, to confidently explore wines evaluated and recommended by their peers. The event is organized by the Lodi Tokay Rotary and is open to wines of every price and style from around the world.

We first started the program using traditional, trained judging panels and then morphed to using a special evaluation process and only untrained, everyday wine consumers. The data you will find in Appendix 1: Vinotype Facts and Figures, was collected in conjunction with the Consumer Wine Awards evaluator application process.

The competition recognizes three primary wine consumer sensitivity segments based on previous research on sensory sensitivity/tolerances and wine preference criteria. Judges were screened via the consumer questionnaire and physical counting of taste buds to determine the taste sensitivity and wine attribute preferences of every judge. Tasting panels included an equal number of judges from each of what we have now determined to be Vinotype sensitivity groups.

The wines are evaluated by every-day wine consumers, creating a peer-to-peer affinity base that is very engaging. People who love White Zinfandel evaluate wine with similar sweetness levels; people who love Cabernets evaluate the Cabernets; and we have a really great range of "adventure" wines – a Virginia Viognier from Jefferson Vineyards was a high award winner in 2010 and Red Ass Rhubarb from North Dakota the year before. At the traditional end, Rocca Cabernet from Napa garnered the Best in Class for that varietal. The diversity of wines that gain Platinum and Gold medals is extraordinary.

Many wine experts and pundits take exception to the idea of wine consumers evaluating and giving awards to wines. I take it all in stride (sniff). Conversations I have had with many top experts have made it clear that consumers are not generally fit to evaluate wines in a formal tasting situation. Here is a quote from the blog of a well-known critic and wine judge, "With this breathless hyperventilation, the producers of the latest get-rich-quick 'wine awards' gimmick announce yet another effort to 'democratize' wine assessment by taking it away from — gasp! — evil experts like me and handing it over to that ever-popular bastion of populism — the Consumer! We're seeing these 'consumer-judged wine competitions' multiply like e coli in a petrie [sic] dish."

The intention of the Consumer Wine Awards is not to take anything away from wine experts or critics, or to detract from the results of any other wine competitions. The Consumer Wine Awards is a way of exploring new ways to make good, personalized, peer-to-peer wine recommendations.

The awards are organized and presented in a number of ways so wine consumers can identify their own Vinotype, sort the award winning wines and find wines particularly suited to their preferences as awarded by people who are similar Vinotypes. This event is getting bigger and better each year and for more information you can visit www.consumerwineawards.com.

Restaurant wine lists, sommeliers and hospitality professionals

Restaurants are places that could benefit immensely from adopting the New Wine Fundamentals principles and the process of Vinotyping. Imagine what it would be like to have a sommelier make highly expert, personalized suggestions based on the wines you like, rather than raising that supercilious eyebrow if you make what he perceives to be a misstep. And imagine too, the benefits for a restaurant, where the guests are not too intimidated to order wines instead of turning to beers or cocktails. Imagine how much more enjoyable and less intimidating it might be if the mission was to get the appropriate wine to the diner, not the dinner – permission to enjoy the wines you know you love with the foods you really want to try from the menu. Also keep in mind that, if the guest prefers, they are completely free to request being "taken to Paris." This means the knowledgeable and eager wonks can regale diners who are interested in hearing about the magical pairings and live vicariously through the experiences and tastings of a great sommelier.

I've been working with restaurants across the U.S. that are interested in creating a new kind of wine list, a progressive list that breaks wines downs by type, sweet, fruity, dry, smooth, intense and so forth. But breaking down the years of misconceptions means progressing one step at a time. Restaurants of all levels of service and types of cuisine employ Progressive Wine Lists, from national chains like Olive Garden, hotels including many Ritz Carlton properties and even top-end fine dining establishments.

Some years ago I met with the CEO of a respected restaurant group to discuss the idea of creating a Progressive Wine List for their small chain of white tablecloth restaurants. During the workshop I was watching his reactions to the wines we were tasting. He was grimacing and wincing with each sip. I began asking him questions about salt (loves lots of salt), coffee (can't stand it), and artificial sweeteners (tastes like biting into aluminum foil). OK – he is a Hypersensitive taster for sure. Then I asked, "What kind of wines do you like?"

"I hate the stuff myself," he admitted. "I am surrounded by wine experts and they are always trying to get me to try this wine or that wine and they are all horrible."

"Wait a minute," I said and I went to the bar. I asked the bartender for a glass of White Zinfandel. It turned out they were too embarrassed to put it on the wine list of a high class place, but they kept a bottle under the counter. I took a glass to the owner who tasted it cautiously.

"This I like," he exclaimed, "What is it?" Turns out none of the experts surrounding him would dare to consider he might like something sweet. He now openly declares his love of wine, orders expensive bottles when he entertains and makes sure there is something on the table for everyone's taste – if the guest prefers.

Retail wine stores

Find your guide! Just imagine if retail wine consultants and employees were trained how to identify each customer's Vinotype and then make wine recommendations for wines selected by someone with that Vinotype? And that there were sections in the store by Vinotype merchandising the special finds, value and prestige wines for diverse clientele tastes?

There are several retail stores and chains set up by flavor categories but none of them really fully understand the full opportunity. These stores tend to get sucked back into the collective delusions of modern wine groupspeak – dry is better, a red wine is a much better choice with your steak, etc. Then they will typically use metaphorical descriptors, like crisp white or sexy reds, instead of more direct and plain words to call out the sections.

The new conversation of Vinotypes, preferences, occasions and expectations not only encourages more interest in exploring and discovering new wines, it helps create loyal, repeat customers who will tell others about the great experience at your store every time they open and share a bottle of wine with others.

Winery tasting rooms

I've seen the same thing happen when I've trained tasting room staffs at wineries in Vinotyping. In every group there are people who tell me they don't really like wine themselves, until they learn about their own Vinotype and try the wines that this knowledge suggests they might prefer.

This translates not only into a more enthusiastic and knowledgeable staff but in happier customers who, when they feel they are accepted on their own terms, are going to have much more fun on a tasting adventure.

The wineries in Indiana, Ohio, Istanbul, Texas and even here in the Napa Valley, who have trained their staffs in Vinotyping, are also seeing a jump in sales.

Jim Pfeiffer of Turtle Run Winery tells tales about watching a customer taste a big, intense red and then making the face that suggests to him a Sweet Vinotype. While her husband tasted the big reds he liked, Jim got her a sweeter wine, with the result that she bought two cases she had never planned to buy.

Vinotypes is a way to engage visitors to tasting rooms in a whole new conversation about wine. One that starts with a discussion and about what you like as an individual. In other words, "What is your Vinotype? If you don't know I can help you find out, then we can focus on the wines that you will really love."

Giving wine as gifts

People have pointed out to me that Vinotyping won't drastically affect the behaviors, confidence or preferences of the Tolerant and Sensitive Vinotypes of the enthusiast, connoisseur or expert genres. They already know what they like and are comfortable with it. But it may help them to understand — and get along better with — the Hypersensitive and the Sweet Vinotypes. No more wasted efforts — and wine — giving a Sweet Vinotype a bottle of intense Syrah or Cabernet Sauvignon that they'll never enjoy or will suffer through politely. Instead, you can find the smooth, delicate and even sweet wine to please them.

Conversely, if you know you are buying wine for a Tolerant Vinotype that loves intense, highly rated wines – no problem. Go to your trusted retail consultant or web site, find the geek-of-the-week selection and you are good to go! Find the right wine merchant to guide you, get a bottle of wine that will knock their socks off and have them declare, "How did you know!"

The trick, of course, is finding a wine retailer, merchant or store wine consultant or Internet wine sales site that you can trust.

Cooks, chefs and other culinary artists

If all this seems to be far too easy a way to pair food with wine, and you feel skepticism rising, you are definitely not alone. And you should be skeptical. After all, this could be another "magic bullet" shot from the rifle of the wine industry. All hype and no substance. Except these simple principles are very different and more practical than anything the wine industry has presented thus far. They are based on years of scientific research with sensory scientists as well as my personal experiences with some pretty formidable skeptics all around the world — people who now wholeheartedly endorse these principles. I was probably the worst skeptic of all, but I had the benefit of experiencing a series of discoveries over a ten-year period. This book is like whacking a died-in-the-wool wine geek over the head with a two-by-four.

One of the early skeptics of the revolution was Jerry Comfort, the executive chef at Beringer Vineyards. Jerry has an impressive resume and loads of direct experience at top levels of food and wine, making him an undeniable expert in the field. Before joining Beringer, he worked for years in great restaurant kitchens such as Domaine Chandon in Napa Valley; Stars, Jeremiah Tower's legendary San Francisco restaurant and Checquers, a small, luxury hotel in downtown Los Angeles.

I was the export and educational director at Beringer at the time, so Jerry called me over to the kitchen. He was mucking around and Beringer cooking up some different cuts of steak and tasting them with some different Beringer Cabernet Sauvignons. This was supposed to be a no-brainer of a match supposedly made in wine heaven. The conventional theory goes that the sensation of astringency in the wine will be lessened by the proteins and fat in the steak. This supposedly softens the tannins in the wine and makes it taste more delicious. Much to Jerry's surprise and concern, he did not have that experience at all. In fact he felt that the steak actually made wine taste even more astringent, bitter and less pleasant than it was by itself.

Again and again we found that the steak made the strong wines – Cabernets, Merlots, blends, Syrah, and so on, taste even stronger. We called in other people to try it out. Same results.

The wines that actually tasted great straight off the bat with the steaks were all the wrong ones – Riesling, Chardonnay and even White Zinfandel. This was not right! The only way we could soften the wines enough to make them a great match with steaks was to salt the steaks. We discovered on that afternoon what makes the combination of red wine and steak work is not the protein and/or the fat of the steak; it is simply the salt that is customarily used to season steak. This has since been corroborated by scientific studies that indicate one of the main reasons humans add salt to food is because the salt suppresses our ability to perceive bitterness in the food.

From that point on, the revolution began in earnest. Here is what Jerry Comfort, former skeptic and now soldier in the revolution, has to say:

"Before I came to Beringer and started working with Tim, I had a tidy little package of wine-matching ideas. These had been formed from listening to the experts and reading current literature from the wine and food gurus. I started compiling my own set of fantasies: Do this because of this; don't do this because of that. When Tim and I started working together everything went haywire. I had to start all over again and, the truth is, it's a blast. I feel for the first time that I actually make sense to myself, and have a great base to work from."

Another skeptic of my ideas was Mercer Mohr. When we met he was the executive chef at the Clift Hotel in San Francisco. One day I asked Jerry Comfort and his sous-chef Eric Tosh to accompany me on a trip to visit Chef Mohr in his kitchens. I was working with the Clift to revise their massive wine list to a Progressive Wine List format, organizing the wines by flavor categories. Mercer, Jerry, Eric and I were joined by the dining room staff and Ahbed Shalout, the food and beverage director at the hotel. We set out all sorts of wine on a table and started tasting a bunch of Chef Mohr's food from the menu. Chef Mohr would turn out to be the one who proposed that Flavor Balancing could be applied to virtually any dish, thus rendering wine and food pairing obsolete! I very honestly thought the ideas was preposterous at the time.

I asked the group of servers and managers, "If a customer orders the roast duckling with cherry compote here, what wine would each of you recommend?" The first respondent suggested a red Bordeaux from St. Emilion and explained that the wine's concentrated fruit characteristics would beautifully match with the compote. The second suggested a Napa Valley Merlot because it too had a rich, concentrated fruit quality that would create a "bridge" to the cherry compote. Another voted for a Carneros Pinot Noir, from the Napa Valley, which all wine geeks know has pronounced cherry fruit flavor - definitely a natural pairing for the compote.

Then I asked each one of them, "What is your favorite wine?" The first server, who recommended red Bordeaux with the duck, said he loved red Bordeaux, especially St. Emilion. The one who recommended the Napa Valley Merlot said Napa Valley Merlot was his favorite. And the one who recommended Pinot Noir said he lived to drink Pinot Noir from the Carneros region of the Napa Valley. Interesting coincidence, I thought.

So we tried the roast ducking with cherry compote with their favorite wines. The unanimous verdict was that each and every combination sucked. The wines they loved on their own were strong and bitter with the food. You might think that their preferences for the wines and the fact that they thought the wines and food "should" match would help them overlook the bitterness, but in this case, the combinations were so obviously bad that each of agreed there was a serious problem.

Chef Mohr suggested he could make a whole new sauce for roast duckling, when Jerry Comfort stopped him and brought a wedge of lime and a salt shaker over from the bar. Jerry squeezed a few drops of lime juice and a bit of salt on the cherry compote. We tasted the food and the wines again, and everything was delicious. Each wine was smooth, fruity and wonderful. The Bordeaux lover loved his Bordeaux. The Merlot drinker loved his Merlot, and the Pinot Noir lover loved his Pinot Noir. When Chef Mohr tasted his cherry compote alone, he said, "You know, Tim, what Jerry just did has made my food taste better, too. Not only does it taste excellent now with the wines. I think it tastes better even by itself. And, you know, I can do this type of balancing with every item on my menu."

"No way," I thought. What a stupid idea. We then tried dish after dish, finding that almost all of the other dishes were in proper balance and all the wines on the table were already delicious with most every combination. A couple of times the dish needed a squeeze of lemon, drop of vinegar, a tad of mustard or a few grains of salt and, *voila, the dish came right into balance.* This was too simple. Couldn't be. And, most unbelievable of all, the fillet of sole was great with strong red wines. This phenomenon with the sole was later convincingly corroborated in an article by Harvey Steiman, wine and food guru for the Wine Spectator magazine and author of the book *Essentials of Wine*, published in 2000.

It was just at this point when I fully realized the true form my search was taking. Imagine this ludicrous scenario – "Welcome to our restaurant. We have a great menu with dishes you will find to be delicious with your favorite wine. The wine list has been laid out so that it is easy to find the wines you like the most and at the same time this layout makes it easy to experiment with some of the lesser-known wines we have sought out. Great to have you here with us tonight."

Get outta here! No way!

It is astonishing how complicated the wine-oriented brain can make this simple proposal, so once again: *When the food is properly balanced, the wine somebody loves the taste of will be delicious with that food, and the food is no different if the guest wants a white Zinfandel, Chardonnay, Barolo, Cabernet Sauvignon or anything else.*

Needless to say, I have met an incredible number of skeptics, some of whom really dislike me for what I am promoting. Oh well. I guess if I did not create a great deal of controversy it means that I am not trying hard enough. Funny thing is that most of the skeptics, and especially the most expert of the skeptics, have listened to me patiently, and questioned me incessantly. Through the discussion and demonstration of the principles I am promoting, virtually all have joined the revolution, and have expressed their uneasiness with the traditional ways we have presented wine and food principles. Let me share a few of these stories with you.

Many really high-end wine authorities confide in me that they feel a huge sense of relief at not having to parade around as wine and food experts. In March of 1999 I hosted a group of thirty-seven Masters of Wine, got up on my soapbox, and launched into my tirade, replete with a wine and food tasting demonstration of my principles. After the presentation, one of the attendees approached me and expressed that he was very happy to hear what I had to say. He was expecting to hear the old "have this with this and that with that" routine, and now he felt a great sense of relief. He was always suspicious of the whole wine and food matching scene, but felt compelled to play the part as was expected of someone in his position. After all, he was the chairman of the Institute of Masters of Wine at the time and the author of several authoritative books on the subject of wine. Anthony Hanson MW is now a soldier in the revolution.

I love working with food and wine professionals, as well as consumers, to introduce an objective look at these conditions and myths that have persisted for many years and lead them to the realization that so much of what we do is unjustified, simply taken for granted to be true.

Trouble in Zurich

Some years ago I was invited to visit the prestigious Dolder Grand Hotel in Zurich, Switzerland, to conduct a seminar and dinner for European wine and food journalists. I was honored and jumped at the opportunity. It turned out that Walter Daubenmeier, the deputy manager of the Dolder Grand Hotel, had heard of my wine and food antics and expertise. He was interested in hosting the press event and dinner featuring my ideas.

It turned out that Walter had obtained some outdated papers I had written many years previously, and an accompanying video, that was filled with the "old" rules of "correct" food and wine pairing—you know; white wine with fish, sweet wine with sweet food, that sort of thing. Hey, there was a time when I not only believed that garbage; I actually promoted it!

When I arrived at the hotel we met and Mr. Daubenmeier showed me the menu he had prepared for the conference's gala dinner. He had "matched" each of the dishes with the "correct" wines in complete opposition to my new way of thinking. I remember him saying to me, "As you say in your video, I have matched the lighter wines with the lighter foods, and the strong red wines with the Beringer Private Reserve Cabernet Sauvignon so the proteins will soften the tannins, just as you say, live and in person on your video."

Uh-oh. That video was many years outdated and not even remotely close to my "new" position on Flavor Balancing and un-pairing wine and food.

An awful lot of the information I had learned over the years since I created those materials was now completely contradictory. I knew I couldn't possibly go in front of these people and promote the same old myths. Trying hard not to alarm Mr. Daubenmeier, I explained, "Well, actually the program has changed pretty significantly over the past couple of years. I am now promoting the elimination of wine and food pairing./"

"What do you mean?" he said with a worried expression.

I went on. "The part about red meat and red wine, for example. Well, none of that is true. It's not the meat that makes the wine delicious. It's simply the salt that makes the wine taste mild. The same thing will happen with a trout fillet. My current program starts with a tasting that demonstrates the 'cause and effect' of flavor interactions, then we serve an array of different wines, serve the food and have everyone discuss the concepts and flavor interactions."

Walter looked around the room furtively, as if he had just been told an ominous secret. "Yah, vell, vee vouldn't vant to tell anyone one that, now vould vee?" he said.

I went into a panic. In a couple of days Switzerland's top gastronomic journalists and wine connoisseurs were coming to the hotel to listen to my perspective on wine and food and Mr. Daubenmeier wanted me to revert to my outdated information. Yikes. I was really proud to have the Dolder Grand Hotel as a partner in this, since it gave my program real credibility, but I had to present the information that I knew was the truth.

The next morning at breakfast Walter sat down, looked at me, and proceeded to blow me away. Maybe he saw the fear in my eyes the day before, but whatever happened, it was magical. "We must change the program, Tim," he said. "This initiative you are bringing us is about change. If we can't change, then we become the problem. So, we will proceed with your new program. What can we do?"

I explained that the dinners I orchestrated with this new premise were much simpler to put together. After my seminar and tasting that demonstrates the principles, we go to the dining room. I would work with the chef to make sure that every dish was balanced to be delicious with wine. All of the wines, ranging from a mild, sweet white wine; a mild, dry white wine; a strong, dry white wine; a mild, dry red wine and strong dry red wine, were poured all at once. The service staff was instructed to simply refill the glasses of the guests as needed. The guests were then encouraged to try all of the wines with each dish and see how each wine retained its integrity of flavor.

Now all I had to do was convince the chef. Right, no problem.

Chef George Angehrn had started his culinary apprenticeships twenty-two years previously at the Grand Dolder Hotel. He had never had a job anywhere else. We walked into the kitchen and he sort of looked like Keith Richards from the Rolling Stones dressed in an impeccable, starched chef's uniform with a tall pleated toque. He looked very stern and the earring he wore, combined with the arms folded across his chest, gave him an ominous, even dangerous look. I thought I was doomed.

George declared, "I received a copy of your new culinary principles video your assistant sent (thanks Elaine!). I have Flavor Balanced everything – this is amazing and I have everything ready to try." He poured us all a glass of red wine and we went through a tasting of all the dishes, sauces and garnishes. George said, "I had a real problem with my butternut squash soup but the addition of lime juice really made it come alive – just try it with the wine. Who would have thought it could work so beautifully with red wine?"

That evening I had a blast. The cynicism from the guests was palpable at the beginning. By evening's end *everyone* was having a complete blast. What might usually be disagreements or even heated arguments became discussions. The guests were trying all sorts of different combinations of the wine and food, many finding their expectations for matching were met as they anticipated. But many faces displayed complete shock when they tried a combination considered to be unacceptable only to find it quite delicious. I was even further honored to present the keynote address for the 100th Anniversary at Ecole Hôtelière de Lausanne, one of the world's most prestigious hotel and culinary school in Lausanne, Switzerland, as a result of the coverage the dinner provided.

To see professionals like Jerry Comfort, Sarah Scott, Jeremiah Tower, Mercer Mohr and countless other wine and culinary professionals take this program to heart is amazing. But what I really love seeing, more than anything else, is consumers breathing a huge sigh of relief that they don't have to toe the line and drink according to someone else's prescriptions. The simple and easy ideas in this book create a completely new operating system for food and wine that encourages the enjoyment of wine at every level and for anyone with the slightest interest and without judgment.

A Rant about Sweet Wines and Sweet Wine Lovers

Mankind has been making wine for 8,000 years, and until the last 50 years, most of these were sweet wines.

I just got off the phone with my mother-in-law, Joanne. She is a Sweet Vinotype of the enjoyer genre who likes White Zinfandel and now Moscato. She shared with me, "I brought that bottle of Moscato to a get together with a bunch of gals – we were all supposed to bring something and mine was the only bottle that was empty at the end. Everyone loved it the most by far. But then, we aren't really wine drinkers."

I stopped her right there and said, "Why do you say you are not wine drinkers if you all brought wine to a get together and everyone drank some?"

"Huh, I never really thought of that," was her reply.

I'll tell you why she said, "We aren't really wine drinkers." Because the wine industry, pundits, geeks and experts are so deeply enmeshed in our collective delusion that "dry wine is real wine and sweet wine isn't really wine and people who drink sweet wines aren't even wine drinkers" baloney that SHE is convinced she is not a wine drinker. Even when she is drinking wine! Now how crazy is that?

You have to learn NOT to like sweet tastes

I met a wine writer who swears that she never, ever liked the taste of sweetness from her time of birth. I don't think she was lying but it certainly seems to be a very isolated incidence. My question was, "If your tastes are so far removed from any normal human being how can anyone relate to your wine evaluations?"

Human beings are pre-programmed to be attracted to sweet and umami tastes, and we all start from this point of attraction. Over time sweetness is more and more associated with childish tastes, bad health, hyperactivity, dental deterioration (and all of the memories associated with dentists and pain) and obesity. You have to "unlearn" to like sweet, and this is an easier task for Tolerant and Sensitive Vinotypes. Sweetness helps to mitigate the intensity of bitterness in foods and beverages and the Vinotypes less sensitive to bitterness find it an easier task to give up sweet things. This is similar to the ability to give up salt as well as it suppresses bitterness – the more sensitive you are the harder it becomes to give it up!

But true Sweet Vinotypes find it difficult, if not impossible, to rewrite their sensory hardware to migrate to dry wine preferences. Sweet Vinotypes are so highly sensitive to bitterness and sourness that they require additional sweetness to enjoy many beverages from coffee to tea and wine. In consequence, they are often punished throughout their lives for their penchant for sweet things and especially when they aspire to become a wine consumer.

History shows these vibrant, expensive and great sweet wines were served with hors d'oeuvres, fish and beef at any fitting occasion.

As Darrell Corti of Corti Brothers Market in Sacramento reveals, "Historically, sweet wines have been considered to be among the finest wines in the world because they were stable and had good longevity. They often required more processing and aging, and they were produced in locations with a history of tradition and practices in place."

Sweet wines were among the most prized wines in the world and price lists show that in the 19th century quality sweet wines - Sauternes of Bordeaux, the Tokaji wines of Hungary, and sweet Rieslings from Germany – cost more than the great dry wines of Burgundy and Bordeaux. Vin Santo, for instance, is made in Tuscany from harvested grapes hung in attics or rafters to concentrate sugar and flavors.

Prior to World War II sweet wines were considered table wines, not dessert wines. Very sweet French and German wines were highly prized and appropriate to accompany any dish if the guest preferred.

So what happened? After the repeal of Prohibition there was a loophole that allowed high-proof spirits to be added to grape juice and sold as wine. This was the cheapest way to deliver the highest level alcohol bang-for-the-buck. The U.S. Feds decided to crack down on this practice and created a category called Dessert Wines. Anything over 14 percent alcohol was taxed at a higher rate. At the time this was about as high a level of alcohol a wine could achieve by natural fermentation so anything above 14 percent was considered a "fortified" wine. Over the past few decades most all sweet wines above 3 or 4 percent started to be included in this Dessert Wine category.

The truth of the matter is that many very, very sweet wines by today's standards were never considered dessert wines until about the 1960s. The dessert wine category was developed by the U.S. Feds decided to close the loophole on cheap, highly fortified wine-like beverages and continues to impose taxes on natural wines that exceed 14 percent alcohol by volume. Sweet wines are not relegated to the Dessert Wine category on wine lists and it is time to restore many of these wines to the main part of wine lists and primary wine sections in wine stores.

It is clearly time to end the ignorance surrounding sweet wines and the unnecessary stigma associated with both sweet wines and the consumers who love sweet wines.

Here is a fascinating look from a New York Times article by the late and great Frank Prial at the value of sweeter wines just after World War II. It clearly shows how much we have devalued the wonderful array of great sweeter wines that could be better marketed to a very wide audience if we can restore the true traditions of wine at the table and offering an array of options.

It includes tidbits on what the relative prices were for sweet and dry wines in 1945, showing clearly that a good quality German Riesling was more expensive than most Bordeaux wines and a fine estate German wine such as the Bernkasteler Doktor noted below, which is currently available for about $60.00 a bottle, was the same price as Romanée Conti, which now sells for thousands of dollars a bottle – if you can even find it!

WINE TALK; A Stroll Through the '21' List, Circa 1945

By Frank J. Prial
Published: January 15, 2003
http://www.nytimes.com/2003/01/15/dining/wine-talk-a-stroll-through-the-21-list-circa-1945.html

> Wine drinkers who are just now beginning to discover German wines would be fascinated by the six pages of German rieslings "21" offered 58 years ago. On average, they were priced two to three dollars more per bottle than the Bordeaux. True, there were 15 Liebfraumilch, but there were dozens of fine estate wines under $15 and a priceless spätlese Moselle, a 1934 Bernkasteler Doktor, Dr. Thanisch, for $18.
>
> The most expensive of the Burgundies was a 1929 Romanée-Conti from the Domaine de la Romanée-Conti for $18.

Looking through old retail price catalogues and restaurant wine lists it is easy to see that the best of sweet wines were typically as, or more, expensive that dry wines. A fine quality German wine would easily fetch a higher price than most quality Bordeaux and Burgundy wines from the finest of estates. Part of the reason we have lost value for so many of these wines, and the reason we are losing the diversity of wine styles and flavors that used to be available, is that we have not focused on the consumer. We have put far too much emphasis on the product and a false, homogenous model of quality.

I propose that the healthiest and most sustainable future of wine will come from celebrating not only the diversity of the wine styles and flavors, but also celebrating the diversity of the preferences of the people who consume the product.

The Future for the Diversity of Wines and Regions of Production

There's another consideration for understanding and accepting different Vinotypes. Today, more and more passionate wine lovers are decrying the loss of many traditional, typical styles of wine and the increasing homogeneity of wine styles from around the world. This is due, in part, to the adoption of a standardized, 100-point wine evaluation system that rewards intensity and higher alcohol levels, and tends to penalize wines that show qualities that were for centuries an integral and wonderful part of the wine landscape.

Many classic wine styles have disappeared or are on the endangered species list due to the increasingly narrow flavor attributes — conforming to the criteria established by the 100 point system and not to the consumer.

Many red wines were historically made with a blend of red and white grapes. This yields a lighter wine more delicate in color with a smoother and less bitter flavor. Wines with more delicate character have trouble garnering the attention or favor of most wine evaluators today.

Even most experts will erroneously say that true red Burgundy wines from the famed Cote d'Or region are required to be made of 100 percent Pinot Noir grapes. In fact, many of the villages in this area allow blending, not of other red grapes, but up to 15 percent white grapes: Pinot Blanc, Pinot Beurot (aka Pinot Gris or Pinot Grigio) and

A cry for help from a classic region

I received this e-mail, reprinted here verbatim, from an organization of French wine producers. They are confounded by the loss of tradition, namely serving fabulous sweet wines with the meal instead of afterwards, and working to restore the rightful place of these wines at any table for the enjoyment of anyone who might favor this style of wine with their meal.

"We are working with the *Sauternais* to *'Liberez les Sauternes'* or free Sauternes from its labeling as a dessert wine, and I instinctively feel that you might be able to help us. The Sauternais drink their wines with fish, roast meats and spicy foods as well as with dessert - they can't understand why the world insists on drinking it only with sweet dishes, cheese or foie gras.

"In reality, because of the extremely powerful, concentrated and complex flavours in Sauternes which are concentrated by up to 100 times by botrytis, the wines are probably the most versatile food wines bar none, capable of standing up to the spiciest curry or the most delicate flavours within traditional French cuisine. The 'anti-sweet' phenomenon is frustrating and confusing to them. They sense that, if left alone to choose, most people would prefer to drink sweet wines much more frequently and your research suggests that this might be the case. If there is anything that you can send to help our mini-movement I would be most grateful."

Many wine enthusiasts and experts decry the movement toward more homogenous global wine styles – here is a chance to ensure the production of these great wines of Sauternes can be sustained and improved. They simply need to be marketed effectively to Sweet Vinotypes – with whatever food they please, as was the tradition for centuries.

Pinot Blanc, the white mutation of Pinot Noir. It was once common for producers of red wines to blend in a portion of white wines to enhance wine. The requirement for darker color has all but eliminated these traditionally styled, elegant wines.

Chianti has morphed from a light, smooth red wine to much darker, more alcoholic and tannic wine with the advent of the 100 point rating system – and now conforms to the trend to become a more homogeneous, less distinctive style for red wines. In the 19th century, Baron Bettino Ricasoli, who would later become the prime minister of Italy, decreed that to qualify for the use of the name Chianti the wine was required to be a blend of 70 percent Sangiovese, 15 percent Canaiolo and 15 percent Malvasia Bianca (the white grape also known as Moscato) or Trebbiano, another white grape. The wines were much lighter in color and very smooth in comparison to modern Chianti wines.

World War II, the globalization of wine and planting the seeds of today's collective delusions

The more I look back at early writings about wine and wine with food, the more proof arises that World War II was a seminal period for shifts in wine and food fashion. Wine marketing, transportation and production were all greatly affected.

On the one hand American soldiers were introduced to French, Italian and German cultures and wines. There was certainly an explosion in American interest in wines from Germany, France and Italy following the war. This also gave rise to a proliferation of wine merchants and wine marketers who, it turns out, also became wine pundits and authors on wine. It is important to keep in mind that wine information began to be disseminated by people who were selling wine. This also coincides with the shift in attitudes and the rise in many of the misassumptions, clichés and collective delusions that now exist around wine today.

A combination of the post-war global transportation and new technologies, such as sterile filtration, that could be applied to winemaking gave rise to an expansion of international wine commerce. And the American market was ripe for the picking. No doubt Americans showed a fondness for German wines, semi-sweet rosé from Portugal and Lambrusco from Italy. The checkered tablecloth and fiasco-clad Chianti bottle became was permanently etched into the American psyche.

Wine started to become fashionable, like never before, in the 1960s. Restaurants like Beef 'n' Burgundy started cropping up, and the delusion that "red wine goes with red meat" began to become mainstream. A big shift was occurring in France, with the introduction *la cuisine nouvelle* having a disruptive influence on regional and traditional French cuisine. Most significantly of all, the wine pundits started to promote the idea that dry wine is good wine, and that sweetness was a means to mask wine flaws and that more "sophisticated" wine drinkers should drink dry wines.

As modern wine tastes turned more towards the dark, concentrated model for red wines in Chianti the laws were changed and by 1996 it became permissible to add to 20 percent non-traditional grapes including Cabernet Sauvignon, Merlot and Syrah. By 2006, the addition of the white grapes was banned and the traditional wines of Chianti are all but lost.

A new category called Super Tuscan wines emerged and are now considered the crème de la crème for the highest quality wines of the region — dominated by the internationally more popular Cabernet Sauvignon and other "invasive" varieties as producers sought to modernize the wines and be able to compete with the expanding trend to make wines that could garner the favor of international wine experts, pundits and geeks. All of a sudden the traditional wines with revered names, geographic boundaries, grape varieties and vinification traditions that were strictly defined by law became overshadowed by a new generation of wines that conformed to the new, global standard – intense, heavily oaked and high in alcohol and flavor.

In the past many regions in Italy, France and Spain would harvest the grapes and leave them to dry – in the sun, in an attic or any dry, safe place, to increase the sugar levels by dehydration. This practice produced wines of rich flavor and enough natural alcohol that the wines could safely contain sweet, residual sugar without the danger re-fermentation and exploding bottles!. These sweet wines were highly prized and served throughout a meal, not reserved for "dessert" or frowned upon as sweet wines are today. In France they were often called *vins de paille*, or "straw wines." In Italy the famous wine of Amarone, the "bitter" red wine made from partially dried grapes, was always made in a sweet fashion up until the mid-1950s.

At one time, at the end of harvest, people used to revel in the newly fermented wines — even before they were completely finished with the fermentation! They were sweet, fizzy and most certainly kept people "regular" given that the yeasts were still active in the frothy, fresh wines. Nouveau in Beaujolais and the wines of Lambrusco in Italy were two that gained international notoriety, but the harvest traditions in nearly every region had a similar celebration and consumption of copious quantities of the new wine.

Wines were mulled, spiced, fortified, mixed with herbs, sweetened with honey, fortified with brandy or grain alcohol and often sweetened by adding a sweet liquor, like Cassis, or even a simple cube of sugar at the table. The list of endangered or lost wine species includes May wines, mulled wines, *vins doux naturale* and vermouth. You may find them around if you try hard enough and new artisan producers are trying to restore many of these lost wines but it is a hard row to hoe for them.

The German wine trade has been struggling for decades to restore the country's place as a producer of great wines. The wines that used to enjoy prices equal or greater than the finest of French chateaux and domains have found the popularity, demand and critical acclaim for the best of German vintages has diminished in direct proportion to the unfounded stigma attached not only to sweet wines but to the people who enjoy sweet wines as well. The latest strategy is to try to convert wine growing and winemaking to kowtow to the great gods of dryness and high alcohol — the style of wines popular for Tolerant Vinotypes and point-hungry crowd. They are oblivious to the bigger opportunities if they could get their act together, and acknowledge Sweet and Hypersensitive Vinotypes.

This is just a partial list but suffice to say we are losing many traditional wines and unless there is a major change in thinking this trend will continue. My assertion is that by disenfranchising sweet wine drinkers and living in the delusion that dry, strong wines are more sophisticated and a sign of consumer maturity we have lost the means to market a wonderful range of wines that were vastly different from today's increasingly homogenous standard for dry, intense wines. There are ways to produce distinctive, modern wines that have character and could delight millions of consumers but the change has to come from the industry and be smartly directed and based on building understanding, confidence and clear communications with the right consumers.

So how do we save the endangered wine species? Vineyards with classic or distinctive grape varieties are being ripped out and replanted with the more commercially acceptable primary varieties like Chardonnay and Cabernet Sauvignon. This is due in large part to market demand favoring predictable flavors. My assertion is that with improvements in understanding consumer preferences and better communication, without today's inherent judgment or stigma, a much wider range of wines can be produced and successfully marketed.

BURGUNDY.

	Per Doz.
Beaujolais	18/6 & 24/-
Beaune	30/- & 36/-
Beaune Supérieur, 1899	42/-
Aloxe Corton	42/-
Santenay, 1904 & 1900 ...	36/- & 42/-
Volnay, 1902 & 1900	42/- & 48/-
Pommard, 1904 & 1902	42/- & 48/-
" 1899	48/-
" 1891	72/-
Nuits St. Georges, 1899 ½-Bots. only	26/-
" " 1898	60/-
" " 1902	42/-
Corton, 1893, Very Fine	96/-
" Clos Du Roi, 1881	108/-
Chambertin, 1900	54/-
" 1892	108/-
" 1886 Very Fine ...	160/-
Richebourg, 1892	108/-
Clos de Vougeot, 1896... ... 78/-	
" " 1898 ... ½ Bots. only	45/-
" " 1887	150/-
Château de Clos Vougeot, 1889	144/-
Romanée Conti, 1895, Estate Bottling	150/-
" " 1891 " "	180/-
" " 1888 " "	200/-
Chambertin, Clos St Jacques, 1904 Monopoly (Very Fine, for laying down)	60/-

CLARET—continued

		Per Doz.
	Vin Ordinaire	12/6, 14/-
	Clos du Prieur, own growth ...	16/6
	St Estèphe	18/6
	Médoc Supérieur	21/-
1900	Ch. Rochemorin	30/-
	Ch. Moulin de Calon Ségur, ½ Bots. only	18/-
	Ch. d'Aiesme Bekker	42/-
	Ch. Chasse Spleen	42/-
	Ch. Mouton Rothschild ...	60/-
1899	Ch. Lafon Rochet	36/-
	Ch. Léoville, Poyferré ...	42/-
	" " Lascases ...	45/-
	Ch. Brown Cantenac	45/-
	Ch. Lafite	72/-
1896	Ch. Lafite	78/-
	Ch. La Mission Haut Brion	72/-
1893	Ch. Léoville, Lascases ...	60/-
	Ch. Cheval Blanc	78/-
1888	Ch. Smith Haut Lafite ...	72/-
1878	Ch. Lafite Ch. Bottled ...	180/-
	Ch. Palmer Margaux	96/-
1877	Ch. Léoville	108/-
1874	Ch. Larose, in Wine Bottles ...	66/-
1870	Ch. Margaux	90/-
1869	Ch. Lafite, Grand Vin, Ch. Bottled	200/-
	Ch. Lafite, probably 1869	108/-

HOCK.

	Per Doz.
St Jacobsberg	20/6
Niersteiner	30/-
Erbach	40/-
Eltville Sonnerberg 1904 ...	60/-
Rudesheimer, Berg, 1900 ...	66/-
" " 1904 ...	60/-
" " Cabinet 1886 ...	132/-
Steinberger, 1893	96/-
Steinberger Cabinet, 1876 ...	90/-
Marcobrunner, Cabinet 1886 ...	190/-
Schloss Johannisberg Cabinet—	
Prince Metternich's, 1893 ...	200/-
" " 1889, 144/-; 1884, 180/-	
Red Hock	50/- & 60/-
Sparkling ditto	50/- & 66/-
Sparkling White Hock	54/- & 66/-

	Per Doz.
1786 Hochheimer	96/-
1865 Marcobrunner	100/-
1865 Steinberger	108/-
1868 Marcobrunner (Hellgrüner Lack)	144/-

Appendix 1: How my cooking changed

Sarah Scott, Chef/Culinary Consultant/Author

I have worked as a chef in the Napa Valley cooking for wineries and wine aficionados for over 30 years. It took half those years to finally learn how to cook food for wine that didn't alter the taste of the wine detrimentally. The biggest learning curve occurred when I learned about the umami taste from Tim Hanni and how this was impacting wine and food interactions.

His idea seemed simplistic at first and I rejected his notion that you could predict wine and food interactions from a cause and effect chart showing the five primary tastes in food and how they changed a wine's flavor. I had been long schooled in conventional wine and food pairing and was still trying to create "perfect marriages" through herbs, bridge ingredients, similarities in weight and texture, color, regional pairings and the "complement or contrast" approach. None of these had ever given me consistent, successful results in creating harmonious wine and food matches. And, as much as I practiced, taught and preached the old ways, I knew they weren't really working.

When I began to experiment with Tim's concept of balancing umami and sweet tastes with acid and salt tastes in a dish, I saw, over and over again, that I was able to create dishes that allowed wines to taste their best. Rather than looking at a dish from the angle of its flavor or protein profile and how that might complement or contrast with a wine, I began to look at the five tastes within a dish: salty, sweet, acid, umami and bitter. What was predominant? What was lacking? How can I bring this dish into balance for the wine? This changed my whole viewpoint on cooking and improved it as an unexpected benefit.

I first had to learn about the basic tastes that were impacting wine and how they showed up in the food. The four tastes that seem to have the most influence on wine are umami and sweet and acid and salt. Bitter tastes are present in some foods and as a result of some cooking methods, but don't exist in most dishes.

The umami taste is present in most the delicious ingredients we use: proteins - aged meats, fish, shellfish, poultry; parmesan and aged cheeses; seasonal, ripe fruits and vegetables, especially tomatoes; tomato paste and sun-dried tomatoes; stocks and broths; sea vegetables; cooked mushrooms; anchovies and Asian fish sauces; soy sauce and aged balsamic and wine vinegars. It also comes into play when foods have been fermented, aged, dried or concentrated in some form or alchemized from raw to cooked.

Sweet tastes come from fruits - dried and fresh, from caramelizing vegetables such as onions, shallots, garlic and carrots and from other sources such as fruit juices, chutneys, syrups, honey, jams and jellies. Often sweet ingredients are combined with proteins when seeking a wine and food pairing to try to match up aromatic similarities. Dried cherries to go with cherry aromas in Pinot Noir or pears with Chardonnay, or berries to match berry-like aromas in a Cabernet Sauvignon.

Salt in a dish comes from adding salt as a seasoning, a finishing touch or in a preserving or brining or pickling preparation. It can also be present in oysters or other briny seafood, but isn't the primary taste in those foods. Ingredients like capers, cornichons, olives and preserved lemons provide a kick of salty taste to a dish along with some acidity.

Acidity in its purest form in cooking comes from fresh lemon juice. Additional sources of acid taste come from; vinegar, *verjus*, lime, yuzu, lemon supremes, wine, tamarind, sorrel, rhubarb, mustard, yogurt, fresh goat cheese and buttermilk. Other citrus fruits can provide acidity, but also will add sweet tastes – Meyer lemons, oranges and grapefruits, for example. Regular lemon juice, used in conjunction with these juices, will bring the acid level where it needs to be.

What I have learned is that when I am cooking for meal that features wine, I have to balance umami and sweet tastes in a dish with acid and salt tastes. Contrary to conventional wisdom, acidity in food is not an enemy of wine. In fact, it is what is needed much of the time to balance the rich, savory umami tastes in a dish that are causing a wine to taste harsh. The addition of acid has to make sense in a dish. It needs to be a natural addition that doesn't change the essential flavor of a dish, but enhances it. Along with the proper dash of salt, the judicious addition of acidity is what makes the difference 99 percent of the time.

So, what does this look like in the kitchen?
In addition to salt and pepper, I now keep fresh lemons and lemon juice by my workspace at all time. When making a sauce, I deglaze the pan with wine or a bit of vinegar or *verjus* to give a hit of acidity along with the broth or stock. If I add a sweet element to the sauce, I know I have to add extra salt and lemon to balance that taste. The simple test of tasting the wine with the sauce will let you know what needs to be adjusted. When the wine tastes harsh and bitter, you know you need to add more acidity and salt to the food. Cream sauces, too, need white wine or Champagne vinegar or lemon juice added at some point to provide the acid taste.

Marinating and brining with ingredients like yogurt, buttermilk, vinegar, wine or a salt-based brine are all ways to both tenderize and infuse flavor as well as introduce the salty/acid taste to an ingredient. I season any meat or poultry a day ahead with salt and pepper so the seasoning has time to penetrate and add flavor. For finishing, I use fleur de sel and a squeeze of fresh lemon juice on the main dish and any side dishes as well. Every element on the plate needs to be balanced for the wine.

Classically difficult ingredients like artichokes and asparagus are not a problem for wine when balanced with acidity and salt. A tangy hollandaise, a lemony vinaigrette or mayonnaise make it possible for these former wine "enemies" to work with wines seamlessly.

Wine reductions used in a sauce or a vinaigrette usually need the added boost of fresh lemon juice to give them the right amount of acidity. Even vinegars like good balsamic or an aged wine vinegar will also need a bit of lemon juice, as they also tend to have umami and even sweet tastes that needs balancing. Lemon zest, while adding the flavor of lemon, does not add acidity. Again, lemon juice will be needed. Unseasoned rice vinegar or champagne vinegar are other sources of clean, bright acidity.

Surprisingly, the foods that pose the most challenge with wine are those that are highest in umami and sweetness. Understanding this is the missing link in working with wine and food compatibility. It's that aged, marbled steak that will make a big red wine taste harsh and bitter if it isn't seasoned with salt and some form of acidity. Or those savory mushrooms, sautéed in butter that will need a good squeeze of lemon and pinch of salt to really work with a Pinot Noir. Or that lobster risotto, layered with stock and butter and savory shellfish that will need the brightness of acidity and balancing with salt to really shine with a Chardonnay. Without the acidity and salt, all of these "classic pairings" will bring out the worst in a wine.

How do you know when you have balanced a dish so that any wine you drink will not be changed? You taste the wine first, so you know what it tastes like on its own. Pay attention to all the elements in the wine. Then taste the food. Now, taste the wine again. If the wine has changed, if it tastes stronger, more bitter or harsh, you know you need to add more acidity and/or salt to the dish. If the wine tastes milder and has lost flavor, you know you have too much acid and salt and the dish needs to be adjusted in the other direction. The wine will always tell you what the food needs.

As your palate gets used to what "balance" tastes like for you in a dish, you will know it instinctively at first bite. Just as I can detect the taste of umami in the sides of my mouth and by its mouthwatering effect, I can now also tell when a sauce or dish is balanced by similar sensations in my mouth. There is a zing, a piquancy that lets me know there is enough acid and salt present.

There is no formula for how much acidity and salt are needed in each dish. Ingredients are different. Palates are different. Umami levels vary, as will sweetness. Learning how to taste and recognize when the balance has been achieved takes practice, time and really paying attention to the wine and food and how they interact with one another.

This is a dramatic change from working with the "old rules" of wine and food pairing. There is no longer a need to have certain wines with certain foods. Building on the foundation of balancing the tastes in a dish, you are freed to enjoy the wines you prefer with the foods you love.

Notes: _____

_____

_____

_____

_____

_____

_____

_____

_____

_____

_____

_____

_____

_____

_____

_____

_____

_____

_____

_____

_____

Appendix 2: Vinotype Facts and Figures

Dr. Virginia Utermohlen, MD

Virginia Utermohlen, MD obtained her undergraduate degree in physics from Washington University in St. Louis, and her medical degree from Columbia University's College of Physicians and Surgeons. After an internship, residency, and chief residency in pediatrics, she was appointed a post-doctoral fellow at Rockefeller University, and thereafter moved to Cornell University, where she is currently Associate Professor in the Division of Nutritional Sciences, College of Human Ecology.

"Ever since I can remember, I have been fascinated with the question: why do people differ? I don't mean obvious differences, like sex or age, but rather subtle differences, for example differences in their likes and dislikes, in their behaviors and personalities, and in their physical and mental performance. As a faculty member in the Division of Nutritional Sciences at Cornell, my fascination with this question has been channeled to an examination of individual differences in taste and smell sensitivity, and how they relate to a number of different aspects of personality and performance."

Wine market segmentation based on taste sensitivity

Dr. Virginia Utermohlen, MD, and Tim Hanni MW

With somewhere in the neighborhood of 80,000 to 100,000 different wines available in the United States, wineries face a huge challenge: How to make their wines stand out in the crowd. For large scale producers, this question translates into, "How do we reach the most people with the right product, pricing and messaging?" For a small specialty producer the question is, "How do I identify and sell to the right consumers in my market niche?"

In order to answer these questions we offer an approach to wine market segmentation that integrates the physiological and psychological dimensions that affect consumer preferences, behaviors, values and, ultimately, wine choices. This approach is the equivalent of defining and targeting consumer "phenotype" segments.

Encyclopedia Brittanica defines a phenotype as, "all the observable characteristics of an organism, such as shape, size, color, and behavior that result from the interaction of the genotype (total genetic makeup) with the environment. The common type of a group of physically similar organisms is sometimes also known as the phenotype." Wine consumer phenotype segments are created by grouping people based on using a combination of physiological taste sensitivity elements and the inevitable changes in wine preferences that occur from interactions with other wine drinkers, social influences, aesthetics, habituation and fashion.

The value that this approach brings lies in a deeper understanding of key elements that define each phenotype segment and ultimately drive consumer choices. This in turn provides the ability to narrow down and target populations of wine consumers with the right products, language and messages.

Why does physiology matter?

The answer to this question is straightforward: Our sensory physiology dictates how sensitive we are to different tastes and flavors. Simply put: Some people have more taste buds than other people, and some people get a stronger message from wine — of acidity or alcohol, for example — than others.

It is easy to imagine that the person with more papillae will get stronger taste messages than the person with fewer papillae, and, typically, this is the case. The total number of taste buds in the tongue ranges according to some estimates from fewer than 500 for some people to over 11,000 for others. It is important to note that more taste buds does not equate to a "superior palate" or better ability to taste wine. It does mean that people with different sensory physiology may experiences sensations differently and research clearly shows that many people sense different compounds that other people are incapable of sensing at all. This information has very important implications ensuring the right product is targeted to the right phenotype segment.

Of course, taste sensations must go to the brain to be experienced, processed and interpreted: this is where physiology meets psychology. Stronger sensations reaching the brain make for stronger impressions — either good or bad. Our personal values, culture, life experiences, habituation to sensations and aesthetics all come into play in assessing and defining what a sensation represents.

If more sensations go to the brain (in other words if you are more sensitive), higher alcohol levels often give a strong, unpleasant, burning sensation. If you are less sensitive, alcohol can give a sweet sensation with a pleasant, gentle burn or no burn at all. Sweetness in a wine can mask the burning sensation that highly sensitive people experience with high alcohol levels — a person who finds a dry red wine with 15 percent alcohol very painful may enjoy a cream sherry with 17 percent alcohol. Bitterness and acidity in a solution also seems to play an important role in defining the intensity at which alcohol is perceived and this is an area of exploration in our research. The point is that many of the arguments over wine quality and appropriateness of alcohol levels is "in the eye of the beholder" and explained inside of our phenotype segmentation applied to wine critics and professionals.

Using these insights into physiology and psychology — coupled with the results of consumer surveys involving thousands of people both in the U.S. and abroad — we have segmented wine consumers into four basic groups or phenotype groups: Sweet, Hypersensitive, Sensitive and Tolerant.

This segmentation allows us to strategically define product qualities, flavor characteristics, language, and messaging. Using the principles developed through this analysis wine producers, sellers and marketers can position wines to appeal to specific segments. These principles can be applied from the ground up with product ideation and development or applied to existing products in the market. It is possible to apply these concepts to an entire portfolio of wines to increase the reach of a winery across segments, or alternatively to burrow deeply into the segment that a winery can best serve.

The Determinants of Wine Sweetness Preference Among Respondents to an On-Line Survey

Amy DuFlo May, 2010
Biology, Health and Society, Cornell University
Dr. Virginia Utermohlen M.D., Ph.D, Cornell University
www.nutrition.cornell.edu/che/bio.cfm?netid=vu10
Tim Hanni MW, HanniCo LLC
www.timhanni.com

Abstract

Purpose: to explore the determinants of wine sweetness preference in a sample of respondents to an online survey.

Background: Wine has become an increasingly popular aspect of the beverage industry in recent years. In 2008, the U.S. produced almost 700 million gallons and imported 217 million gallons (Hodgen 2008). The increased importance of wine has both spurred and been caused by related occurrences, such as the advent of formal wine education. Wine education is designed to move people away from a purely hedonic appreciation of wine to an understanding of wine features and their origins. In general, wine educators consider high levels of sweetness are considered a less desirable characteristic of a table wine, so we can expect that people with greater levels of wine education would prefer drier wines. At the same time, the perception of sweetness intensity depends on biological factors, such as age and gender. These biological factors therefore may also contribute to wine sweetness preferences.

Methods: The creators of the Lodi International Wine Awards in California posted an online survey concerning wine preferences and consumption frequency, demographic characteristics and level of wine education on December 6, 2009. The survey was advertised by word of mouth, television interviews, newspaper articles and related events. Data collected from 1,143 respondents as of February 1, 2010, were received; 548 responses provided complete data for this analysis of sweetness preferences in wine. Due to multicollinearity among the variables, partition analysis was used to determine the primary factors involved in sweetness preferences.

Results: The most important determinant for sweetness preference was frequency of wine consumption, with respondents who drank wine less often than twice a week preferring sweeter wines. The respondents who drank wine at least twice a week could be further divided into two groups, with those younger than 40 years of age preferring sweeter wines. The older group of frequent wine drinkers could be further divided into males and females, with the females slightly more likely to prefer sweeter wines. The younger group could be divided into two groups, one with higher wine education and lower preference for sweet wine, and a second group with the opposite preferences. People who preferred sweet wine also preferred to put sugar in their coffee or tea.

Conclusion: The more frequently one drinks wine, the less likely one is to choose a sweet wine; however if one drinks wine frequently, biological factors (age, gender) determine the preferred sweetness level before wine education comes into play in the analysis, suggesting that biological characteristics may play a significant role in determining wine preference, and wine education level is less influential.

ABOUT THE SURVEY

This report offers a brief overview of a survey of the preferences, attitudes, and behaviors of two groups of wine consumers

~ SWEET and TOLERANT ~

with wine stylistic preferences at the
extreme ends of the spectrum of wine styles.

The data presented in this report come from an on-line survey conducted in conjunction with the CONSUMER WINE AWARDS at LODI 2010.

Filters were created to cluster respondents who preferred sweet wine types versus those with a preference for more intensely styled red wines —the tolerants.

This report contains comparative charts demonstrating significant differences between 'Sweet' and 'Tolerant' groups in:

- Gender
- Age
- Preferences for wine by variety/type
- Wine selection attitudes and confidence
  Adult beverage consumption frequencies
- Desirable characteristics (flavor descriptors)
- Adult beverage preferences by occasion (home, fine dining, social/bar)
- Beer style and coffee preferences

For more information or to order the full report, contact: Tim Hanni, tim@timhanni.com or call 707-337-0327

SURVEY STATISTICS

Collection period:
December 2009 — March, 2010

Total started survey: 1,597

Survey response total for this analysis: 1,485

'Sweet' respondents: 324

'Tolerant' respondents: 341

Contact: tim@timhanni.com   707-337-0327

A FEW WORDS ABOUT TASTE (AND SMELL) SENSITIVITY AND WHY DIFFERENCES IN SENSITIVITY MATTER

What is taste?

Strictly speaking, taste is made up of the sensations coming from the mouth, and smell those from the nose, but our brains assign both taste and smell to the mouth. Therefore we commonly call the result "taste," though "flavor" may be the more correct term.

What is taste sensitivity?

Taste sensitivity refers to the intensity with which you perceive tastes and flavors.

We differ considerably in what we each can taste and smell, and in how intense different tastes and smells are to us. People with high taste sensitivity experience tastes, and usually smells, too, as being very strong. They are also able to distinguish individual flavors in a mixture very well.

Is one taste sensitivity level better than another?

No! Greater (or lesser) sensory sensitivity does not make a person more expert or capable—just different.

Does taste sensitivity influence wine choice?

Yes!

Why does taste sensitivity influence wine choice?

The nerves that bring sensations from the nose and the mouth to our brain are closely linked to our emotional centers, our memory centers, and our centers for evaluation, judgment, and decision-making. Our taste sensitivity depends on the interactions of signals from taste and smell nerves with these centers in the brain.

Consquently our experience of taste—and therefore our wine preferences—are affected by the strength of the taste signals coming from the mouth and smell signals from the nose, as modified by life experiences, aspirations, family, culture, learning/education, peer dynamics, just to name a few important influences.

All of these influences can contribute to shifts in preferences, attitudes and behaviors, but the physiological starting point is your fundamental taste sensitivity.

A common misconception is that "one's palate matures and becomes more sophisticated over time". The reality is that little children are generally *physiologically* more sensitive than adults, and that taste (and smell) sensitivity decreases with time, more sharply in some people than in others. By the end of adolescence we reach a plateau, the level of which varies from person to person. As we age, sensitivity can continue to drop, but normally at a much slower pace—though here again people differ.

At the same time, as we grow older, we accumulate our psychological experiences—these in turn further modulate our experience of the taste of wine, so that each us will have a different "take" on the same wine.

Does this mean that wine professionals should expand their definition of high aspiration wine?

Absolutely!...because each level of taste sensitivity brings with it a different palate—and with each different palate a fresh gamut of possibilities for the appreciation of excellence in wine.

AFFINITY GROUPS

A brief overview of traits, preferences and opportunities of the four consumer groups

SWEET

Highest level of taste sensitivity ~ needs sweetness to offset other tastes

Prefer sweet wines by declaration

Preferred wines: Riesling, White Zinfandel, Sangria, fruit & sparkling wines, Chardonnay

Language: Sweet, smooth, fruity

Sell opportunities: Moscato, sweet Riesling and other sweet wines

Avoid: overplaying wine-food pairing, selling dry wines

HYPER-SENSITIVE

Very high taste sensitivity

Primarily prefer dry and slightly off-dry wines by declaration

Preferred wines: Pinot Grigio, dry Riesling, light reds, sparkling wines

Language: dry, light, fruity, balanced

Sell opportunities: dry, less intense whites or rosés and very smooth, lighter intensity reds.

SENSITIVE

Moderate taste sensitivity

Wine preferences run a complete spectrum of styles and flavors

Language: dry, balanced, fruity

Sell opportunities: very open to exploring, have very wide range of flavor acceptability

TOLERANT

Least likely to have problems with taste sensitivity ~ the stronger the better

Prefer big red wines

Language: point ratings, complex, bold, intense

Sell opportunities: big reds

We have identified four primary consumer groups, who span the spectrum of wine style preferences, from light & sweet to intense & red.

CLOSE-UP OF THE TIP OF A TONGUE SHOWING AN ABUNDANCE OF TASTE PAPILLAE

This is a close-up of the surface of the tongue of a hypersensitive taster.

The large rounded bumps are the fungiform papillae, which house the taste buds. The black dots on the top surface of the bumps are the taste pores, entryways to the taste buds.

Photograph by Tim Hanni

We experience taste when a food or beverage molecule falls into a taste pore, where it makes contact with the taste bud cells and with the nerve endings in and around the taste bud.

There are two kinds of nerve endings in the taste buds. One set gets messages about the taste molecules via the taste bud cells, while the other set makes direct contact with the taste molecules as they come through the taste pores.

At the level of the tongue, the type and strength of the taste messages sent to the brain depend on two main factors:

- the types of receptors on the taste bud cells and nerve endings;
- the number of taste buds a person has.

Taste receptors are under genetic control: for example your ability to taste a bitter chemical called PTC (phenylthiocarbamide) is determined by the form of the receptor gene that you have.

Some people have the gene for a receptor that can bind to PTC, so they find the chemical extremely bitter.

Some people have the gene for a receptor that can't bind to PTC, so they can't taste the chemical at all.

Still others have a gene that is effective in binding PTC when they are young, but becomes less effective as they age—in fact this type of change may occur for other receptors as well. This switch in receptors may explain why children tend to find many foods intolerably bitter, that grown-ups find quite mild.

THE TAKE-HOME MESSAGES

THE 'SWEET' CONSUMER

There's a new market opportunity for wine out there: primarily female—but with a signficant percentage of males as well—young, adventurous, and willing to try new wines—on their own terms. They are put off by the emphasis on dry wines, all the jargon surrounding wine-speak, and easily embarrassed when confronted by wine authority.

Trying to move them to dry wines on the theory that dry wines are inherently better or more appropriate with food will simply backfire.

You will have to engage them and build up their confidence in their wine preferences if you want to lure them away from cocktails and light beer and towards wine.

You will have to help them figure out how to pair wines with food in a new, friendly, and free-form way. They're not sure how to do it and would love to learn—but your advice needs to be personalized to meet their expectations—no dogma, please.

Preferred wine types include sangria, fruit wines, white zinfandel, and Riesling—especially Riesling—and sparkling wines. You must take care to get the right product to the Sweet consumer: sweet Riesling and Moscato in the 2-5% residual range are very desirable, not the dry, less fruity examples.

Among the reds, the best bets are Shiraz/Syrah, zinfandel, and pinot noir, but they aren't liked as much as the whites—low alcohol with very little bitterness or astringency is mandatory, whether the wine is red or white. Pinot can be problematic for these Sweet consumers due to bitter phenolics commonly associated with this variety.

THE 'TOLERANT' CONSUMER

By contrast, if you have big red wines, then the Tolerant consumer will love them.

Who are the Tolerants? More likely to be male, a little older, and much more confident in choosing wine and in pairing wine with foods—maybe a bit cocky about wine, all told. They like jargon and they like authority.

They look for dry wines, complex wines, balanced wines and full-bodied ones, and will order wine even in a bar or non-dining social situation—in fact they drink wine almost every day. They tend to think of themselves as connoisseurs of wine.

Why do we call them Tolerants, then? Because they are physiologically predisposed to *tolerate* the bitterness and astringency of intense red wines and are relatively impervious to the burning sensation caused by wines with high alcohol content. In fact, alcohol often tastes "sweet" to the Tolerant group.

Tolerants choose a very narrow range of wine types. They go primarily for Cabernet Sauvignon and Cabernet Sauvignon based blends.

Interestingly, they share a liking for Pinto Noir and Shiraz/Syrah with the lovers of sweet wines—so if you offer rich yet very smooth examples of these varietals, you can catch both audiences.

> *Remember, coffee companies struck gold with the 'Sweet' consumer:*
>
> *sweetened and flavored coffee often sells for 3 to 4 times the price of a regular cup of coffee.*

THE NEW MARKET OPPORTUNITY:

UPSCALE PRODUCTS FOR 'SWEET' CONSUMERS,

WHO ARE TASTE SENSITIVE AND PREFER SWEETER WINES

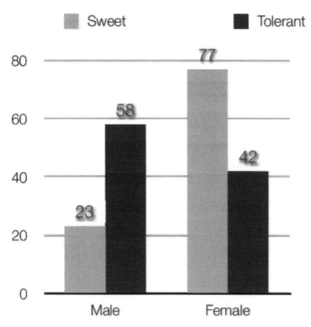

Percent of males and females in each taste group

GENDER AND AGE DISTRIBUTION 'SWEET' VERSUS 'TOLERANT'

People who like **sweeter** wines are more likely to be **female** and **younger**

~

People who are **tolerant** are more likely to be **male** and **older**

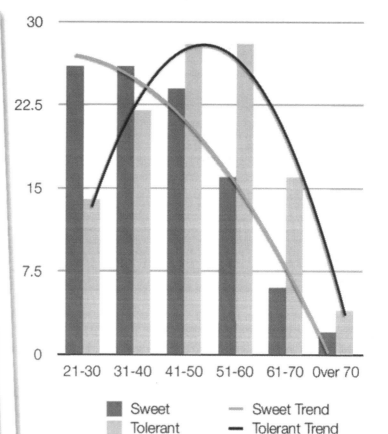

Percent of participants in each age group, with trend lines for each taste group

CONFIDENCE CHOOSING WINE

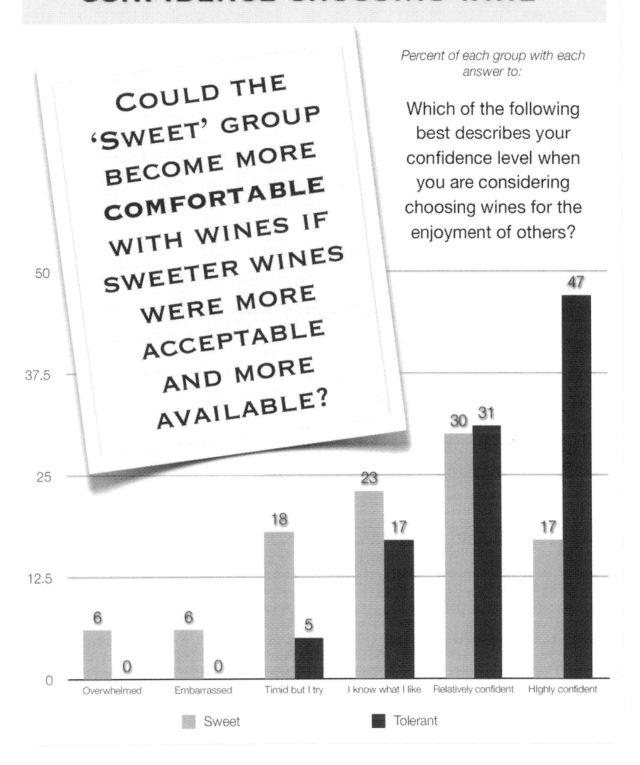

COULD THE 'SWEET' GROUP BECOME MORE COMFORTABLE WITH WINES IF SWEETER WINES WERE MORE ACCEPTABLE AND MORE AVAILABLE?

Percent of each group with each answer to:

Which of the following best describes your confidence level when you are considering choosing wines for the enjoyment of others?

	Overwhelmed	Embarrassed	Timid but I try	I know what I like	Relatively confident	Highly confident
Sweet	6	6	18	23	30	17
Tolerant	0	0	5	17	31	47

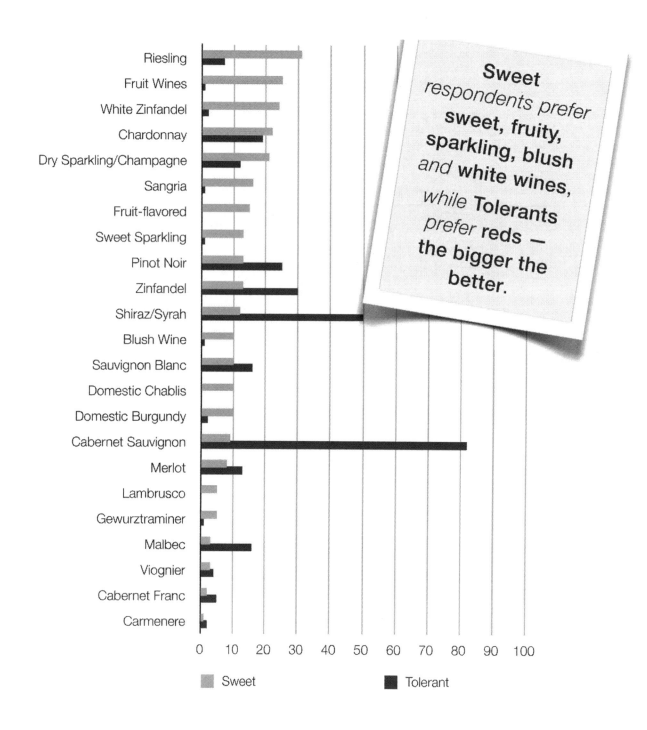

Sweet respondents prefer sweet, fruity, sparkling, blush and white wines, while Tolerants prefer reds — the bigger the better.

Percent of each phenotype citing Pinot Noir among their top three wines

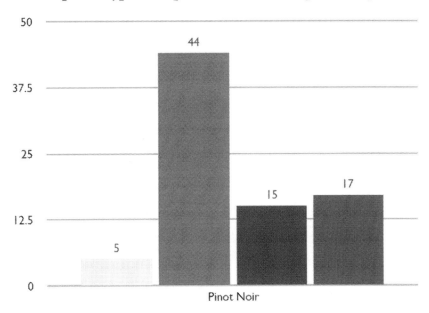

Percent of each phenotype citing Dry Sparkling Wine among their top three wines

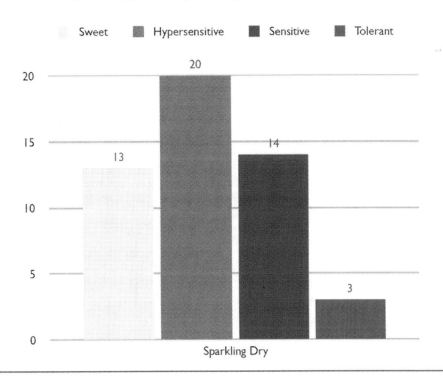

Major wine preferences by variety/type: percent of each phenotype citing the wine among top three. *Values at 20% or above are colored deeply; values at 12% to 19% are colored more lightly.*

	Sweet		Hypersensitive		Sensitive		Tolerant	
	Males	Females	Males	Females	Males	Females	Males	Females
Sangria	38	29	0	3	2	1	2	1
Lambrusco	19	7	3	3	0	0	0	0
Fruit wine	52	50	1	1	2	1	0	1
Sweet sparkling	10	16	4	6	0	1	1	1
Fruit flavored	14	24	3	3	0	3	1	0
White Zinfandel	48	49	0	2	4	3	1	3
Other blush	0	12	5	7	1	4	1	0
Riesling	24	17	21	14	2	3	5	3
Dry sparkling	14	13	15	22	9	18	0	6
Pinot Grigio	5	3	9	13	4	8	0	4
Sauvignon Blanc	0	2	24	28	7	8	7	2
Chardonnay	5	12	13	13	53	61	10	6
Pinot Noir	5	5	48	43	14	16	13	21
Zinfandel	14	15	38	29	38	30	45	44
Merlot	19	3	5	6	59	59	8	15
Cabernet Sauvignon	0	3	61	42	60	49	65	59
Shiraz	10	2	5	10	14	12	82	81
Malbec	0	2	7	6	4	1	34	29

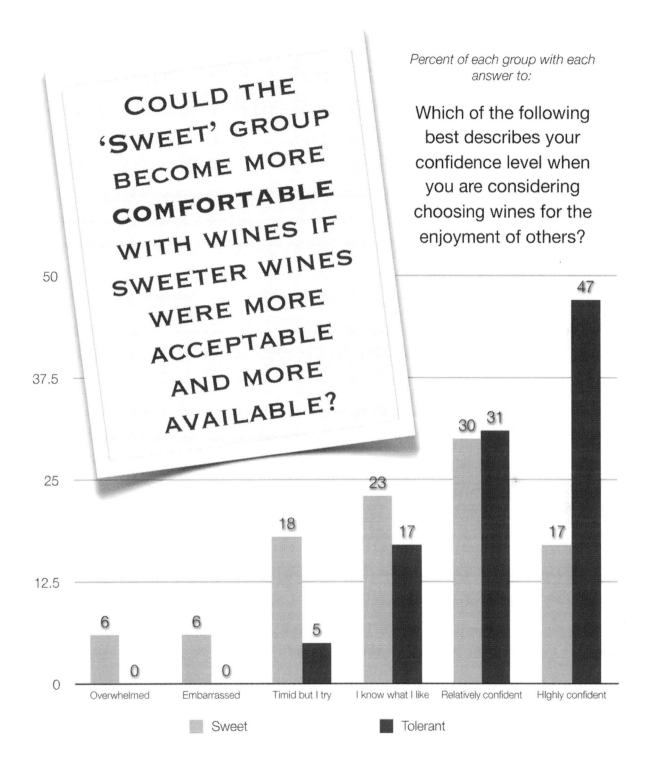

COULD THE 'SWEET' GROUP BECOME MORE **COMFORTABLE** WITH WINES IF SWEETER WINES WERE MORE ACCEPTABLE AND MORE AVAILABLE?

Percent of each group with each answer to:

Which of the following best describes your confidence level when you are considering choosing wines for the enjoyment of others?

Sweet

Tolerant

Overwhelmed · Embarrassed · Timid but I try · I know what I like · Relatively confident · Highly confident

FREQUENCY OF WINE CONSUMPTION

Percent of respondents consuming wine at each frequency for each taste group.

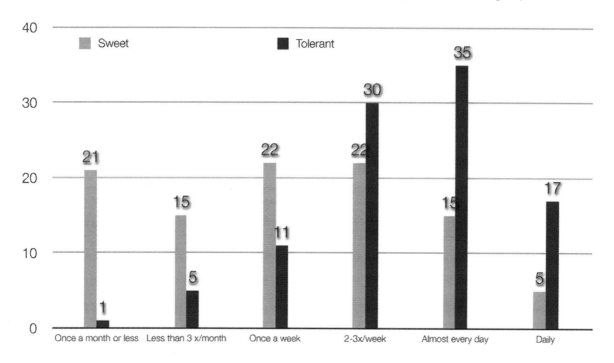

Respondents
in the
Sweet *group*
drink wine
far less often
than do
Tolerants.

HOW DO WE ENCOURAGE 'SWEET' CONSUMERS TO DRINK WINE MORE OFTEN?

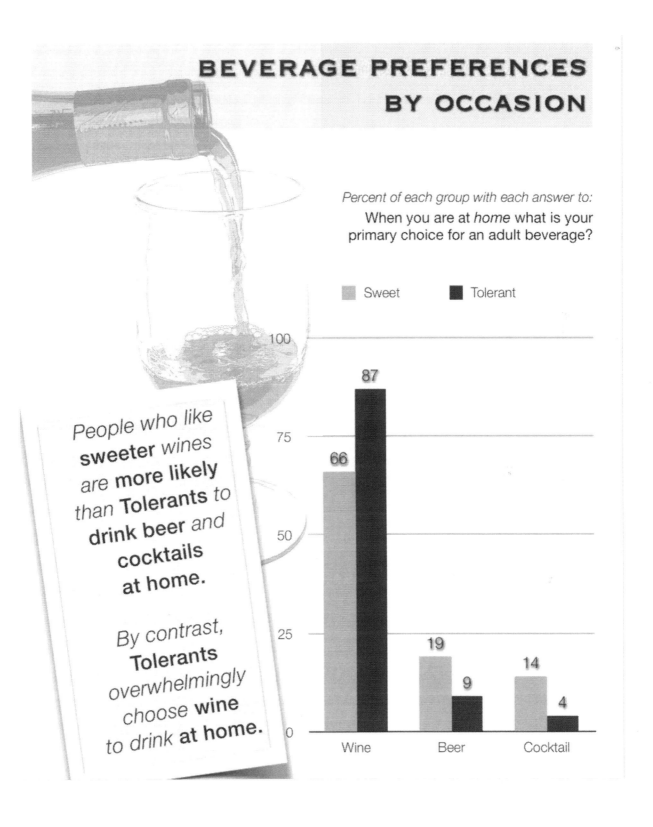

BEVERAGE PREFERENCES BY OCCASION

Percent of each group with each answer to:
When you are at *home* what is your primary choice for an adult beverage?

Sweet   Tolerant

People who like **sweeter** wines are **more likely** than **Tolerants** to **drink beer** and **cocktails at home.**

By contrast, **Tolerants** overwhelmingly choose **wine** to drink **at home.**

Wine: 66, 87
Beer: 19, 9
Cocktail: 14, 4

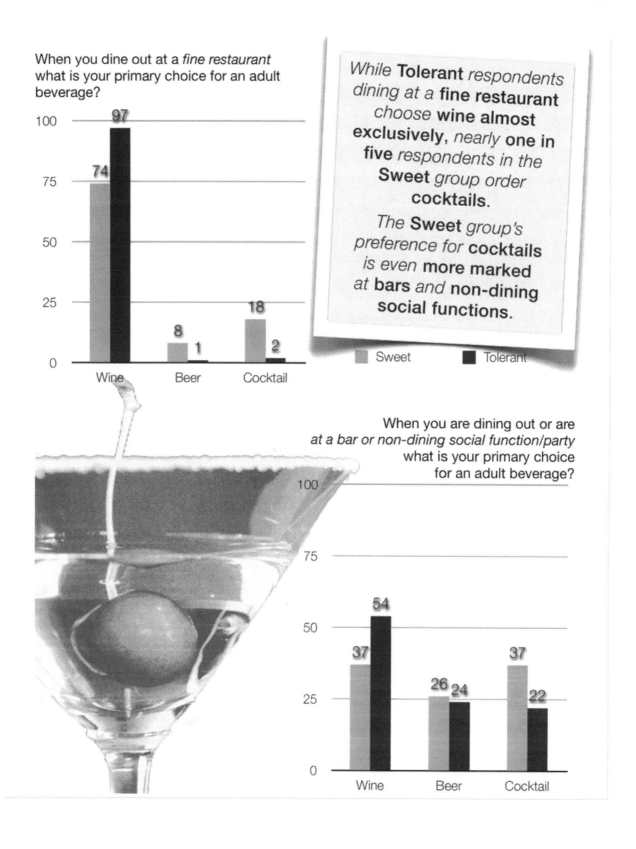

When you dine out at a *fine restaurant* what is your primary choice for an adult beverage?

While **Tolerant** *respondents dining at a* **fine restaurant** *choose* **wine almost exclusively,** *nearly* **one in five** *respondents in the* **Sweet** *group order* **cocktails.**

The **Sweet** *group's preference for* **cocktails** *is even* **more marked** *at* **bars** *and* **non-dining social functions.**

Sweet | Tolerant

When you are dining out or are *at a bar or non-dining social function/party* what is your primary choice for an adult beverage?

> *The* **Sweet** *group's preferences for* **light tastes** *extends to* **beer...**
>
> *...while the* **Tolerants** *taste for* **intensity** *and* **alcohol** *leads them to choose beers they consider less watery, diluted, and "wimpy."*

THE 'SWEET' GROUP'S PREFERENCE FOR LIGHTER TASTES MEANS THAT THEY EXPERIENCE THE SAME DISENFRANCHISING ATTITUDES WHEN IT COMES TO BEER!

BEER PREFERENCES

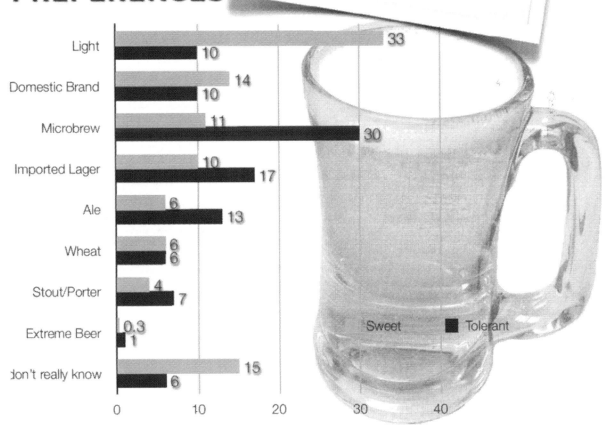

	Sweet	Tolerant
Light	33	10
Domestic Brand	14	10
Microbrew	11	30
Imported Lager	10	17
Ale	6	13
Wheat	6	6
Stout/Porter	4	7
Extreme Beer	0.3	1
don't really know	15	6

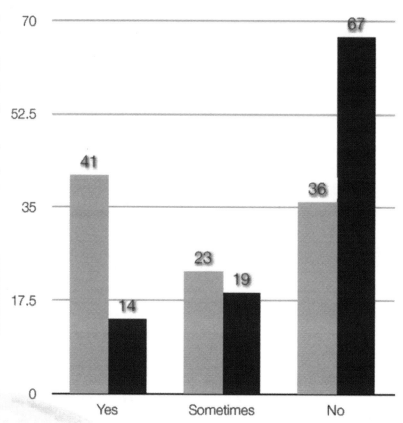

Percent of each group with each answer to:

Do you ever add flavored creamers or shots like almond, hazelnut, vanilla, caramel or Irish cream to your coffee?

COFFEE FLAVORING

Two thirds of the Sweet group use sweet upgrades for their coffee, while two thirds of the tolerants do not.

Sweet respondents are **spending extra** to have **flavorings** added to their coffee.

Report design by VU Designs

Appendix 3: Redefining critical wine terms

Many of the most important terms in the wine lexicon are poorly or vaguely defined. This is the source of a great deal of confusion for wine consumers, wine professionals, wine educators and people in the hospitality industry that recommend and serve wine. The following definitions are important to understand and use when addressing the interactions of wine and food.

- **Taste:** a primary sense comprised of the basic sensations of sweet, sour, bitter, salty and umami.
- **Flavor:** a composite of the sensations of olfaction (smell), taste, touch, chemesthesis (chemical irritation of the trigeminal nerve endings such as the burning irritation of capsicum and many spices) and psychological factors that may affect perceptive attention or acuity.
- **Aroma:** a single, identifiable smell, such as the aroma of lemon, butter, oak, vanilla, oxidation/aging, spice, fruit in general or specific fruit.
- **Bouquet:** the combined olfactory effect of the aromas. A wine that has one single, dominant aroma would be considered to have a simple bouquet, whereas a wine with a wide variety of aromas would have a complex bouquet.

Here is an example of how these definitions would be applied when describing a wine:

The FLAVOR of a great Cabernet Sauvignon construes the net effect of many sensations. A concentrated and complex BOUQUET with AROMAS of cassis, cedar, licorice and spice combined with the more subtle AROMAS of bottle age (olfaction). On the palate the wine demonstrates a firm yet supple tannic structure (touch), a perceived sweet TASTE with moderate acidity (taste) and richness imparted by the alcohol without the burning pungency associated with high alcohol (chemesthesis). The tasting was conducted "blind" (meaning I did not know the identity of the wine) so that my judgment would not be affected by seeing the label (psychological predetermination).

Taste the sensation versus vs. taste as in fashion or aesthetics

In discussing wine and food an important distinction should be made between two common definitions of the word "taste" (from Roget's II, The New Thesaurus):

1. A distinctive property of a substance affecting the gustatory sense.

2. A liking or personal preference for something.

The first definition is of the physical sensation of taste; the second is a definition of taste as an expression of opinion.

One of the great failings in wine and food pairing is that we discuss the gustatory interactions between wine and food with the assumption that everyone will reach the same conclusion or should share the opinion of an "expert." We rarely make allowances for the fact that everyone has his or her own opinion as to the desirability of any given combination of wine and food.

The premise of the Cause and Effect of Wine and Food is to gain a greater understanding of what occurs in the interaction of wine and food and then communicate the occurrence without necessarily passing judgment on the desirability of the interaction. We can develop certain generalizations about acceptability of different combinations but should not assume there is or should be a unanimous agreement.

The arguments that go on about the qualities of one wine versus another or the suitability of a given wine with a certain food are nothing more than the expressions of individual preference. People with more similar cultural, regional and psychological experiences will tend to be more in agreement on the desirability of specific flavor characteristics than people from very diverse backgrounds.

To best understand gustatory interactions between wine and food, it is important to have a foundation on the sense of taste in general. Our sense of taste, as well as our other senses of touch, sight, hearing and smell, is constantly changing.

Flavor

The flavors of a wine or food dictate whether or not an individual will find the sensations desirable. This desirability of a wine or food, or combination of the two, is completely subjective. The expectations and tolerances for flavor sensations by an individual determine the acceptability of the flavor. These expectations and tolerances come from the cultural, regional and psychological experiences of that individual.

As our bodies go through these changes our senses of taste, smell and touch change. To get a handle on sensory adaptation we need a foundation of understanding about our senses in general.

The Sensory Aspects of Taste

The sense of taste is comprised of five primary groups of sensations. I am of the opinion, supported by researchers on the subject, that there are many more than five basic tastes. For example, there are many substances that provide the sensation of sweetness yet they are different compounds, require different taste receptors and the perception of the sensations can vary dramatically from one person to the next. My work with umami taste uncovered a spectrum of sweet-tasting amino acids as well, many of which are found in wine and account for the "sweet" taste found in wines that contain virtually no sugar. This suggests that they are different primary tastes that fall under the categorical heading of "sweet."

Another example is sodium chloride (salt) which has bitter-suppressive qualities while potassium chloride provides a similar salty taste for most people, a bitter taste for others and does not possess the bitter-suppressive quality of sodium chloride. This is important to understand since the people who crave salt the most – the Sweet and Hypersensitive Vinotypes, are most likely to find potassium chloride bitter-tasting and it does not provide the attributes of bitter suppression that have them crave salt in the first place.

This being said, here is the list of generally accepted primary tastes:

- Sweet
- Sour
- Bitter
- Salt
- Umami

Our sense of taste was possibly developed as a survival mechanism for humans to ascertain the wholesomeness of certain foods. The taste of a food gave an indication as to whether or not the food could be safely eaten and also function to begin the processes necessary to assimilate certain food compounds.

The five basic tastes are considered sensory signals that provide the body with the first indication of the arrival of nutrients and prepare the body for appropriate physiological reactions to follow.

Umami taste may be the signal that announces the intake of protein to prepare the body to digest and absorb protein by stimulating the secretion of digestive fluids, the motion of digestive organs and the provision of metabolic reactions regulated by neurons and hormones. Sweet taste may be the signal for carbohydrate intake as energy source. Sour taste may be the signal for the intake of organic acids like citric acid in order to promote energy generating metabolisms through the citric acid cycle and at the same time to serve as a warning that bacterial deterioration has spoiled the food. Salty taste may be the signal for mineral intake to keep maintaining osmotic pressures in the body fluids. Bitter taste may be the signal to prevent poisonous substances from entering the body. Thus it is possible that the five basic tastes may be the signal for either maintaining life or protecting the body from external danger."

Sweetness
Sweetness is found in many foods and wines. Sometimes we do not really think of certain types of sauces or foods as "sweet" when in actuality they are, such as teriyaki, cocktail and many tomato sauces. Often vegetables and certainly fruits can add a degree of sweetness to a dish and must be considered when making a wine selection.

There is a wide range of sweetness levels in many beverages and foods. Our individual expectations will dictate the desirability of levels of sweetness. This is expressed in many ways: how we take our coffee or tea, what kind of chocolates we like, the balance of a wine, etc.

The desirability of a wine and food combination that affects the sweetness of the wine depends entirely on the preference of the individual experiencing the combination. A combination that raises the sweetness of a wine may be delicious to someone who appreciates a sweeter wine while the same combination is considered unsatisfactory for someone who prefers a drier wine. When food is sweet it will suppress the sweetness of the wine served with it through sensory adaptation.

Sweetness in food will increase the perception of sourness, bitterness and astringency of the wine while making the wine appear less sweet (more dry), stronger and less fruity.

Acidity

Natural acids impart tartness or sourness of food or wine. Most wines that have sweetness, such as White Zinfandel and many Rieslings, also have a very high acidity to keep the wine from tasting flat or cloying. If a food reacts in a way that suppresses the sourness of such wines, they will taste very sweet in comparison.

Dry wines tend to taste more acidic because they do not have the sweetness balancing and covering the sour taste. White wines tend to be higher in acidity than red wines.

Foods with high amounts of acidity will decrease our perception of sourness in the wine and make the wine taste richer and mellow. If the wine is sweet to begin with it will seem to taste sweeter in comparison to the taste of the wine before the acidity.

Sweetness and Sourness Combined

Many foods have a combination of sweetness and sourness, such as honey/mustard sauces and other "sweet and sour" or *aigre-doux* preparations. The balance of one to the other will dictate the reactivity with the wine. The sweetness and sourness can actually be balanced in the food to be neutral with the wine. This is very important in dishes where one does not naturally expect sweetness, as in many tomato sauces, which is also high in umami. Fruit relishes and garnishes can be made much less reactive by judiciously adding citrus juice or vinegar. Look out for things like teriyaki sauce or other meat glazes.
Combining sweetness and sourness in food can have the effect of cancelling each other out depending on the concentration level of each. If one or the other dominates the wine will react according to the basic formula.

Bitterness

Bitterness is often confused with astringency and is similar to astringency in its interaction with food. A bitter taste is commonly found in some green vegetables (endive, arugula, radicchio) and herbs, many spices, some fruits, or food charred during the cooking process. Bitterness is extracted from many foods during cooking, especially at high temperatures. This also occurs when you boil tea instead of gently steeping it.

Food with bitter components seems to increase the bitterness of a wine served with it. Make sure that the herbal-smelling Sauvignon Blanc chosen to serve with the dish with lots of fresh herbs does not push the bitterness of the wine over the top.

The umami taste in food seems to be responsible for increasing the perception of bitterness in wine or leaving a bitter or metallic aftertaste. This is common with caviar and dry white wines (including sparkling wines), with many bleu cheeses and even tomatoes. A bleu cheese will have the effect of softening the astringency of tannic red wines but leaving a bitter taste impression, which has been accentuated by the umami taste of the cheese. Saltiness or sourness, in the form of vinegar or citric acid from lemon or lime, in the food will help to eliminate the bitter taste in the wine.

Bitter, sweet and umami flavors in food will increase the perception of bitter elements in wine. Sourness and salt in the food suppress bitter taste in the wine.

Saltiness

As foods become more salty, they tend to increase in their own flavors and neutralize bitter and sour tastes of the wine tasted after the salty food. Saltiness in the food creates an impression of less bitterness in the wine. Saltiness will negate the effect of umami in the food - if the food is high in umami compounds <u>and </u>salt, the salt will negate the umami's usual effect of making the wine more bitter.

Some people make a habit of putting a little salt on Granny Smith and other "tart" apples. This is done to soften the sourness and bitterness, making the apple seem more mild in taste. Proper seasoning of meat-based sauces is important to negate the umami compounds produced in the cooking process which can unfavorably impact the taste of the accompanying wine. This practice is usually a sign of a Sweet or Hypersensitive Vinotype!

The judicious addition of salt to food, especially to sauces and other foods high in umami, can be useful in some cases to tone down bitterness and astringency of some wines. You may find that salty foods make sweet wines taste sweeter.

Umami

You like umami. It is the fundamental "good" taste of foods as diverse as meats, seafood, vegetables, chocolates, stocks, broths and soups.

Umami has gained acceptance by food scientists as a fifth taste, separate from the tastes sweet, acid, salty and bitter. The prototype for umami taste is monosodium L-glutamate (MSG) and is found naturally occurring in almost all food to some degree. MSG is added to foods that are of a low quality to make up for the natural compounds that may be lacking.

Umami was identified by the Japanese researcher Ikeda in 1908 as the taste in *laminaria Japonica* seaweed, used as a component of soup stocks in Japanese cuisine, and was associated with glutamate (monosodium L-glutamic acid). Later, ribonucleotides were discovered as having umami taste and also having a synergistic effect with glutamates that greatly enhance the perception of the umami taste.

Umami taste is associated with a "savory" characteristic in foods. Umami is more prevalent and found generally in higher concentrations in Asian cuisines. The word *umami* in Japanese actually translates to "delicious" or "savory." Western palates do not as easily recognize Umami because we have never been taught to identify it. As with other tastes, the umami taste may be hidden behind stronger tastes like saltiness. The umami taste of a food can have an effect on taste elements of a wine that is served with it, bringing out bitter and often metallic tastes. The reaction between umami and the wine can be negated by salty tastes in the food.

Examples of Umami

The umami taste is associated with everything from steak to ham and seafood (sea urchin, abalone, crab, scallop, shrimp and lobster), tomatoes, asparagus, meats and cheeses. Oily fish (sardines, bonito, mackerel and tuna) seem to have more of an umami taste than lighter fish. The "sweet" taste associated with many shellfish is actually the umami taste. Shiitake mushrooms have umami, especially when they are dried.

Aged beef is preferred over fresh beef due to the higher levels of umami taste after the beef has been aged. During the curing process the umami taste is greatly increased in making ham from fresh pork.

The drying or fermentation of foods with umami concentrates the compounds to over four times the level in the undried product. An example of this is dried shiitake mushrooms. Sauces, stocks, broths and bases are very high in umami taste, as well as tomato products from catsup to marinara sauce. Oyster sauce, fish sauce from Thailand and "tan" broth (from China) are all sources for umami taste, as is Worcestershire, soy, A-1 and other sauces.

Compounds responsible for the umami taste are found in different concentration levels according to seasons in many types of seafood. Scallops are highest in umami compounds in the month of June, when they are considered the most palatable to Japanese diners. European chefs and diners recognize the same flavor superiority of scallops during this season, especially when the scallops have the roe. They are lowest in these compounds during July and the scallops are considered less desirable.

The Umami and Wine Hypothesis

There are many "unexplainable" aspects of taste interaction between wine and food that may be directly linked with the umami taste. It is important to point out that the cause and effect reactions that occur between foods high in umami and wine deal mostly with bitterness, the least understood and most unpredictable of all tastes. Not everyone will find these reactions to occur.

Foods high in umami seem to increase our sensitivity to bitterness in wines and create a "metallic" taste. This is true with many soup and sauce stocks; strong, oily fish; oysters, and many dried or preserved foods including caviar, all of which have umami taste. Saltiness in food high in umami compounds neutralizes the bitter or metallic taste in the wine that follows.

Soft-ripened bleu cheese is a classic example of this phenomenon. A taste of the bleu cheese followed by a taste of tannic wine will generally lower the perception of astringency in the wine, but very often there will be a bitter or metallic aftertaste. The protein, fat and acidity alone of the cheese would normally soften the bitter taste along with the astringency. The theory is that the bitterness is heightened by the umami compounds in the cheese.

Dry or aged bleu cheese seems to create less of a decrease in astringency. The proteins are bound (coagulated) by each other and less effective in binding the tannins of the wine, but the umami taste is still strong and increases the bitterness of the wine.

This theory would go a long way in explaining the generally undesirable taste reactions that can occur when you serve caviar with sparkling wines, fish with red wines (many Pinot Noir and salmon or tuna combinations) or oysters (especially during the spawning months) with dry white wines.

Acidity naturally occurring in or added to food with strong umami taste will reduce our perception of sourness and bitterness in the wine accompanying the dish and will tend to neutralize the reaction of umami.

Umami in food will increase our perception of bitterness in wine. Saltiness in conjunction with umami in the food will neutralize the effect.

Touch

There are tactile sensations, such as astringency, imparted by wine and food, which can react in combination. Astringency (mostly from tannins in wine, fruit and vegetables) is the most prevalent of these sensations. These sensations of touch are important along with taste in determining the basic reaction potential between different wine and food combinations and were once thought to actually be a sensation of taste.

Astringency

Sensory adaptation and residual compounds from food and the physical condition of the taster affect the degree of astringency one perceives in a wine. The physical condition of the taster will affect the amount of saliva (with salt and protein) in the mouth. If you are fatigued or under a great deal of stress, the amount of saliva you produce will be reduced, increasing your perception of astringency. The "tannic" taste of a wine is actually a sense of touch and not of taste. Tannins coagulate proteins in the saliva and the tissues in your mouth and create a puckering or drying sensation known as astringency. Consumers who think that this sensation is what is meant by a "dry wine" very often misinterpret this sensation. A "dry" wine is simply not sweet.

Astringency in wine is accentuated by food that is sweet or "hot" (spicy) and is suppressed by foods that are acidic and/or salty.

Increased perception
Sweetness in the food will greatly increase the perception of astringency in the wine. Tannin (from nuts, fruits or certain herbs and vegetables) in the food can also amplify the perception of tannin. The prototype for astringent taste is a persimmon.

The amount of saliva in our mouth has an effect of how we perceive astringency and acidity. Saliva is made up of protein, salt and other compounds that affect how we taste. People may react differently due to the fact that they are "high flow" or "low flow" producers of saliva. Tasters who are fatigued or under a great deal of stress may also experience an increase in the perception of astringency of a wine as a result of having less saliva.

Chemesthesis
The sense of chemesthesis is an irritation associated with pungent or "hot" characteristics in some food, even to the point of pain if the food has high concentrations of some of these compounds. The heat we feel from peppers and other spices come from the effect of chemesthesis. Other sources of chemesthesis are certain acids and carbon dioxide.

Foods that contain enough of these compounds tend to sensitize the mouth of the taster so that the perception of bitterness and astringency in the wine will become heightened. The effect of chemesthesis tends to be cumulative; the first sip of wine after a hot pepper may not seem reactive and may even make the wine taste smoother and fruitier. By the time the chemesthesis starts to sensitize the mouth, the same wine tastes strongly bitter and astringent.

Olfaction (sense of smell)
There is a great deal of confusion over the rudimentary terminology used to describe the smells of wine. The following clarification is offered:

Aroma "The quality of something that may be perceived by the olfactory sense." Roget's II, the New Thesaurus, 1988
This would indicate distinct, identifiable smells found in wine such as primary grape smells, specific fruit smells, smells from fermentation, oxidation or spoilage, smells from oak aging or treatment, smells of spices or herbs, etc.

Bouquet refers to a *group* of aromas (as a bouquet refers to a group of flowers, from the French *bousquet* for a thicket). The bouquet may therefore be considered as a group of smells, either in young or old wine, as a group. As the bouquet increases, the singular aromas tend to become less distinct or identifiable.

Many of the sensations we ascribe to "taste" are actually aromas. This is why we tend to say we cannot "taste" things when we have a cold. There are potentially over 2,000 different compounds found in wines. About 1,200 to 1,400 have been identified.

The Cause and Effect of Wine and Food stress the fundamentals of taste rather than aroma. This is because the most predictable reactions occur with taste. There are only five basic variables of taste involved and literally hundreds of aromas potentially in wine. Aromas tend to be much more difficult to describe and analyze.

A great deal of work has been done to create a more specific language using common words, such as butter, black pepper, or certain varieties of fruit, to describe the smells of various wines. Many of the compounds in wine are actually the same or similar compounds which give rise to the smell in the food or other item used as a descriptor:

- Butter is the compound diacetyl (a by-product of malo-lactic fermentation)
- Cloves is eugenol (extracted from oak barrels during aging)
- The smell of bell peppers is a pyrizine found in Sauvignon varieties as well as bell peppers.

As with taste, there are sensory adaptations that increase the intensity of certain aromas and suppress the intensity of others. When someone wears a cologne or perfume regularly, they may become oblivious to the fact that they are slathering on more and more to compensate for their sensory adaptation to the smell. The same is also true for developing a certain regard or disdain for wine aromas. One person is used to a regional characteristic of a wine and cannot figure out what another taster is talking about when they find something that they construe as a flaw in the wine.

Our tolerance for certain aromas is very subjective, even more so than our tolerance for tastes. One taster may find a particular aroma completely offensive and pronounce the wine in question as commercially unacceptable, while another equally expert taster may find the same odor typical and completely acceptable, even desirable.

On the other hand, many people are very sensitive to some smells that others may not even smell at all. We all have our own thresholds of sensitivity and this may vary a great deal from one person to the next.

Our sense of smell is very closely linked with our memory. Certain odors may provide olfactory triggers that can evoke memories. Sometimes the memory that is triggered is vague and shapeless or strong and vivid. We then form an opinion as to whether or not we like the smell.

For the individual offended by the smell of a certain wine, the best food match would be one that suppressed the offensive odor. The individual who found the odor to be attractive may prefer a food combination that seemed to increase the intensity of the smell. The person with a high threshold may not even be able to distinguish the smell. As they say, beauty is in the nose of the beholder.

Notes: _____

_____

_____

_____

_____

_____

_____

_____

_____

_____

_____

_____

_____

_____

_____

_____

_____

_____

_____

_____

_____

_____

Appendix 4: Wine Lists in the Future

This article was written for, and is reprinted with the permission of, **In the Mix Magazine**. In the Mix is a national publication that focuses on providing information for restaurants, bars, hotels and cruise ships. The reason for the inclusion of this article in **Why You Like the Wines You Like** is to provide hospitality professionals with an outline for creating wine lists that are simple for consumers to navigate and consistent with the concept of Vinotypes. This article can also provide readers with insights into what goes into a "Vinotype" wine list and if your favorite restaurant does not use one make a copy of these pages and take them to the manager! The intention is to create wine list categories that are based on primary flavor attributes that match to different Vinotype flavor preferences.

SUCCESSFUL WINE LISTS AS EASY AS 1-2-3-4

Tim Hanni MW offers new strategies for wine list creation. Over two decades of research conducted with scientists in the field of taste perception has resulted in an identification process he calls Vinotyping – a means of segmenting consumers using newly known physiological and psychological factors that determine personal wine preferences. Combined with his popular Progressive Wine List strategy, the result is a complete breakthrough for increasing wine sales, forging the modern wine list into a tool for inclusion and increased customer satisfaction.

The perfect wine list. You've dreamed about it since you were a little oeno-tyke. "Someday, when I get to be the boss, I'll have the biggest list *ever*…," has hung over your head in a little thought bubble for so long that it casts a shadow on your coffee cup strewn desk. Now, for better or worse, you *are* the boss, at least of the wine list. You have also learned that with more selections on the list comes more inventory, more logistics headaches and more intimidation for your staff and guests. So, what is the perfect number of wines for a list, and how do you determine what that number should be for your list?

In my twenty years leading seminars with wine trade professionals in the Napa Valley and all over the world, this question has been the source of more heated discussion than portion control, hot plates waiting in the window, or the all-time best vintage of *Clos du Bec d'Or*. And, after the knockdown, drag-out battle is over, a clear answer always emerges about how many wines would appear on the perfect wine list: one. Which one? The one everyone wants. How much does it cost? As much as anyone is willing to spend.

OK, so that's not very realistic. The fact of the matter is that every extra selection *after* the first one increases inventory, storage, maintenance, training and expenses accordingly. If you only had one wine to program, price, stock, place an order for, inventory, train the wait staff on, etc., life would be a lot easier. Multiply that one wine by two, by ten, by twenty, by a thousand... and you get my point.

So how do you determine the magic number for your wine list?

Think Beyond Your Own Palate

The first thing you need to know is that old marketing saw, "You are not the market." You have good taste. You love wine, you are well educated on the subject, and most importantly, *you know what tastes good.* Right? Think again. You are the expert on what tastes good to *you.* If you've attended one of my seminars, classes, or lectures, you know that there is a spectrum of palate profiles that fall into four basic categories. (See sidebar.) You'd be doing a disservice to your potential clientele—and your bottom line—if you left any one of these groups out.

If you're arranging your list in the Progressive Wine List fashion, which I recommend you do, you'll start with lighter-intensity, sweet and slightly sweet wines, like sweet Riesling, White Zinfandel and Moscato, providing a range of price points. A Progressive Wine List will "progress" to off-dry, delicate wines, drier whites with more intensity and gradually increasing in intensity and fullness to wines with substantial structure, such as Syrah and Cabernet. Good wine managers and sommeliers buy what's considered good by devoted wine lovers, peers and critics. *Great* wine managers find something special for customers across the entire spectrum of taste and price preferences. This includes offering wines for the more adventurous among them to try something new that fits within their realm of preferences along with well-known standards for those who a more conservative in their tastes. Tasting with this in mind will open your eyes to a world of possibilities for featuring great wines of every price and style.

What if you've got what we term a B.A.L. (Big Ass List) with more than 60 selections, maybe even hundreds of selections? Use what I call a "Strategic Progressive List" on the first page or two. A strategic Progressive Wine List is a carefully designed Progressive Wine List, interspersed with your wines-by-the-glass selections, to highlight wines you want to sell. This can be wines that are purchased on promotion and offer a higher margin, inventory you want to highlight and move, and selections that you and your staff are most passionate about. Research has shown that as much as 90 percent of sales from a B.A.L. come from a relatively small number of wines. A carefully crafted, flexible Strategic Progressive Wine List, will allow you to maintain a larger selection of wines, organized in traditional fashion, for the guests who are interested in more esoteric selections while focusing your staff and your guests on the wines that will help you derive more profit and better manage your inventory.

What other factors do you need to consider in crafting your list?

Logistics

How much wine can you properly store and easily access? How much wine do you want to inventory each month? Perhaps you work for a deep pockets billionaire who doesn't mind lingering verticals of Mouton aging gracefully in the temperature controlled mega-cellar. How nice for you. Or maybe you are a mom-and-pop startup, and your cold whites share reach-in space with the cheese. A well-designed list does not require a huge allotment of temperature-controlled space yet will meet the needs of the widest range of guests palates and pocketbooks.

Profitability

You'll want to include wines at a variety of prices in each flavor category. It becomes a new challenge to find exciting wines at slightly higher-than-the-lowest price in the sweet or off-dry category, but trust me, these are the consumers who are most neglected, least understood, and most appreciative when they're treated with respect and not condescension. Include big name, high-scoring wines in the medium-weight and heavy-weight categories, as folks with those palate preferences are the most likely to be influenced by scores and ratings from Robert Parker or the Wine Spectator. Take it easy on the esoteric and flowery wine descriptions – most people put little stock in the imaginary language of the wine cognoscenti.

The key is to understand the guests' needs, embrace them, and never impose your will without permission. You'll create customers for life and can cultivate them over time as you gain their trust in the fact that you know, and respect, their personal tastes.

Trainability

One of the less obvious benefits of a well-constructed Progressive Wine List is that it is a valuable tool that simplifies staff training. Have no more wines on your list than your staff can confidently sell. Listing wines in flavor categories takes the guesswork out of which wines are drier, more tannic, smoother or more sweet. Say you have a full-time sommelier. What happens when that person is not available? Does everything fall apart? Do servers cower and guess, or push their personal preferences rather than trying to find the right wine for the guest? When you have a great Progressive Wine List you can first train the staff on how to use the "tool" quickly and effectively while continuing to cultivate their deeper wine knowledge.

Hospitality professionals should be trained to understand and respect personal wine preferences. Courtesy of Bob Johnson

Using the sidebar see where everyone in the front of the house falls on the Vinotype sensitivity scale. Taste through the wines being considered for inclusion on your list with your staff to see where their personal taste preferences fall in relationship to their Vinotype. Then personify your guests – who are they, what are some of the common questions that come up over and over, what kind of wines would light them up? Pay special attention to the guests who seem the most ill at ease with the wine conversations. Recognize individual differences positively, especially for those who are Sweet and Hypersensitive Vinotypes, and encourage staff members of all taste preferences to participate. Make this strategy a part of the culture of your restaurant and you'll have an empowered staff engaging your customers.

One of the huge advantages of a Progressive Wine List, including the use of a Strategic Progressive Wine List in conjunction with a B.A.L, is that your list becomes a tool. Training is focused on how to use the tool to get your guests to the wine that will be delicious and memorable. Training on the tool, combined with traditional wine education, is confidence building and easier to execute during service and will make your wine program more profitable. Over time your guests will become more confident and comfortable with the list as well and will love sharing their knowledge with others at their table.

Aspirations

Do you want to (and do you have the budget to) win a prestigious award for your wine list? Amass the largest selection of Russian River Pinot Noirs or wines rated 90+ points? Become known for your reasonably priced wines and knowledgeable staff? Just want to provide a great, inclusive dining experience for your guests? Write that goal out and post it above the desk where you sit (or stand, wolfing down the team meal) to place your wine orders, to keep you on track. Share it with your servers, your chef and your boss, and not only will it become reality, but you'll soon hear it repeated back to you by people outside your walls.

It is as easy as 1,2,3,4:

1. Determine the appropriate number of wines for your clientele (all of them, not just a narrow range!), logistics and marketing your wine program.
2. Pepper the list with very carefully selected wines you and your staff are passionate about.
3. Arrange the wines in a fashion that is intuitive, forwards sales and is easy to use for guests and staff.
4. Train more on your guests, how to use the well-organized list as a tool and focus on everyone being respected and honored for their personal preferences and only then dive into traditional product knowledge.

Ultimately, the perfect wine list can be 50 carefully selected wines that cover the needs of your clientele or hundreds of wines that bring in the wine cognoscenti to marvel at the range and diversity of wines you have collected. A great wine list is one that meets its goals, is inclusive, practical, profitable, and accessible enough that staff—all staff—can confidently provide *every guest* with the most enjoyable experience *for them.*

Appendix 5: Sensory Evaluation: Science and Mythology

Sensory Evaluation: Science and Mythology
Reprinted with permission from an article by Herbert Stone, Ph.D.

A former director of Stanford Research Institute (SRI), Dr. Stone was president of the Institute of Food Technologists (IFT) from 2004-2005. With a Ph.D. from U.C. Davis, he has lectured worldwide, is the author of over 125 publications, and holds six patents. Dr. Stone is co-author with Joel Sidel of *Sensory Evaluation Practices*, now in its fourth edition, and one of the most respected texts in the industry. Along with Mr. Sidel, Dr. Stone founded Tragon® in 1974.

Stone and Sidel, a trained psychologist, collaborated to understand why consumers perceive product differences and similarities. Together they defined the standard on advancing sensory evaluation as an industry method of measuring and understanding customer perception. From this, Quantitative Descriptive Analysis (QDA) was born—a new way of understanding and using sensory evaluation. Their book, *Sensory Evaluation Practices*, is one of the most respected texts on the subject. The company has grown to comprise a highly educated, motivated staff, 90 percent of whom have earned technical degrees in related fields. We maintain our reputation for excellence by keeping operations completely internalized, subject to rigorous management controls. Such experienced personnel in our facilities and in the field make a tangible difference when it comes to briefing panels, conducting research, and analyzing the results.

SENSORY EVALUATION: SCIENCE AND MYTHOLOGY

Sensory evaluation has had a long and active relationship with the food industry. Most of the earliest work on methods development and applications was supported by the industry, which came to appreciate the relationship between a product's sensory characteristics and market success. Over the past three decades sensory professionals made considerable strides in achieving acceptance from its scientific peers. A variety of misconceptions and myths about sensory evaluation had to be challenged; including, for example, the traumas of organolepsis and triangulation (both diseases of the mind) and the tyranny of experts (tongue, nose, etc.) stating what to perceive, what to call the perceptions, and what the consumer would like. With increased acceptance by their peers, sensory professionals were able to participate in the product decision making process, as well as provide procedures for marketing and quality oriented tests. In more recent years, however, these gains have become in danger of being lost with the re-emergence of experts; the proposition that people can be trained to be invariant; sameness testing a curious but flawed concept that posits that products not perceived as different must be the same, as if products ever are the same; universal scales; and the use of statistical terrorism; e.g., using complex algorithms as a substitute for a well-organized and fielded test.

Sensory evaluation is a science that measures, analyzes, and interprets the reactions of the senses of sight, smell, sound, taste, and texture (or kinesthesis) to products. It is a people science; i.e., people are essential to obtain information about products. With that product information in hand, business decisions are made often with major economic impact. This people testing process may seem simple enough; however, there are numerous ways by which one goes about deciding who in the population will participate, how they will be tested, and what kinds of questions will be asked. Much research has been done to understand consumer behavior and there is no doubt much more will be done before we have a better understanding of consumer choice behavior.

In this work, one regularly encounters myths about consumer behavior that defy established knowledge about the anatomy and physiology of the senses and observed response behavior.

One of these myths is the proposition that consumers can be trained to be invariant. Subjects providing the same response each time a specific stimulus is presented is used as evidence of the validity of this approach, where as it is confusing reliability with validity and using a form of behavior modification to fool us into thinking that individuals trained to provide the same response to a stimulus is realistic response behavior. For statistical wimps this concept of subject invariance has the added advantage of avoiding statistics entirely.

Perceptual skills vary considerably; about 30percent of any population cannot differentiate at or above chance among products that they regularly consume. This knowledge is either ignored or summarized in ways that mask differences, and leads to sensory evaluation being labeled as an inexact science. Another myth focuses on the use of lists of words that describe a product, often referred to as "lexicons" and the implication that the use of such lists will yield a universal language (the aura of a periodic table of the sensory elements for products).

This has enormous appeal as it avoids the difficult task of asking a panel develop its own language, avoids translations, and has an aura of scientific respectability as such lists are usually prepared by professional committees. Requiring a panel to use only certain words has numerous faults. To a considerable degree, it is nothing more than the reappearance of language that used in product standards of identity about 50 years ago. It ultimately was found to have little or no relationship to consumer preferences or purchase behavior. Words used to represent sensations are nothing more than labels and assumptions as to causality are not sustainable without appropriate experimentation. The idea that with such a list the sensory evaluation of products is easily achieved impugns the science of sensory evaluation, the perceptual process, and raises questions as to the role of sensory evaluation within the business environment.

The idea of a universal scale in sensory evaluation is another myth that has considerable appeal but is equally false. It ignores the most fundamental of issues, namely, that each person is uniquely different.

Mathematically, one can produce a universal scale but at what expense?

Human sensory behavior is far more complex than what some might like to believe. Any population will exhibit a wide range of sensitivities and preferences; trying to eliminate or mask such differences does not do justice to the science of sensory evaluation nor does it provide confidence in business decisions.

Sensory professionals and food science professionals as well, need to recognize these myths and respond to them as they would to snake oil, with all due respect for reptiles.

Notes: _____

_____

_____

_____

_____

_____

_____

_____

_____

_____

_____

_____

_____

_____

_____

_____

_____

_____

_____

Appendix 6: Umami, a taste unto itself

Dr. Stephen Roper, University of Miami School of Medicine, sroper@med.miami.edu

Many scientists believe that there are only a few basic taste qualities--sweet, sour, bitter, salty, and *umami*. The notion of a limited number of basic tastes stems from antiquity. Aristotle summarized the common beliefs of the day regarding taste qualities in his treatise on natural philosophy, *De Sensu*. He described 7 basic tastes. Sweet and bitter formed the polar extremes on a linear scale. Salty was positioned near bitter. Additional tastes included harsh, pungent, astringent, and acid (sour). Further, Democritus, a contemporary of Socrates, concluded that the "atoms" that gave rise to these different qualities had characteristic shapes and consequently exerted distinct physical actions on the tongue. For instance, sweet tastes were smooth and round. Bitter tastes were rough and jagged. This was remarkably prescient insofar as scientists have recently been able to identify and actually view "binding pockets" in receptor molecules, into which taste molecules insert. I will discuss more about receptor molecules later.

Aristotle, Socrates, and their contemporaries did not recognize umami as a taste. However, umami has been an element in oriental cuisines for centuries. Umami taste is imparted by certain additives such as dried seaweed or bonito flakes that impart a rich, full, savory flavor to cooked foods. The notion that umami is an independent taste quality on par with sweet, sour, bitter and salty received a strong impetus at the beginning of the 20th century. Specifically, in 1909 the Japanese scientist Kikunae Ikeda published his findings that a simple amino acid, l-glutamate, isolated from dried seaweed, is the active ingredient that elicits umami taste. In the following decades, the nature of umami as a fundamental taste quality was hotly debated in academic conferences and research publications, with the alternative viewpoint being that umami was simply a synthesis of other fundamental qualities such as salty and sweet.

Whether umami is a basic taste is an important question. The answer provides important insights into how gustatory sensory organs respond to chemical stimuli and how the nervous system is organized to process gustatory data. It is believed that each basic taste quality is explained by a distinct molecular mechanism. If umami were merely a combination of other fundamental tastes, there would be no impetus to search for separate molecular mechanism to explain how glutamate or related umami tastants stimulate sensory cells in taste buds. The debate regarding umami as a fundamental taste occupied chemosensory researchers until 2000.

In 2000, researchers working in Nirupa Chaudhari's laboratory at the University of Miami Medical School identified a possible molecular mechanism to explain umami taste. They discovered a particular receptor molecule that was synthesized by taste sensory cells and that interacted with glutamate in a manner consistent with umami taste. Shortly after, Nicholas Ryba at NIH and Charles Zuker at UC San Diego identified additional important receptor molecules for amino acids, including glutamate, that were key to umami taste. These findings put an end to the debate over whether umami was a fundamental taste quality, and attention was focused on characterizing the umami taste receptor molecules.

Taste buds, taste cells, and the sensory organs of taste

Before proceeding further, it is important to describe how tastes, generally, are sensed. Chemical compounds in foodstuffs (salts, sugars, proteins, amino acids, etc.) are dissolved in saliva and interact with peripheral sensory end organs—taste buds—distributed throughout the oral cavity. The highest density of taste buds is present on the surface of the tongue but there are also collections of taste buds on the soft palate, the epiglottis, and even the upper esophagus. In all, there are roughly 5000 taste buds in the oral cavity. Interestingly, there is a population of individuals, so-called "supertasters", who have a much greater number of taste buds. This was described by L. Bartoshuk who is now at the University of Florida. Supertasters are more sensitive to gustatory stimuli than the average individual. Supertasters form about 25 percent of the population. Supertasting is a genetic trait.

Each taste bud is a tightly packed collection of 50 to 100 elongate cells that form a structure resembling a clove of garlic. The apical tips of the taste bud cells protrude into a shallow cavity that opens onto the lingual surface. This cavity is the taste pore. It is here where dissolved chemicals interact with the tips of the taste bud cells to initiate gustatory sensations. For the most part, chemical stimuli do not penetrate from the taste pore cavity deeper into the main body of the taste bud. Exceptions include sodium ions, which may permeate into the interior of the taste bud and stimulate salty taste.

Individual taste buds respond to more than one taste quality. That is, a given taste bud is not dedicated to sweet, or sour, or bitter, etc. Nonetheless, individual cells within a taste bud can differ in their taste sensitivities. For instance, one cell may respond to sweet and an adjacent cell will respond to bitter. Many taste bud cells are "specialists" and respond only to a single taste quality, such as sweet or bitter or umami. A minority of taste bud cells are "generalists" and respond broadly to several taste qualities. Importantly, there is no strict "map" of taste such that the front of the tongue senses only sweet and the back senses only bitter. The flawed argument of tongue maps stems from a faulty translation of an early German scientific publication. Instead, there are slight regional preferences for different tastes over the tongue surface.

Many cells in the taste bud are primary sensory cells. When they are stimulated, they transmit signals across a cellular junction (synapse) to sensory afferent axons, the pathways that lead to the brain. Bundles of axons from taste buds travel first to the base of the brain (specifically, to the Nucleus of the Solitary Tract), where they relay their gustatory signals to neurons located there. Those neurons, in turn, send their axons to a higher brain center (thalamus) which then distributes the signals to the overlying cerebral cortex (specifically, the gustatory primary sensory cortex). Finally, information from the gustatory primary sensory cortex is next passed along to a region in the front of brain named the orbitofrontal cortex. This last brain region also receives converging input from the olfactory system. The orbitofrontal cortex thus appears to be a key site where perceptions of "flavors" are generated. That is, the neuronal basis for the intimate relationship between taste and smell (i.e., "flavor") may first be formed in the orbitofrontal cortex.

Umami taste transduction

The conversion of a chemical taste stimulus (such as glutamate for umami taste) into an intracellular response within a taste bud sensory receptor cell is termed *transduction*.

Returning to the biology of the taste bud, it is important to understand that the initial event in taste transduction consists of the interaction of a taste chemical with molecular receptors on the apical, chemosensitive tips of gustatory sensory cells. Molecular receptors for bitter, sweet, and umami have been cloned and characterized. Consequently, we now know many of the proteins and genes for these tastes. Less is known about receptors for sour (acid) and salty tastes. The taste receptors for umami are G protein-coupled receptors (GPCRs). The best evidence to date suggests that there may be several GPCRs for umami. Among them, in order of their date of discovery, are (1) a modified synaptic glutamate receptor mGluR4 that has a truncated extracellular N-terminus; (2) a heterodimer consisting of T1R1 plus T1R3, two of the T1 (taste, family 1) receptors; and (3) a modified (N terminal truncated) form of another synaptic glutamate receptor mGluR1. Heterologous expression of all of these receptors in non-taste cells (HEK293 and CHO cells, *Xenopus* oocytes) produces cells that respond to umami taste compounds (glutamate, other amino acids). Further, genetic knockout of T1R1 or T1R3 expression in mice produces animals that have subnormal responses to amino acids, including glutamate, strongly supporting the notion that the two proteins T1R1 plus T1R3 form an *umami* receptor. Comparable genetic mutation experiments with the metabotropic glutamate receptors is complicated by the fact that mGluR1 and mGluR4 are important transmitter receptors at synapses in the brain. Thus, knocking out these genes would not only affect peripheral gustatory reception but also might alter central pathways involved in the perception and behavioral responses to umami tastants. Indeed, mGluR4 knockout mice manifest altered behavioral responses to umami taste, but, as explained, this does not necessarily support the hypothesis that mGluR4 is an umami gustatory receptor in taste buds.

However, even given the above identification of candidate umami receptors, the physiological responses of taste cells when stimulated by glutamate do not completely match the characteristics of any single one of the aforementioned receptors. Moreover, knocking out any one of the above umami receptors does not entirely abolish behavioral umami taste responses. Collectively, the data suggest that combinations of molecular receptors, or possibly the involvement of yet-undiscovered receptors, underlie a full explanation of umami taste reception.

The events that occur when umami taste receptors are stimulated are understood fairly well. When an appropriate taste chemical (e.g., glutamate) interacts with umami taste receptors, this releases intracellular G protein βγ subunits that normally are bound to the receptor. The βγ subunits that are freed from the umami receptor interact with and activate an enzyme, phospholipase C β2. This enzyme cleaves membrane phospholipids into inositol trisphosphate (IP3) and diacylglycerol. IP3 is a diffusible messenger that moves through the cytosol to intracellular caches of calcium, typically endoplasmic reticulum. IP3 acts on receptors on the endoplasmic reticulum to release calcium into the cytoplasm. This flush of intracellular calcium triggers transmitter release from the activated umami taste sensory cell.

Other taste transduction pathways involving gustducin (a G protein α subunit) and cAMP degradation may also be involved, but the link to eventual transmitter release is not established.

The transmitter(s) released by gustatory sensory cells is(are) not known with certainty, but ATP and serotonin appear to be leading candidates. Other transmitters that have been identified in taste buds include acetylcholine (ACh), adenosine, and γ-amino butyric acid (GABA). ATP-sensitive postsynaptic axons innervate taste buds and provide a connection between the peripheral sensory organs and neurons in the brain, mentioned above.

Unanswered questions about umami taste

The above survey of umami taste makes it clear that there are several unknowns and uncertainties. Principal among these are (1) how many molecular receptors are there for umami taste? None of the proposed receptors on their own appears to fully explain umami taste responses in taste cells. (2) how is neurotransmitter release triggered from taste cells stimulated with umami tastants? Unconventional synaptic release mechanisms appear to operate and little is known about them. (3) what is/are the neurotransmitter(s) that taste bud cells release? ATP, serotonin, ACh and GABA have been mentioned, but are there others? (4) Finally, what is the coding for umami taste in the nervous system? Are there specific gustatory sensory cells that are "tuned" to umami tastants and that convey this information along dedicated "umami" axons to specific clusters of umami-responding neurons in the brain (the notion of "labeled line")? Or, is there some more complex activation of groups of neurons such that gustatory information is encoded as patterns of activity in larger groups of neurons (the notion of combinatorial or temporal coding)? These and other questions are currently being intensely investigated in laboratories world-wide.

Dr. Stephen Roper

Appendix 6a: Umami Taste in Wine

Tim Hanni MW

There is little doubt that amino acids and 5'-ribonucleotides add primary taste constituents in wine. Glutamate and 5'–ribonucleotide, which is known to synergize the intensity of umami taste of glutamate, are found in sufficient concentration levels in wine to play an essential role in forming the taste and flavor profile and intensity of quality wines. The correlation of these compounds to desirable taste and flavor characteristics of wine has been referred to by Emile Peynaud[1] and has just being fully analyzed of late. Additionally there are several amino acids that have been identified that add a sweet taste to foods, notably proline, arganine and alanine that are found in sufficient concentrations to be considered as taste contributors.

A preliminary review of existing studies shows sufficient levels of naturally occurring umami taste substances in both wine grapes and finished wine to warrant further study of this hypothesis. Glutamic acid, a natural compound found in wine grapes and a precursor to glutamate taste substances, and 5'-ribonucleotides, which are associated with yeast fermentation and the enzymatic decomposition of ribonucleic acid from yeast cells. The contribution of glutamic acid (more correctly glutamate) to the taste of wine is acknowledged by Emile Peynaud in his books Knowing and Making Wine and The Taste of Wine: *"Among the amino acids, however, glutamic acid should perhaps be accorded a special mention. Its appetizing flavor is well known, salty, and mellow at once. If some 200 mg/l were present in a wine, its effect on the taste would not be negligible."* Synergized by 5 –ribonucleotides, lesser amounts of glutamic acid would contribute significantly to the taste and flavor of wine.

Alanine, proline, glycine and arginine have been found to contribute a sweet taste in various foods and are associated with the "sweet" taste of crab and other seafoods (Umami, the Fifth Basic Taste[2]). These amino acids are found in significant levels in wine grapes and wine as well. Understanding the importance of the umami taste in wine, now recognized as the fundamental taste of seafood, tomato, asparagus, mushrooms and cheese, will lead to a better understanding of standard of viticultural and winemaking processes. Implementing practices in the vineyard and winery that create higher concentrations of the appropriate precursors and optimize umami taste intensity in wine can maximize desirable taste characteristics.

---

[1] E. Peynaud, Knowing and Making Wine, 48, (1981) The Taste of Wine
[2] Umami, the Fifth Basic Taste

Correlation of umami taste to bitterness suppression

Increased amounts of free amino acids and ribonucleotides in food products have been correlated with reduced bitterness and acidic "bite." This effect is similar to the flavor enhancement achieved when wine is aged for extended period on the lees deposited during and after fermentation.

Wine descriptors consistent with umami taste descriptors:
- Sweet, savory, brothy, creamy, mouthfeel, mellow, rich, etc.
- Wine flavor descriptors –
    - Red Wine: body, extract, ripe, beefy, sweet, mushroomy
    - White Wine: creamy, mellow, sweet, smooth, rich, ripe

Fermentation and umami taste enhancement

Yeast contribution from yeast types and contact with yeast after fermentation and during yeast autolysis.

Red wine fermentation is conducted with the inclusion of grape solids. The pumping over or submersion of the cap keeps yeast cells constantly moving during the maceration period. Extended maceration of red wines creates a flavor profile consistent with umami taste characteristics, and may explain the softening and reduced bitterness and astringency of red wines made with extended maceration.
White wine fermentation is generally shorter in duration and conducted in the absence of grape solids. The umami flavor enhancement occurs during the aging period of the wine in contact with the lees resulting from fermentation and also my be enhanced during malo-lactic fermentation.

The aging of Champagne and sparkling wines on the lees, or spent yeast cells, after secondary bottle fermentation creates flavor distinctions consistent with enhanced umami taste characteristics: reduced impression of bitterness, rich, mellow, creamy, etc. The lees would provide a source for 5'-ribonucleotides that would act as the potentiometer to synergize existing glutamates in the wine.

The relationship of flor yeast formation and increase in ribonucleotides are additionally important in increasing the rich, mellow flavors of traditional Sherry wines.

Appendix 7: The Color of Odors

Gil Morrot *Unite´ de Recherche Biopolymeres et Armes, Centre INRA de Montpellier, Montpellier, France,* Frederic Brochet and Denis Dubourdieu *Faculte´ d'oenologie de l'Universite´ de Bordeaux 2, Talence, France*
Published online August 28, 2001

Synopsis

The interaction between the vision of colors and odor determination is investigated through lexical analysis of experts' wine tasting comments. The analysis shows that the odors of a wine are, for the most part, represented by objects that have the color of the wine. The assumption of the existence of a perceptual illusion between odor and color is confirmed by a psychophysical experiment. A white wine artificially colored red with an odorless dye was olfactory described as a red wine by a panel of 54 tasters. Hence, because of the visual information, the tasters discounted the olfactory information. Together with recent psychophysical and neuroimaging data, our results suggest that the above perceptual illusion occurs during the verbalization phase of odor determination. ©2001 Academic Press

Comparative Tasting

The two wines used for the experiment were Bordeaux wines (AOC ''Bordeaux,'' vintage 1996), containing Semillon and Sauvignon grapes for the white wine (wine W), and Cabernet-Sauvignon and merlot grapes for the red wine (wine R). Part of the white wine was colored red (wine RW) with 2 g/L of purified grape anthocyanins (E 163, ANTOCIAL, SEFCAL, 30760 Saint-Julien de Peyrolas, France). Wine W was treated in the same way as wine RW (stirring and oxygenation) except coloring. The neutrality test of the dye was carried out by 50 people

Excerpt from the conclusion:
The hypothesis that the identification of an odor results from a visual identification of the mental representation of the object having this odor could be the reason why humans never developed specific

olfactory terms to describe odors. Indeed, if odor identification results from a visual process, it is logical that the odor is identified using visual identifiers. Our results tend to confirm that sense of smell is, by itself, unlikely to provide sufficient information to allow for a consciously reasoned decision. The capacity to identify odors could only be an accessory aspect of the olfactory function. The true function of smell is probably sought elsewhere.

Excerpts from the discussion:

From a sensory viewpoint, the fact that the authors used a different vocabulary to describe white and red wines is relatively surprising. Indeed, tests carried out with opaque glasses show that identifying the color of a wine without the assistance of sight is not an easy task (Sauvageot & Chapon, 1983).

Evidence of the relationship between the perceived odor and the color of a wine initially led us to hypothesize that the color of a wine directs the identification of its odor. We tested our hypothesis by asking 54 subjects to identify in parallel the odors of a white wine and the same white wine colored red. The results of our experiment were consistent with our hypothesis. The white wine was perceived as having the odor of a red wine when colored red. The wine's color appears to provide significant sensory information, which misleads the subjects' ability to judge flavor. Moreover, the mistake is stronger in presence than in absence of access to the wine color. The observed phenomenon is a real perceptual illusion. The subjects smell the wine, make the conscious act of odor determination and verbalize their olfactory perception by using odor descriptors. However, the sensory and cognitive processes were mostly based on the wine color.

Index

Z

Notes: _____

_____

_____

_____

_____

_____

_____

_____

_____

_____

_____

_____

_____

_____

_____

_____

_____

_____

_____